Women in Welsh Coal Mining

Women in Welsh Coal Mining

Tip Girls at Work in a Men's World

Norena Shopland

First published in Great Britain in 2023 by
Pen & Sword History
An imprint of
Pen & Sword Books Ltd
Yorkshire – Philadelphia

Copyright © Norena Shopland 2023

ISBN 978 1 39907 522 0

The right of Norena Shopland to be identified as Author of this work has been asserted by her in accordance with the Copyright, Designs and Patents Act 1988.

A CIP catalogue record for this book is available from the British Library.

All rights reserved. No part of this book may be reproduced or transmitted in any form or by any means, electronic or mechanical including photocopying, recording or by any information storage and retrieval system, without permission from the Publisher in writing.

Typeset by Mac Style
Printed in the UK by CPI Group (UK) Ltd, Croydon, CR0 4YY.

Pen & Sword Books Limited incorporates the imprints of Atlas, Archaeology, Aviation, Discovery, Family History, Fiction, History, Maritime, Military, Military Classics, Politics, Select, Transport, True Crime, Air World, Frontline Publishing, Leo Cooper, Remember When, Seaforth Publishing, The Praetorian Press, Wharncliffe Local History, Wharncliffe Transport, Wharncliffe True Crime, White Owl and After the Battle.

For a complete list of Pen & Sword titles please contact

PEN & SWORD BOOKS LIMITED
47 Church Street, Barnsley, South Yorkshire, S70 2AS, England
E-mail: enquiries@pen-and-sword.co.uk
Website: www.pen-and-sword.co.uk

Or

PEN AND SWORD BOOKS
1950 Lawrence Rd, Havertown, PA 19083, USA
E-mail: Uspen-and-sword@casematepublishers.com
Website: www.penandswordbooks.com

Contents

Acknowledgements vi
Introduction vii

Chapter 1	Degrading Labours	1
Chapter 2	The 1841 Census	11
Chapter 3	A Great Many Girls	20
Chapter 4	Lucy Thomas and Eos Vach	31
Chapter 5	They are Murdered by the System	41
Chapter 6	Getting around the Act	55
Chapter 7	Unsexing Themselves	69
Chapter 8	The 1851 Census	83
Chapter 9	Should Female Labour be Employed?	90
Chapter 10	The Clayton Images	103
Chapter 11	Sackcloth and Ashes	117
Chapter 12	1881 Census	132
Chapter 13	Angels of Humanity	139
Chapter 14	Rough Grace	152
Chapter 15	Diminishing Numbers	165
Chapter 16	Endings and Beginnings	178

Notes 185
Bibliography 195
Index 197

Acknowledgements

This book would not have been possible without the expert knowledge of Ceri Thompson and his wonderful work on increasing the knowledge of women in Welsh coal mining. My thanks also go to my wife Julie Carpenter; my father Robert Shopland for his continuing support; Susan Edwards for her advice; Rhian Diggins at Glamorgan Archives; Benjamin Price; the staff at the Big Pit National Coal Museum; Walter Waygood, Rhondda Cynon Taf Libraries, and John Peel, Manchester Art Gallery.

This book is dedicated to all the forgotten women who worked in the Welsh coal industry.

Introduction

The development and decline of the coal industry are, arguably, the most important event in modern Welsh history. At the beginning of the nineteenth century, around three-quarters of the Welsh population were living in the Welsh coalfields. By the First World War, there were around a quarter of a million Welsh mineworkers in both the north and south Wales coalfields producing 60 million tons a year.

Coal mining is seen as a very masculine affair, but women and girls have worked in the industry from early times. Unfortunately, most published histories of the Welsh coalfields have tended to ignore female labour and women are usually only mentioned as miners' wives keeping their male family members clean and fed or as supporting their husbands on the picket line.

This is perhaps understandable as women were usually a small proportion of the workforce and not every colliery employed them. In 1841 they were around 3.5% of the UK colliery workforce but, following female labour being banned underground in 1842, they fell to 2.5% in 1851 and around 1% after 1861.

Despite their small numbers, women formed an important part of the workforce, often doing jobs that the male miners found degrading. They sorted coal and pushed drams at the top of the pit and, before 1842, also worked alongside men underground, occasionally at the coal face, but more often on the transport roads.

Accounts of their working lives raised outrage among the Victorian middle class. They were accused of heavy drinking, swearing, and working almost naked. They were seen as having low sexual morals and being unfit to be wives and mothers. Many trade unionists, male miners and social reformers campaigned to prevent women from working in the collieries. These campaigns met opposition from the female mineworkers themselves who valued the independence that working in the collieries gave them.

Their numbers dwindled up to the Second World War, but they were then replaced by other female colliery workers who played the role of medical, clerical, and scientific staff. The introduction of pithead baths complexes

viii Women in Welsh Coal Mining

also added to their numbers as the canteen facilities within these were mainly run by female labour.

This is the first major study of Welsh female colliery workers and will prove invaluable to students of the coal industry.

Ceri Thompson, Curator, Big Pit: National Coal Museum

Chapter 1

Degrading Labours

The earliest records of using coal as a burning agent date back to ancient China – archaeologists have discovered surface mining dating to 3490 BC. Indeed, until the industrial revolution, beginning in the eighteenth century, coal mining was mostly surface or small-scale operations that consisted of picking pieces from the surface, digging shallow pits, or driving low horizontal tunnels into a rock face. Records of these low-level mining operations in the UK date back to Roman times and cover outcrops existing throughout the country – however, the main coalfields areas are in Northumberland and Durham, North and South Wales, Yorkshire, the Scottish Central Belt, Lancashire, Cumbria, the East and West Midlands, and Kent.

Many of these early, low technology mines would have been small affairs run by groups or families in which everyone would have taken part as it made economic sense for the whole family to work a smallholding rather than pay someone else.

The most consistent evidence of mining dates from sixteenth-century Germany with Georgius Agricola's (1494–1555) influential book *De Re Metallica* (On the Nature of Metals), published a year after his death, probably the most well-known. Agricola detailed different types of mining and the book was to remain a standard reference for over a century. The first English translation appeared in 1912 by Herbert Hoover (1874–1964), later president of the USA, and his wife Lou (1874–1944). When geologist and mining engineer Hoover travelled the world, Lou went with him becoming an expert linguist, particularly in Latin and it was her idea to translate *De Re Metallica* – but as the *National Mining Hall of Fame & Museum* explains:

> Previous attempts at translation had never come to fruition, for Agricola—the Father of Mineralogy—had simply invented new Latin expressions (hundreds of them!) to describe processes and substances for which no Latin equivalent existed. In 1906, Lou decided to take on the task of translating the tome, unaware that the project would turn into more than five years of strenuous exertion for both of them; consuming all free time and over $20,000 of their own money.[1]

However, in 1914 the Hoovers were rewarded for their work when they both received a Gold Medal from the *Mining and Metallurgical Society of America*, and Lou was the first woman to be so honoured, and the last woman for another eighty years. Their version remains the most important translation to date due to its clarity of language and extensive footnotes detailing the classical references to mining and metals.

De Re Metallica details how men, women, and children worked in and around a variety of mines where the work could be horrendous at times:

> No care at all is taken of the bodies of these poor creatures, so that they have not a rag so much as to cover their nakedness, and no man that sees them can choose but commiserate their sad and deplorable condition. For though they are sick, maimed, or lame, no rest nor intermission in the least is allowed them; neither the weakness of old age, nor women's infirmities are any plea to excuse them; but all are driven to their work with blows and cudgelling, till at length, overborne with the intolerable weight of their misery, they drop down dead in the midst of their insufferable labours.[2]

One of the most frequently reproduced images of women in early mining is taken from *De Re Metallica* and while it concerns the sorting of iron ore the principles were the same as that of sorting coal. The illustration features a group of women in a wooden building who are separating valuable lumps from the surrounding earth and rock and it is a lively scene, one woman at the back appears to be wagging her finger at another, perhaps admonishing her, while on the left a woman appears to be threatening a man with a sharp piece of rock.

Agricola describes the work as:

> They throw the mixed material upon a long table, beside which they sit for almost the whole day, and they sort out the ore; when it has been sorted out, they collect it in trays, and when collected they throw it into tubs, which are carried to the works in which the ores are smelted.[3]

A similar image, also from Germany, is in *Münz- und Mineralienbuch* (Coin and Mineral Book, 1594) by Andreas Ryff (1550–1603). The beautiful coloured images, showing mining in various fields, include two rather nicely dressed women working at the sorting shed.

The sixteenth century also saw one of the earliest references of coal mining in Wales. George Owen of Henllys (1552–1613), a Welsh antiquarian and writer commented on coal mining for local domestic use in his *An Essay on the History of Pembrokeshire* (1570). This was reproduced in *The Cambrian Register* in 1796:

> The digging of this cole is of ancient tymes used in Pembrokeshire, but not in such extent and skilfull sorte as now it is; for in former tyme they used not engins for lifting up of the coles out of the pitt, but made theire entrance slope, soe as the people carried the coales uppon theire backes along stayers, which they called landwayes; whereas nowe they sinke theire pittes downe right foure square, and with wyndeles turnid by foure men, they drawe upp coles a barrell full at once by a rope; this they calle a downright dore ... In one pitt there will be sixteen persons, whereof there will be three pickaces digging, seaven bearers, one filler, four winders, twoe ridlers, who riddle the coles ... These persons will lande about eight or a hundred barrells of cole in a day There tooles about this work are picaxes with a round pole, wedges and sledges to batter the rockes that crosse theire worke.[4]

While Owen does not specifically mention women, he uses the term 'persons' not men, causing the *Haverfordwest and Milford Haven Telegraph*, when it reproduced parts of the essay in 1917, to remind readers that the workers were 'workmen and workwomen (because in those days women worked underground)'.[5]

The Eighteenth Century

One of the earliest direct references to women working at mines in Wales also comes from Pembrokeshire but dates to the eighteenth century. George Edwards in his 1863 paper on the coal industry in Pembroke cited papers from 1777 concerning the Moreton Colliery where thirty men received 8d or 9d a day and eight women received 4d. However, it is not specified what the women were doing. In the same year at the Begelly Colliery seventy-seven people, including eighteen women and a few boys were employed. Again, the nature of the work is not mentioned. By 1806 men were receiving a shilling a day and women, mainly engaged in winding coal and filling carts, received 6d to 8d – about the same as male agricultural labours so they were a lot better off than most female workers.[6]

In 1791, Ceridwen Lloyd-Morgan, a visitor to Pembrokeshire wrote that there appeared almost as many women employed in the mines as men.[7]

For those small mines located in remote areas where the roads were poor, there are minimal records during the eighteenth century. One reference illustrating the difficulty of transporting the coal is from *A Collection of*

Welsh Tours (1798) by an anonymous writer who noted that the coal had to be conveyed on the backs of horses or donkeys by the poor of Hawarden whose women would go 'with their asses laden to Chester, knitting as they went, setting a laudable example of industry to the sluggard and the beggar'.[8] Francis Elizabeth Wynne (1836–1907) from Denbighshire, a prolific lay artist, sketched *Welsh lady carrying coal, 1859* on 12 October at Dolwydelay – the place name cannot be located but it may be Dolwyddelan in Conwy.

Often the only way we can know about women miners is through death records. Work done by Jon Mein (listed on the website GENUKI) covers coroner's records for Pembrokeshire and includes a number of women – some who died in horrendous accidents.[9] Most seem to involve falling out of the 'tubs' or buckets that people would travel in up and down the shaft.

In 1794 the St. Issells coalfield was owned by Ann Callen, a widow who had inherited her husband's properties. It was at this coalfield, in the Wim Pit that Sarah Phillips, a single woman, died trying to climb into a secured tub. She lost her footing and fell twenty-four fathoms (about forty-four metres) to the bottom dying instantly of a broken back. Two years later at another pit in the St. Issells coalfield, the Beacon Hill, Elizabeth Morris, a single woman, died.

Often the only way to travel up and down a pit shaft was for one, or two people, to sit on an iron bar attached to a rope that was then wound up and down via a winch or windlass, a job most often done by women. When a report was published in 1842 showing two young people, Ann Ambler (13) and William Dyson (14) from Elland, Yorkshire, sitting on an iron bar, crotch-to-crotch, their arms around each other, the public was horrified. It was while Elizabeth Morris was being drawn up in this fashion at St. Issells that the rope slipped off the bar and she fell to the bottom of the pit – thirteen fathoms or more. She was taken to the house of someone named Thomas Howells where she died. Elsewhere, at the Jeffreston mine, Rebecca Davies, a single woman, died in 1797 when she was employed in the Timber Croft field 'turning druke of air' (a method of air conditioning). The 'stander' [wooden bar] on the druke gave way and she fell to the pit floor twenty-three fathoms, breaking her back.

Some women are known about not because of their deaths at mines, but because their occupation is mentioned, such as Sarah Parcell, a single woman, who was 'working as usual at the Hean Castle coal works' in 1800 but on the way home drowned in a rivulet near Coppet Hall.

At the Amroth pit near Tenby, four women died. The first in 1807 when Mary Cozens 'slipped into a coalpit where she worked'; in 1812 Mary Hilling was going down in a tub in a mine owned by Lord Milford when she fell out and dropped ten fathoms; in 1815 Elizabeth Childs 'fell out of a tub onto her head while working in a coalmine'; and in 1823 two women, Mary Griffiths and Ann Evans died when 'the rope holding the tub in an Amroth coalpit gave way' and they fell thirty fathoms to their death. Elsewhere, Ann Jenkins (12) from the Graig Collery, Pontypridd 'fell into a coal pit' in 1839.[10]

These deaths show how dangerous the occupation was for both women and men. It was not only dangerous it was laborious. Usually, it was the men who hewed the coal out of the rock and the women and children who either carried it out on their backs or dragged it along in tubs. At the surface, women, children, and the elderly, or men with disabilities, would clean and sort the material usually by size and quality ready to be taken away for sale. Most of the work was done by hand with only small tools for breaking the ore from the surrounding dirt producing consistently sized pieces.

Women were rarely named in the official accounts of the mines if accounts existed at all, but it is worth bearing in mind that this kind of work was being done by women in countries around the world. An exhibition in 2020 at the Big Pit Museum showed Japanese women working underground much later than was permitted in the UK.

In 1799 Edward Daniel Clark (1769–1822), a clergyman and mineralogist, set out to travel through Europe and Russia and visited a number of mines including an iron mine in Persberg, Sweden. In his book *Travels in various Countries of Europe, Asia and Africa* he described:

> In the principal tin-mines of Cornwall, the staves of the ladders are alternate bars of wood and iron: here they were of wood only, and in some parts rotten and broken, making us often wish, during our descent, that we had never undertaken an exploit so hazardous. In addition to the dangers to be apprehended from the damaged state of the ladders, the staves were covered with ice or mud; and this rendered so cold and slippery, that we could have no dependence upon our benumbed fingers, if our feet failed us. Then, to complete out apprehensions, as we mentioned this to the miners, they said, - "Have a care! It was just so, talking about the staves, that one of our women fell, about four years ago, as she was descending to her work." "Fell!" said our Swedish interpreter, rather simply; "and pray what became of her?" "*Became of her!*" continued the foreman of our guides, disengaging one of his hands from the ladder, and slapping it forcibly against his thigh, as if to illustrate the manner of the catastrophe – "*she became (pankaka) a pancake.*"[11]

A footnote to the piece added, 'females, as well as males, work in the Swedish mines'. This is similar to work done in Scottish mines for the same period.

Women and girls would carry coal baskets on their backs held in place by a leather strap around the forehead to which a lamp was attached. For balance, they would wear a large lump of coal on their breast to counter the weight on their back. Some would have to climb ladders in excess of a hundred yards and if a strap or rung broke, or they were overbalanced, they could easily fall to their death. [12]

As limited work on tip girls in Wales has been done, many of the coroner's records of this time have not been examined – but the possibility of discovering more women is there. For example, in the 1842 *Children's Employment (Mines)* report, on 9 June 1820 at Cwmgwrach in Neath, Elizabeth Pendry aged six and Annie Tonks aged twelve died in a gas pit explosion.

The Nineteenth Century

At the beginning of the nineteenth century, Britain was producing about 80% of the world's coal but evidence of women in Welsh mines remains scant. One reference comes from the Rev. John Evans' (1779–1847) account when travelling through Pembrokeshire in 1803:

> The mine contains diggers and bearers: the first, men who, by candle-light and in a sitting posture, with pickaxes dig out the coals; the second, consisting of women and children, who carry the coals in baskets, each an allotted distance, relieving each other till it is borne by the last to the door of the pit ... since they have found the best coal at twenty and thirty fathoms deep, they have adopted a method used in other deep collieries, that of sinking a perpendicular shaft about six or seven feet in diameter, and drawing up the coals in baskets by a rope and winch, turned by four men or women: In a few places they make use of a machine called a jenny, worked by a small horse drawing in a circular direction.'[13]

Given the Reverend made no comment about the working women it must have been standard practice.

In the same year, women from Neath sent a petition to Prime Minister Henry Addington (1757–1844) in response to rumours about a French invasion. They requested permission to:

> defend ourselves as well as the weaker women and children amongst us. There are in the town about 200 women who have been used to hard labour all the days of their lives such as working in coal pits, on the high roads, tilling the ground etc. If you would grant us arms, that is light pikes ... we do assure you that we could, in a short time learn our exercise.[14]

Another rare example is from 1822:

> On Christmas Eve 1822, the funeral of Elizabeth Drew took place at St. Peter's Church. She had died a couple of days earlier in an accident, having slipped on ice while working at the coal patches – she was carrying a basket of coal on her head.[15]

Burial records for Monmouthshire show Elizabeth was 20 when she died. Artist Jon Pountney in his series of videos entitled *Blaenavon: stories from an industrial town* filmed an imaginary scene of Elizabeth carrying the coal on her head which can be seen on YouTube.

One story of the 1830s appears to have come from the pages of a Charles Dickens novel. Henry Crawshay (1812–1879), son of William Crawshay II, the influential iron-master and owner of Cyfarthfa Ironworks was reputed to be a kind man who was good to his employees. However, he enraged his prominent family when he had a relationship with a woman, Eliza Harris (1815–1895) of Penderyn, near Hirwaun. Eliza is often described as a 'working woman' however, the *Glamorgan Gazette* refers to her as a 'mine-girl'.[16] After having eight children out of wedlock, they were eventually married in 1844 when Eliza was 29 but Henry had been disowned by his family, particularly his father, William Crawshay II meaning he did not inherit the Cyfarthfa Ironworks, but was made manager of the Cinderford Ironworks in Gloucestershire where Henry became known as the *Iron King of the Forest of Dean*. It appears Henry and Eliza's marriage was a happy one; they remained together for 35 years and had 12 children – she died on 6 March 1895 in Awre, Gloucestershire aged 80 and a portrait of her hangs in the galleries of Cyfarthfa Castle Museum & Art Gallery.

After the 1840s the expansion of coal mining in Wales was rapid and people poured into mining areas, exploding the population. With this increase in employment, there was also a rise in social commentary with regard to the working conditions of labourers. Women and children had been hired in large numbers in mines throughout the country, particularly in the metal mines of lead, tin, copper, and iron and this began to cause concern among the public.

Direct evidence of Welsh tip girls/women working in collieries is rare prior to the publication of *The Condition and Treatment of the Children employed in the Mines and Colliers of the United Kingdom* 1842 report, and as mining became more intensive the restricted passages were better suited to children either working in pairs or one strong lad. In Wales, boys were taken underground as soon as possible, earlier than anywhere else in Britain, as fathers could claim for them but girls had no value so went when required.

One woman on whom there are some details is Ann Howells who supposedly lived to 105 years old. As she reached this advanced age the media began to take an interest in her and so parts of her life were related. She was born in 1798 at Abercwmboy Farm, near Aberdare, and worked for many years as a pit girl doing heavy work unloading trams of coal, and screening slag and refuse at the pit head of the old Abernant Collieries. The first article to appear about her was in 1903 when she was supposedly 105 years old and states she worked at some of the ironworks in the Aberdare Valley.[17] A second piece, which included a picture of Ann, mentioned she had moved in with her daughter and son-in-law Job Williams, who was well-known as the hero of Tynewydd when he saved the lives of five miners 'entombed in the bowels of the earth for ten days' by wading through a flooded pit.[18] When she advanced another year in age the papers were keen to cover her life story again this time stating that Ann married in 1831 at the age of 33,[19] much older than was usual for this period. Throughout the nineteenth and early twentieth century, there were many claims of centenarian people mainly because records were not always kept and people could be mistaken about their age. Tracing Ann through the genealogical records has not been successful but allowing that the birth date of 1798 is correct and she married aged 33, this gives a window of between 1808 and 1831 when she was at work. Ann died on 18 June 1904 four days off her supposed 106th birthday.

The 1842 Report

Throughout the first part of the nineteenth century, there were growing concerns over the general working conditions of the working classes and changes to labour laws came about initially from a desire to protect children. Lord Ashley (1801–1885), a philanthropist and social reformer, was horrified by the use of child labour and set up a commission to examine the situation in a number of industries. He campaigned for the right of factory children which led to the 1833 Factory Act banning the employment of children under the age of nine; restricted their working hours to nine hours a day; disallowed them to work at night; and allowed them to have some education; among other restrictions.

However, it took a disaster to bring things to a head in the mining industry. In 1838 at the Huskar Pit, a coal mine on the South Yorkshire Coalfield, twenty-six children aged seven to seventeen were drowned. One of the first men who led the rescue was James Garnett who discovered among the bodies that of his eight-year-old daughter Catherine. The public was horrified and the resulting inquiry revealed that a large number of children and women were working underground. Queen Victoria was equally shocked and tasked prime minister, Lord Melbourne, to hold an inquiry into the working conditions in Britain's factories and mines which was subsequently chaired by Lord Ashley.

The royal commission was originally intended to look at the working conditions of children in mines but some of the sub-commissioners who were employed to carry out the investigations were deeply disturbed to see women working in such harsh conditions and included details on them.

The report was intended to:

> collect information as to the ages at which the objects of it are employed, the number of hours they are engaged in work, the time allowed each day for meals; as to their actual state, condition, and treatment; and as to the effects of such employment, both with regard to their morals and their bodily health.[20]

While the information collected was copious, amounting to two thousand pages, it should be borne in mind that some of it may not be reliable as people were named in the report and employees certainly would not say anything to jeopardise their jobs. Also, the term child is a fluid one as a 'child' was defined as someone dependent on others such as parents, relatives, or official guardians however, a number of those aged around 15–16 were orphans and self-employed. Nevertheless, the *Children's Employment (Mines)* 1842 Report is one of the most important documents in British industrial history.

Originally there were eight men employed as Sub-Commissioners, but realising there was too much work, that number was extended to twenty. There was a delay in starting work in Wales, due to it being:

> deemed essential that the Sub-Commissioners for these important mining districts should be acquainted with the Welsh language, no information collected under this Commission being considered satisfactory unless derived, in part at least, from a person examination of the Children and Young Persons themselves.[21]

For Wales, Rhys William Jones took South Wales, and Hugh Herbert Jones took North Wales and its borders. Rhys William Jones (1804–64) was a Welsh-speaking civil engineer who in 1846 worked with the great Isambard Kingdom Brunel on the South Wales Railway through Glamorgan and Carmarthen and it had been Jones' idea to add a branch line to Swansea. He was also an engineer for the Swansea Vale Railway as well as working on Brunel's Vale of Neath Railway, and an engineer to the Llanelly Harbour

Commissioners working on various harbour schemes such as Saundersfoot Harbour and proposals at New Quay.

Jones seemed slow to carry out his work, and 'had allowed so much delay to interrupt his labours that the Commissioners were anxious as to the success of the investigation in this very important district' so Robert Hugh Franks was directed to assist him after carrying out investigations in the East of Scotland. Franks took the western side of South Wales and Jones the eastern.

The Commissioners were directed to write to all mine owners asking them to complete forms, detailing those employed, both men and women, at their works. However, even as the evidence was being collected mine owners were seeking to distance themselves from what was now being seen as a discreditable practice. They claimed women and girls were not employed underground in any of the Swansea pits, and that they did not 'subject females to such degrading labours as that imposed upon them in the mines of the eastern districts'. The Swansea Coal Company admitted that twenty-nine women and five girls were employed but, in a further effort to distance themselves from blame, it was because they were 'immigrants', women who had come from other areas 'from places where this laudable respect and consideration for the female sex was not observed'. They were surface workers picking out rubble and stone from the coal on the banks at the pithead and worked a twelve-hour shift earning from 4d to 1s a day.[22]

In the 1842 Report, a table was produced comparing the fifteen areas in Wales, Scotland, and England that had been studied and in general, the Scottish areas employed far more women and girls than either England or Wales:

Scotland	3,054
Wales	612
England	291

Pembrokeshire had the highest number of women to male ratio in the UK – for every 1,000 men, there were 424 women and Glamorgan had the lowest – 19 women to 1,000 men. For those employing children under 13 Pembroke and Glamorgan had the lowest figures while for those aged 13–18, Scotland had the highest figures.

Given the possible unreliability of the 1842 Report, and in order to test out some of these figures, parts of the 1841 census were examined.

Chapter 2

The 1841 Census

The earliest concerted effort to record the names and details of the national population was made in 1801 but the accuracy of this and subsequent returns were called into question. Nevertheless, from 1801, every ten years a census form was, and still is, sent to every household in the UK (Ireland was not included until 1821, and from 1921 only Northern Ireland) for the purpose of providing a complete picture of the nation to aid the Government in their policies.

Due to the inaccuracies of earlier recordings, the Population Act 1840 aimed to revolutionise the method of collection and the questions asked, so that the revised 1841 census is now regarded as the first 'modern' census and set a precedent that was used in every subsequent census including those of today.

The Census Form

The head of the household, who usually fills in the census form, is required to provide all the names of those on the property on a certain night. For 1841 this was Sunday 6 June and the forms were collected on 7 June by the enumerator, the individual responsible for that area. For the first time, it was made an offence to refuse, or fail to supply, the information or to provide false information and if the head of the house was illiterate the enumerator would help complete the form, or someone else, such as a neighbour could be asked. One of the difficulties with this was if the person did not know how to spell, not an uncommon problem at this time, it was left for those filling in the forms to interpret the information given, which means names could often be misspelt.

Areas of roughly equal size were divided into County, Civil Parish, Sub-registration District, and Enumeration District (an area where all returns could be collected in one day by an enumerator – women were not allowed to be enumerators until 1891) and the information recorded people's names, age, sex, occupation, if they were born in the county of their residence, or if they were born anywhere other than in England and Wales. The completed forms were then transcribed by the enumerator into a book which was checked by local officials and then signed off by a Superintendent Registrar before being sent to London where they were made into the tables which are used today. In towns, the number of houses in a district was about 200 but in the rural areas where enumerators often had to travel further, there may be fewer houses.[1]

The 1841 census comes with a number of difficulties that need to be borne in mind when analysing the results.

The ages of infant children were supposed to be recorded accurately, while those over 15 were to be rounded down to the nearest 5 years, however, not all enumerators did this and often logged exact ages. This leaves a difficulty when checking the ages of those named in the 1842 Report and in building an accurate picture of the working population.

Further difficulties emerge due to enumerators often writing in thick pencil which, when the census is photocopied, makes some details illegible. When tallying up, they would often mark the forms with crosses which can also obliterate details and faded records, so that when they are copied, it makes them almost impossible to read. Numerous mistakes were made on the thousands of forms, and spellings of people's names and place names can vary particularly if the enumerator was filling in the form on behalf of the head.

Another difficulty with the 1841 census (and indeed most digital census records) is that it cannot be searched using occupational keyword searches, such as 'collier' (to do so returns thousands of hits of people with the surname Collier). However, analyses of some census returns were published, such as the Occupation Abstracts,[2] and these can be used to provide a generalised view of some occupations in Great Britain.

Occupation Abstracts

In these abstracts, mining is divided into two categories, those relating to subsidiary coal occupations and those relating to all other mining industries. According to these figures, out of a total of 17,976 individuals working in coal-associated industries, 1,063 women were employed with the largest groups described as coal 'labourer, heaver, and porter' (616) and coal merchants and dealers (441). When split into the three countries the 'labourers' amount to England (371), Wales (57), and Scotland (188).

The second category covers mining occupations – namely those directly involved in recovering ore. There are thirteen branches of employment and females are included in eight of these – miner not specified, coal, copper, iron, lead, manganese, salt, and tin. In this table of the 194,221 people involved in those areas of mining, females account for 6,133. Once again, the terms are generic with 'coal miner' accounting for 2,350 women and girls throughout Great Britain. When these are broken down into countries they account for England (1,321), Wales (262), and Scotland (767).

The Occupation Abstracts are further broken down into counties and districts. Only the *coal miner* category has been included here although another, *coal labourer*, was also included but no definition of this term was supplied so it has not been included.

Despite these figures, the accuracy of the Occupation Abstracts has to be called into question because the calculation of 262 females in Wales as previously stated, increases to 412 in the Welsh tables.

1841 Census Results

As all these results are questionable, it was decided to take a closer look at the 1841 census, to recover more details and to try and flesh out the lives of some of these women in Wales.

This raises a number of difficulties not least the choice of which areas to concentrate on. As there are thousands of files per county searching just one district manually can be an enormous task. For example, the Merthyr area alone has twenty-eight districts with pages ranging from just a few to between twenty and thirty meaning an average of 600 pages have to be examined. Pages are also missing and it is common to find a complete range absent, for example, Aberavon returns only districts nine and ten. Results from the 1841 census, therefore, need to be taken as a rough guide rather than exact figures.

From the 1842 *Occupation Abstracts* tables above, the number of women involved in Welsh coal was given as 319 (57 in coal-associated industries and 262 coal miners). Those taken from the 1841 census returns for this work amount to 206 named females from twenty-one districts in three counties, Pembrokeshire, Glamorganshire, and Breconshire – which shows there is a lot more work needed in locating female coal workers from the 1841 census.

The *Children's Employment* 1842 Report gave Monmouthshire zero results for females in coal mining yet the Welsh *Occupation Abstracts* give 127 females, and a cursory examination of the Tredegar area, where small-scale coal mining operations had been carried out since 1794, returned only four names from Districts 1–15. Due to the low returns, the search was halted. It was not until the 1870s that Tredegar became more involved in coal mining.

Pembrokeshire

As Pembroke was mentioned in the 1842 Report as having the highest number of women to male ratio in Great Britain, it was decided to examine a few records from this county. The areas selected were taken from known examples as mentioned earlier in this chapter and consist of Amroth, Begelly, Jeffreston (modern Jeffreyston), and St. Issells and these were checked using the records on the genealogy site *Ancestry*. Not all district records for these areas are complete but what was recovered includes Amroth districts 1 & 2; Begelly, 4–7 & 9; Jeffreston, 6 & 8; St. Issells, 1–3.

Nevertheless, ninety-eight named women were recovered, Amroth (10), Begelly (24), Jeffreston (6), and St. Issells (58). The *Occupation Abstract* lists 167 females from Pembrokeshire (119 over 20s and 48 under 20s) so over half of those possible individuals have been recovered.

The census does not mention which mines they worked in, but two notable collieries were the Thomas Chapel Colliery – where according to the 1842 Report three trammers Eliza Prout (15), Mary Day (11), and Sarah Davies (15) worked as well as Hester Callan (18) a windlass woman. The same Report mentions the Broad-Moor Colliery which had just opened in 1842 and employed fifty-six men and forty-seven women. Elizabeth Lawrence (15) was a 'wheeler'; Hannah Bowen (16) worked a windlass, and when Benjamin Thomas (8) was interviewed he told the Commissioner he had been working underground for a year and the only meat he ate was some bacon on Sunday. His father had died and his mother, sister, and three brothers all worked in the same pit.

What is interesting from an analysis of the 1841 census records is that they bear out some of the figures in the Report.

The women recovered from the census were identified by their occupation. The most common word in the Pembrokeshire data is the word *collier* next to a woman's name, and these account for eighty-one of the ninety-eight women; other descriptions include 'collier woman' or simply 'coal mines'; twelve use a variation of the phrase 'employed at colliery' or 'employed at coal mine/ing'.

The word *collier* was originally intended to indicate those who worked underground in coal mines but this was flexible and often interchangeable with *miner*, for example, men were often called *coal miners* and were separated out from surface workers who were referred to using other terms such as *labourer at coal mine*. The term *miner* usually referred to those who dig in mines and in early censuses miners were also separated out from non-digging occupations, although this is not always adhered to throughout the century.

Sarah (15) and Ann (15) Marsh (possibly twins) from Llanelly, Breconshire were both described as a *miner* in a household where the head Johnson Morgan (50) was a collier (the two girls do not share surnames with any other members of the house so may have been lodgers or living with an extended family member).

In this first modern census, it was simply recorded if the respondents had, or had not, been born within the county and this allows a modicum of analysis with regard to movements but without their place of origin it is difficult to say where they came from. In the Pembrokeshire data, none of the ninety-eight women were born outside the county and most had classic Welsh surnames such as Thomas, Morgan, Williams, and Davies.

One of the public concerns with regard to the 1842 Report was how young the children were, but for Pembrokeshire, it was stated that few children under 11 were employed and the census data for St. Issells appears to support this. Hannah Williams (9), is the only example and she lived in a household of seven people where both her mother and father were colliers. The next youngest was Ann Buttersfield (11), from a household of five where both her parents and her 16-year-old sister Sarah were colliers. In all, the average age of the Pembroke women was 35 with the oldest being Mary Williams (75) who was the head of a household of four people where she and two other females were colliers.

Mary was not alone in being the head and of the ninety-eight women who lived in eighty-two households, fifty (61%) have a woman as the head. Twelve (20%) of these worked in the collieries with the others consisting of the widow of an agricultural labourer, two female grocers, and three pauper women. Only six of these were widows. In the later census returns marital status was included but not here so no answer can be found in the census why forty-four women (54%) were recorded as heads of households when the enumerator visited. As it was not usual for people to work on Sundays it is not known why so many of the husbands were not present, it is possible they were lodgers in other houses further afield in the search for other jobs in other industries such as agriculture. Three households specifically record agricultural workers such as Elizabeth Williams (60) who lived with Dorothy Williams (50) who was a farmer in St. Issells. James Williams (20) Dorothy's son was also a collier. Ann John (20) at Begelly was a lodger to the widow of an agricultural labourer.

Where a man was the head, only nine females were their wives and these tended to be older women with an average age of 47. The youngest of the wives were 32 and 35 but the rest were in their 50s with the oldest being Elizabeth Williams (60), a collier whose husband was a farmer. Occupants of these houses were predominantly those working in collieries so it would seem the wives were going back to work at a later age.

The average number of people living in a house for the ninety-eight women is five with the highest housing eleven and the lowest being one – five women lived alone and they tend to be older from 45–60 with only one woman aged 20.

Thirty-nine of the women were presumably daughters (no familial relationship is stated on the form but where the makeup is obviously a family, and the surnames are the same, it can be assumed the individuals are daughters) with thirteen having a collier father as head and nine having a collier mother as the head. The rest of the fathers consisted of two blacksmiths, a carpenter, four labourers, and a tailor, while the mothers consisted of four widows, and four paupers with just one with no given occupation.

The remaining females were lodgers, namely those individuals whose surnames differ from the head, however, the definition of a lodger in early census returns is problematic in that the word was ascribed to any individual who was not of the same surname as the head. There are thirteen, of which six were living in houses where the heads were female colliers. Only one woman lodged with a male head, who was a mason.

From these results, it can be seen that in these particular Pembroke districts most of the women working at the coal mines were locally-born, heads of their households (62%), and often housed other collier women. Very young children do not appear to be employed, as the 1842 Report stated, in fact, the average age was 35. Due to the use of the general description of the word collier, we cannot know exactly what work the women were doing and whether it was below or above ground.

Glamorganshire

The other county mentioned in the 1842 Report is Glamorgan and three areas were examined, Aberdare, Aberavon, and all the Merthyr Tydfil districts. From these seventy-one women were recovered, fourteen from Aberdare and fifty-seven from Merthyr.

Unlike Pembroke where the average age was 35, in Glamorgan, it was 19. Here too, few children under 13 were employed, just six with the youngest being nine. Despite the enormous publicity generated about children working as underground doorkeepers the terms rarely appear on the censuses but for the Merthyr area there are two. Glamorgan-born 'door girl' Gwenllian David (9) was living at Nant-yr-Odyn in a house of ten people headed by her collier father and housekeeper mother. Three of her brothers, aged 11, 14, and 15 were colliers and her eight-year-old brother Thomas was also a door boy. The other girl, in this case, referred to as a 'door keeper in level' was Jane Jones (10) also born within the county. She lived in Wellington Street with four other people, her father being a miner in the ironworks so Jane too probably worked in the iron mine.

The largest single group per age is those aged 15 of which there were eighteen, followed by the 20-year-olds of which there were seventeen – making the majority of the workforce approximately half the age of their Pembroke counterparts. After the age of 25, records dwindle with only five women aged 30 (2), 45 (1), 50 (1), and one at 70, Ann Morgans who lived alone in Plymouth Street, Merthyr, and cleaned the mine. Therefore, of the seventy-one Glamorgan women, fifty-six (40%) are aged between 15 and 25.

In Pembroke, all the women had been born within the county but in Glamorgan, it was roughly half – thirty-seven in the county and thirty-four elsewhere.

The seventy-one women lived in fifty-seven households where the average occupancy was six people with twelve the highest number which was about on par with Pembrokeshire where the average was five-eleven people. Twenty-four were lodgers to male heads of which eighteen worked in coal. Compared to Pembroke, where 61% of women were the heads of the household there were just nine women in Glamorgan (16%) and of these only four worked at the coal mines; two mine cleaners aged 30 and 70, a 50-year-old mine loader, and a coal worker. The rest consisted of a beer retailer, and four with no occupations stated.

Thirty-six of the women were daughters of the head and of these twenty-three had fathers working in the coal mines with the remainder a bricklayer and an iron miner.

In regards to their occupations, eight women were mine cleaners; various forms of 'filler' such as 'mine fillers' 'filling carts' 'coal fillers' or an equivalent of 'mine loader' made up thirty-two of the occupations – although it is not known if they were filling carts above or below the mine; there were three coal hauliers; three weighers of coal; while fifteen used a generic 'mine works', 'coal works' or labourers in coal works. Only one was referred to as a tipper which was an occupation that was to feature highly in future years, and one oiled trams.

Breconshire

In the Breconshire area of Llanelly, thirty females were recovered. Five of these came from District 3 (3) and District 8 (2) with the remainder from

District 4 which covered the Clydach Iron Works near Gilwern at the foot of A465 Black Rock Hill. Coal mines were further up the hill at Gellifelen and Llam-march and it is from here the data for female workers is taken.

Of the twenty-five females from District 4 identified as working in coal, eight (27%) cleaned the mine and tended to be young between 10 and 15 with the oldest being 20. Five were mine fillers, a description that covered all the females from Districts 3 and 8. Two were 'tram markers' a description that had not appeared elsewhere in this survey and the remaining seven were generically described as 'works in coal/mine' or 'labourer in coal.'

Another rare example of a doorkeeper is Ann Jones (13) from Darenfelin a location associated with the Clydach Ironworks. She lived in a family of six with the only other working member her father John (35) although they had four lodgers including a William Lewis (13) who was a haulier, a male labourer, and Rachel Lewis (15) who was a *mine worker*. None of these people were identified as being in coal or iron mines.

Four were born outside the county along with three from District 3 and one from District 8. Immigration figures, when counting individuals can be misleading as in a number of cases these are family members. For example, collier Thomas Powell (35) and his wife Elizabeth (35) had eight children and a lodger (a collier) in their house. Most of the children were infants except Mary (9), Elizabeth (13), and Ann (15) who all 'works in coal' and who would have been relied on to bring in a much-needed income to support the family. They had all, including the lodger, moved to District 4 from elsewhere. Some family records are mixed, for example, Walter Lawrence (50) and his wife Elizabeth (40) had nine children and while the couple with their eldest daughter Margaret (20), who 'works in the mine', came from outside the county the rest of the children were born within it. Elizabeth (10) and Jemima (12) may also have worked in the mine but the records are difficult to read as in many cases the word *do* (an abbreviation of ditto meaning as above or the same) is used frequently and so hurried were the enumerators that these can be reduced to a squiggle which can be difficult to interpret, in these cases, such as Elizabeth and Jemima they are not therefore counted.

When the figures are adjusted to represent families like the Powell's and the Lawrence's the eight individuals born outside the county are reduced to four households.

Of the thirty females from all three districts in Breconshire, the average age was 17. Five were lodgers with all the rest being daughters predominantly to men who worked in coal as only two heads of household were women for whom no occupation was given.

Obviously, these are only small samples but it does leave it open for more work to be done in this field of research. Particularly as it seems the accuracy of the information in the census and the Report is questionable. For example, the Report states that few females were employed in North Wales and research in the 1841 census seems to support this – few examples were found with the exception of three from Chirk, Denbighshire. The Report also stated that where employment did exist it was mainly around the Wrexham area but unfortunately, most of the census records for this area have been lost. However, Val Lloyd in her paper *Attitudes to Women at North Wales Coalmines c1840–1901* notes that in the 1841 census fourteen women in Denbighshire and seventeen women in Flintshire were *coal labourers* but according to the Report seventy-five females were employed at just one colliery in Denbighshire.[3]

The collection of information for the *Children's Employment* Report had begun in 1839, so when the census was taken two years later people working in the coal industry would have been aware of general disapproval of certain working conditions. This, therefore, casts a shadow over the reliability of the data in the 1841 census as the work of some children and women may have been neutralised. There are a number of examples of women's work generalised as 'labourer' while it can be seen from other family entries that fathers and brothers worked in collieries. Some are defined further by the mention of coal or collieries but these often remain vague such as 'employed at colliery' or 'labourer in coal works' leaving no idea as to the nature of the employment.

The final analysis of all districts from the 1841 census examined for this book resulted in 206 females in coal works. It can therefore be seen that the Occupation tables issued by the Government in 1842 which gave the figure of 262 for the whole of Wales are suspect. Only twenty-one districts were examined for this book out of the hundreds available for the whole of South Wales, so it would be interesting to see if more results can be recovered in the future.

Chapter 3

A Great Many Girls

The 1841 census sets the scene of some of the women's lives prior to the publication of the 1842 *Children's Employment* report and when it was published (it was the first Government report to include pictures) it became a best seller mainly because it shocked the nation. People were horrified by the deplorable conditions children were working under and because women were being subjected to arduous labour. The 'appalling facts' brought to the public notice by the Report had 'inflicted a great shock on the humane feeling of the country':

> That woman – and women in that situation, of all others, which must claims sympathy and demands exemption from severe toil – should be subjected to the task of dragging loaded cars in coal mines – that children, mere infants, should be employed in the same inhuman and laborious toil – and that, owing to the parsimony, or otherwise criminal indifference, of many of the owners, the machinery by which the labourers were drawn up and down the mines should be either of imperfect construction or intrusted to the care and working of mere boys, by which fatal accidents had frequently been caused.[1]

For the first time the report provided detailed accounts of women and girls' lives in and around coal mines – and that, demanded the public, had to change.

Evidence collected for the *Children's Employment (Mines)* Report showed that 19–40% of the workforce in coal and metal mines in the UK were those defined as children. In coal mining, the majority worked underground but at the metal mines, they worked primarily on the surface.

At the time of the 1842 Report, most UK mines had less than a hundred workers,[2] but it provided detailed accounts of the working conditions of women and girls in Welsh mines, allowing us to look in detail at certain aspects of their lives.

Ages

According to the 1842 Report girls generally began from seven to ten years of age – some were even younger but those instances are rare. The last, according to the Report, generally did 'belong to the poorest population in the neighbourhood'.[3]

In North Wales nine and ten were common ages.[4] Jones, in the introduction to his report, said the youngest in South Wales was between six and seven and some were so small they could not walk the long distances to work – Ann Bowcot (19) Dowlais, remembered her father carrying her to work, and Frederick Evans, a clerk at the Dowlais Collieries, said he had known instances of a father carrying his child of four on his back.

In Pembroke, sixteen out of ninety-eight females were under 18 (16%) but in Glamorgan, it was thirty out of seventy-one women (42%).

Abraham Rowlands, surgeon to the Nantyglo and Beaufort Works said, 'the children go to the works very young – about seven or eight years old – girls and boys the same'. P. Kirkhouse, overman to the Cyfarthfa collieries and ironstone mines in Glamorgan disapproved of the practice saying, 'The youngest are employed at the air-doors, and are taken below at very infantine ages, which cranks [stunts] their growth and injures their constitution, as well as keeping them in a state of ignorance of a very deplorable kind.'

Susan Reece (6) from the Plymouth Works at Merthyr Tydfil said she had 'been below six or eight months' and Mary Davies (nearly 7) was described as:

> a very pretty little girl who was fast asleep under a piece of rock near the air-door below ground. Her lamp had gone out for want of oil; and, upon waking her, she said the rats, or some one, had run away with her bread and cheese, so she went to sleep. The overman who was with me thought she was not so old, though he felt sure she had been below near eighteen months.[5]

Young women would usually continue to work until they married, usually in their late teens or early twenties but some continued to work until they started a family. Others, often widows or older women were also present – the 1842 Report noted a widow of eighty who was clearing ironstone on the surface in the Dowlais district,[6] and in the 1841 census Ann Morgans (70) who lived on her own, cleaned the mine.

However, there is the possibility that ages in the 1842 Report could be falsified, due to public disapproval, or the girls simply did not know them. For example, Mary Benjamin, from Aberdare is aged 16 but in the 1841 census only one Mary Benjamin can be found for the Aberdare area, living with her haulier father (someone who works with pit ponies), the same occupation given for Mary, but her age is 13 making her 14 in 1842, not 16. In the Report, she says she had been working for five years making her nine when she started. From the 1841 census data recovered for this book, only three females are listed as hauliers: Catherine (20) and Mary (15) Edward and Ann Griffiths (15) were all 'coal hauliers' and all four, including Mary Benjamin, were from the Aberdare area.

A further difficulty in assessing accurate ages arises when looking for individuals in the Report by backtracking them in the 1841 census. In this census, the ages of people over 15 were usually rounded down to the nearest five years making someone who was actually 24 listed as 20.[7] However, even these difficulties cannot account for some discrepancies. Ann Bowcot from Dowlais is listed as 19 in the Report but the only 1841 census finding in Dowlais is of an Ann Bowcott (with two *t*s), giving her age as 16. If the rounding down rule had been applied, she should have appeared as 15. Checking the accuracy of ages in the report, therefore, becomes extremely difficult although some do conform, such as Catherine Enock (15) whose baptism records show she was baptised on 21 August 1827 so her age in the 1842 Report is correct.

Confusingly, her sister Mary Enock is given the age of eleven in the Report but there are two records in that name, both born to William and Margaret, Catherine's parents. The first Mary was born on 20 December 1829 but not baptised until 23 December 1834 making her 13, not 11, in 1842. The second Mary, to the same parents and both baptised at the Salem and Ebenezer and Nebo Independent chapel at Aberdare, is born on 15 June 1830 and baptised on 12 October 1830, so the first child was supposedly alive when the second child was given exactly the same name. The second Mary would be 12 in 1842 and is closer to the age given in the Report.

The recording of ages is a consistent problem in census returns as many families at this time, only had an approximate idea of birth dates.

On the whole, where age discrepancies do exist, those given in the Report are generally higher than those shown in the 1841 census but the opposite does occur. For example, there is only one entry for Rachel Enock from Aberdare in the census (she has a different father from Catherine and Mary so is possibly a cousin) and her date of birth is given as 28 December 1828 and she was baptised on 21 January 1829. Her actual age is therefore 13, not 12 as given in the report.

Jane Dudlick is aged nine in the Report which would give her year of birth as 1833 but she has not been located in the 1841 census and there could be any number of reasons for this, simply that she was not in when the census was taken or the name could have been recorded differently. The 1851 census and baptism records show she was born in Merthyr and baptised there on 3 November 1833 but she told the commissioner that her mother was dead and her father, along with his ten-year-old son, was working at Blaina and that she lived with her grandmother and aunt Jane Evans with whom she worked. In the 1851 census, she is living with 70-year-old John Evans and his 69-year-old wife Mary who are probably the parents of Jane Evans.

For those females who had sole occupancy of a property, they were usually older women. Seven have been recovered from the 1841 census, most aged between fifty and seventy with one exception, Eliza Samuel (18) a coal filler living on her own. Eliza Evans (19) interviewed in the Report also lived alone. She worked underground at the Aberdare colliery helping fill trucks and boring holes for explosives. She had no dependants and her money was paid directly to her.

Types of Work

The types of work done by girls and women as outlined in the Report varied. Richard Painter (18), a collier at the Swansea valley Clydach Collieries and Mines, said, 'There are a great many girls working underground here, keeping doors, and helping the miners and colliers' while John Millward, a constable in Merthyr Tydfil, said, 'Girls do the same description of work as boys in the mine, and coal levels, and patches, but not generally under ground, although a great many are employed in filling trams in the levels.'

Arguably, the most well-known work done by children in mines was that of doorkeepers. As Ceri Thompson, curator of the Big Pit explains:

> In order to ensure that the air current reaches all parts of the underground workings a series of 'air doors' are set up. These have to be opened and closed one at a time to prevent the air flow short circuiting. Because this takes time it was the practice to employ small children to open and close the doors to allow the passage or horses and drams.[8]

At the time of the report few girls were employed as such, but a number said they had previously done that work including Jane James (16) Dowlais, who had kept an air door when she was nine and Ann Bowcot (19) Dowlais had kept a door for six years before leaving to stack coals. Elizabeth Williams (10) with Mary Enock (11) and Rachael Enock (12) were door-keepers and worked at the Upper Four Feet Level, Dowlais. Elizabeth had been working for a year, Mary for two, and Rachael for four years. They started at six in the morning and were supposed to come out at six in the evening but were often kept late when the horses were hindered in getting the coal out. On those days it meant they couldn't come out until seven, sometimes even nine in the evening. Mary Reed (12) at the Plymouth mine was similarly affected, saying she could not leave until the last cart was drawn past by the horses. She had worked in the mine for five years generally from six am to four or five pm and would often run home very hungry. When she left, she would either run along the level or hang on to a cart as it passed by – but one slip could cause a serious accident. She did not like the work in the dark and said she would not mind daylight work. During winter, those working underground often did not see the light of day except for Sundays.

Elizabeth Evans (11) told the commissioner:

> I keep a door in the collieries at Evan Jones's pit. I have been working for a year. My father is a collier and he come from Llanidloes. He has four children. I was in school at Llanidloes and could read Welsh but I cannot read much now. I have a brother working. He drives out cinders. I get 6d. per day, Evan Jones pays me. He is the master of the pit. I do not know exactly how long I work in the day. I go at six in the morning or sooner and come home before six in the evening. I have met with no serious accidents but my father was hurt in the pit where I am. The trams broke his arm by the horse going rash. He was driving it. I was with him at the time. It was four months ago and he is not quite well yet. The door I keep is nearly a mile from the pit but I come down to the pit with the trams and hauliers four of five times a day. I would rather go to school than to the works if I could. There are no good schools here. I was in one for four months and that is all the school I had for four years except the Sunday Schools. I go to them every Sunday. There are more girls in the pit with me.

Occasionally girls and women would speak of working at the coal face. Eliza Evans (19) Aberdare had worked a year in the underground mine level filling trams and helping the miner:

> I do nearly the same kind of work as he does,' she said, 'He takes the hardest work and uses the powder for blasting but I can bore the holes and I help to push the trams out. We work in the level about 10 hours. We sometimes come out once or twice and sometimes not once during the turn.

Eliza's father and mother were dead and she lodged on her own in the neighbourhood of the works.

Mary Ann Williams (13) at Ebbw Vale and Sirhowy, also said, 'I work the same as the colliers.'

In Pembrokeshire, one form of work unique to that county was *pouncing*, another name for boring. As Robert Brough, manager of the Begelly Colliery explained:

three women and two men placed opposite to each other and pressing the ends of two long acting logs acting as levers which operated a circular bore. It certainly was not proper work for females although it appeared to me less irksome than the other kinds of labour which women submit to in these parts.

Ann Thomas (17), described as a very healthy, intelligent girl, was a pouncer at Kilgetty Colliery. 'I have been only six months at these works and usually wind up the coal below ground. Pouncing is much harder work than the windlass. It hurts my back. We only pounce when sinking a new shaft and rest frequently, indeed we could not continue long at such hard work. I have not long been away from home. I can read, knit and sew.'

Some girls carried tools to and from the blacksmith to have them sharpened. Mary Clement (13), Aberdare, had been working for three years during which she carried the tools of the colliers from the top of the balance pit to the forge and back, a distance of about a quarter of a mile. She started work between 6–7 am and would make one trip in the morning before going home at 9 am. She returned at 4 pm during which she made three trips before she knocked off again between 6–7 pm. Mary Jones (11) also from Aberdare had been at work for a year and a half and she too carried tools for the men on 'ten one level' about a mile to the blacksmith, four or five times a day. Although she did have time to go home for meals.

The most common work underground for girls was moving the coal from the seam which had been cut by men, to the surface. Prior to the installation of trams and rails, this consisted of pulling or pushing containers full of coal through low, dark, uneven levels.

Samuel Singleton, underground steward of Kilgetty Colliery at St. Issells in Pembroke, told Franks their youngest girl was thirteen and both boys and girls 'work hard and regular and few holidays are taken. Girls and boys do the dramming [dragging coal carts]'.[9] Elizabeth Williams (9) had been below ground for six months assisting her father by filling trams. He had taken her to work because it meant he could have an extra tram and therefore earn more money. She worked six to eight hours but did not like the work at all. 'A good many girls besides me,' she said, 'work in the mines, at pushing the trams and tipping.'

The depths they worked at varied according to the mine, some were around 300 feet (about the height of Big Ben) while others were 200 yards (slightly taller than Blackpool Tower). Going up and down the shafts was via a ladder, dangerous in itself, or being hauled up and down in a tub – a method which had seen the deaths of a number of women.

In North Wales, many of the mines were described as low and narrow, the air foul, and the places where people worked, dusty, dirty, and damp, with imperfect ventilation. In South Wales conditions were no better. In the Blaenavon and Clydach Iron and Coal Works, near Abergavenny, the thickness of the coal seams varied from 2½ feet to 3½ feet (76–106cm) and the lane in which the horses worked were 5½- 6 feet high (167–182cm). Henrietta Frankland (11), a drammer, complained that the mine she worked in was wet, 'as the water passes through the roof, and the workings are only 30 to 33 inches high' (70–83cm). The Report was critical of some mine owners who continued to work their mines in 'modes which have become obsolete in all other districts' and so had inflicted 'grievous suffering' on 'many persons of tender age and of the female sex'.[10]

The obsolete practice he was referring to was the dragging of carts on all-fours with a girdle that passed around the body with a chain between the legs. A system that caused great damage to young bodies. Richard Hare, agent to Kilgetty Colliery, Pembrokeshire, admitted they used the girdle and chain method. One unnamed girl in the 1842 Report complained, 'we are worse off than horses: they draw on iron rails, and we on flat floors'.

Most of the girls worked with family members. Margaret Thomas (11) Ynyscedwyn Iron Works, worked with her father underground in the coal level where she and her sister (over 12) would move the coal out of the stall down to the horse road. She had been there for six months but prior to that had worked briefly at Tredegar helping to clean the mine banks but it had not worked out so she spent three months at the Covin Level at Ystalyfera. She, her sister, and her father left the house at 5 am and usually came out of the level at 4 pm however if she had to take the tools to be sharpened, she often left earlier. Margaret made a point of telling the commissioner that she did not work barefoot as she always had shoes and that sometimes she stayed at home to help her mother with the housekeeping and could not say which she preferred.

Mary Jones (14) had been working underground with her father for two or three years filling the trams. Normally she did not push them but would help out if needed. There was one other girl working on the same level and she knew of others on different levels. She too worked from six to six and occasionally went to the surface with a tram. She took bread and cheese with her and ate it when she liked as there was no set dinner hour.

Not all girls worked with family members – Ann David (13) was ten when she was first taken underground and she, and her sister Mary (16), worked for John Nash, a contractor. Together they pulled downhill, six scores of skips daily, three scores each, and the more they drew the more money they received. Their father, a collier, was laid aside with 'shortness of breath' and their mother had died six months previously.

The weight of the carts the children had to push or pull varied. Richard Hare, of Kilgetty Colliery, said it never exceeded 1½ cwt (1 metric ton – an average family car weighs about 1.4 metric tons). However, for those pushing trams on rails, the weights were higher. P. Kirkhouse, of Cyfarthfa collieries, said pushing trams, 'requires great strength. The main-roads are made as easy as the work will allow, by iron rails being run to the ends of the workings; but this does not alter the nature of the employment, which is certainly unfit for women.' Henrietta Frankland (11) said she drew 'drams' or carts containing 4 to 5 cwt. of coal, from the heads to the main road' and made about forty-eight to fifty journeys. Her sister, who was two years older, said, 'The work is very hard, and the long hours before the pay-day fatigues us much.' Mary Day (11) said her coal trams weighed 7 cwt. Lewis Thomas, proprietor of the Broad Moor Colliery in Pembrokeshire, said it was roughly between 18 to 25 cwt for a distance between 400 yards to one mile.

Most would have had to achieve a set number of loads per day and any extra would bring in more money but some, such as Elizabeth Lawrence (15) at the Board-Moor Colliery, had no idea as to 'how many loads I wheel.'

The distance carts were hauled, or trams were pushed, also varied according to circumstances. Mary Davies (11) had to drag seven hundredweight loads (355kg) along roadways that were never less than sixteen inches (40cm) high. Richard Hare of Kilgetty Colliery said that the distance their boys and girls dragged carts varied from two to thirty fathoms (1.8–54 metres – the width of an average UK football pitch is 45–90 metres). Thomas Stokes, proprietor of Thomas Chapel Colliery gave evidence that eight girls from eleven to fifteen pushed wagons, often in pairs, along the main roads on rails for about 1005 fathoms (1,838 metres).

Once the coal was dragged or pushed out from the narrow tunnels leading from the coal face to the 'road' it had to be moved to the shaft to be hauled to the surface. This was usually done by horses and most of the horse driving was done by boys but Mary Benjamin, from Aberdare was an exception. She had worked for five years and was driving a team of three horses on the tram road, 'Driving horses,' she said, 'is very hard work as the road is steep in some places. I have not been at this work very long. I worked before at the Gadley's Mine Patch. Girls do not often drive horses but they do here sometimes. I do not like the work.'

Girls and women also oiled and maintained trams. Margaret Morgan (20) at Dowlais, had worked for eight years keeping doors but was now oiling trams. Catherine Enock (15) Dowlais who had worked for four years explained what a laborious job it was, 'I have to upset the tram off the road to get to the axles and it is heavy. I can do it myself but I get help sometimes.' Ann Bowcot (19) Dowlais agreed, 'Oiling trams is hard work for I have to turn them off the road to get to the places to be oiled and some of them are heavy.'

Dramming took place both below and above ground. As the coal came to the surface it had to be wheeled away and at Blaenavon, it was moved on the surface level either by horses or women and children from twelve to eighteen years. Jane Dudlick (9) had been working for three months alongside her aunt Jane Evans (19) near Tyle Dowlais Pit where Jane senior had been for several years. They spent most of their time filling the trams by hand on the banks. 'Some of the pieces are too heavy for me to handle,' said Jane junior. She lived with her grandmother and aunt as her mother was dead and her father worked at Blaina.

Once the coal had reached the surface it was trammed to a sorting area where it would be sieving or riddled (raked) mainly by the women, to separate it from the coal dust (culm) as clients would not buy bags of coal if part of that weight was worthless coal dust. Other surface jobs included oiling, cleaning, and maintaining the trams and brushing the roads known as 'polling' which Jane James (16) Dowlais had been doing, arriving between 6–7 and leaving at 6 pm, sometimes sooner.

In some parts of North Wales girls and women were only employed in surface work. Richard Wood, General Manager of the British Iron Company's Coal and Iron Works, Denbighshire said, 'Girls and women never go below the surface in this or in any of the works in this district.'[11]

Jones, the sub commissioner for the report, was satisfied that this was true 'I have,' he said:

> great satisfaction in reporting, though girls find work at the pit mouth, that they never go underground; such a practice has not yet found its way into the northern parts of the principality. The number who work on the surface is comparatively few, and the custom of employing females at all is confined to the districts around Wrexham. At each pit two females are placed to assist in *banking* the coal, and where there is no steam-engine or horse-whimsey, also in turning the winding-barrel, by which the coal and ironstone are brought to the surface. In most cases the females employed exceed the age of eighteen; as strength is required there are but few under that age, and rarely any to be found under eighteen. There is nothing in the employment of banking coal which is repugnant to the feelings; and the manner, conduct and dress of the female so engaged appear respectable and decorous.

In Pembrokeshire, the coal was called anthracite, or stone coal due to its hardness, and in many of the workings, the angle of the shaft was highly inclined. These 'pitching veins' were generally about 45^0, although Franks noted he saw one upwards of 55^0, and they demanded a unique form of labour to remove the coal from the mine.

In small mines, this consisted of simply winding up tubs of coal from below. In other, more complex mines it could consist of a series of windlasses fixed at convenient distances on the incline and the coal, in carts or skips, moved up and down accordingly. At some levels, the carts were dropped by the windlass chain to the flat level where a horse and cart moved them to another windlass to be hoisted to the surface. This was illustrated in the Report.

Windlasses were worked primarily by women, often in pairs due to the great weight, the Report noting that 'their labour is certainly severe', but adding, astonishingly to us today, 'though only of eight- or ten-hours duration'. Hugh Owen, trustee to Landshipping Collieries said, 'Females riddle the coals, and wheel above and wind below; adults can only perform this operation, as it requires great strength.' The weight of the carts being drawn upwards by the women, according to the report, was 4cwt (203 kg, about the weight of three average women). For children, it was 1½ cwts. Captain Child, a mine proprietor, stated that women worked in the mines and on the banks, harder than the slaves in the West Indies.

Often girls would start work at the mine by sorting the coal and then progressed to the windlass as David Morgan, manager of the Board-Moor Colliery explained:

> Boys commence working as early as seven years of age and females about 12. The latter are first employed above for a few years in separating coal from culm and when arrived at full strength they went to the windlass. The women here wind from the deep, and some of the veins are nearly upright, nearly 500. Strong women will haul up by windlass 400 loads in a day's work and their week's wages rarely exceed 3s. 6d. to 4s. It is true they do not work the long hours which the women do in Carmarthenshire but they are more patient and enduring. Many married women work below and they do not object to the labour. There is much fire in the mines of Broad Moor. One died a short time since from explosion. We have no medical man attached, nor do the men subscribe to any medical fund. Many of them belong to a society held in the neighbouring village. Colliers here are disabled from 50 to 55 years of age. They are satisfied with little earnings as they work short hours. Nearly one third of them keep cows and do a little gardening. None

speak Welsh. The women and girls about here will not haul the skips, neither will the boys or men work at the windlasses. The lads earn 3s. 6d. to 4s. a week, girls who pick culm, 2s. a week, windlass women, 3s. weekly and the men are satisfied if they earn 18d. to 20d. per day. If business be brisk we work night as well as day on eight hour shifts.

Hannah Bowen (16), a windlass-woman at the Broad Moor Colliery, had been working at the mine for two years and had never been off work. She described it as 'good hard work' from seven in the morning till three and four in the afternoon and on average she drew up 400 loads of 1½ to 4 cwt per day. In the mornings she had her breakfast at home and was able to eat 'nearly every day' but if they were planning to work extra hours, they took bread and butter with them. Her father had been a collier but was off with 'bad breath' and had been disabled for two years while not very old, although he did not know his age. To support the family, he took their cows to graze on the roadside. They paid 40s a year for the cottage they lived in and while Hannah could knit and sew, she could not read or write and had never been to school but had attended a Sunday School.

Hester Callan (18) had been at the windlasses for three years and her father was a collier in the same mine.

Ann Thomas (16) was not happy with her work below ground. She described it as 'very hard' pulling up 400 loads a day. She had been working for eleven months because she could not find any other work. The hours depended on how much coal was removed and Franks noted she was 'very strong, and although working below, from the character of the coal, was not very dirty'. Ann added with perhaps a hint of bitterness, 'men do not like the winding, it is too hard work for them'.

Many of these stories horrified the public, but there was a lot worse to come.

Chapter 4

Lucy Thomas and Eos Vach

Much of the information about women and girls at the coal mines is dominated by statistics and their work which provides only a narrow glimpse into their lives. Occasionally though, for a few individuals, we can build a more detailed life and two examples of this are Lucy Thomas and Eos Vach.

Lucy Thomas

Women occasionally owned mines and probably the most famous coal mine owner is Lucy Thomas, often referred to as the Mother of the Welsh steam coal trade. Not a great deal has been written about Lucy but what does exist consists of disputed accounts of whether she was, or was not, the first person to kickstart the highly lucrative Welsh steam coal trade.

No birth date has been traced for Lucy, née Williams, but she was baptised on 11 March 1781 in Llansamlet, Swansea and as the age was given as 0, she must have been born in 1780/1. Her parents were Job Williams and Ann (née James) and she married Robert Thomas at Llansamlet, Swansea on 30 June 1802 aged 20–21. They were married for thirty-one years and had eight children, six sons, and two daughters.

At some point, after they were married the couple moved to Merthyr where Robert supplied fuel for Cyfarthfa Ironworks. He then struck out on his own and on 30 December 1824, took out a mining lease at Waun Wyllt, Abercanaid near Merthyr, on a yearly tenancy from the Earl of Plymouth at one shilling per ton royalties. However, he was banned from supplying coal to the four main ironworks in the district which had their own collieries and Robert's lease stated he was 'to open a sale colliery without power to sell to any of the ironmasters, and not to interfere with works which may be erected for the smelting of the Earl of Plymouth's iron mines which may be in that quarter.'[1]

Despite these restrictions, Robert seems to have flourished and at an unknown date, he opened a rich level of coal that was to become famous as the Four Feet Seam which he sold to households, first in Merthyr and then in Cardiff.

In 1901 an unnamed writer in an article entitled *Pioneers of the Industry* for the newspaper *Tarian Y Gweithiwr* outlined Robert's career according to documents that had been shown to him by his descendants. He stated that at first Robert tried to ship his coal via Glamorganshire Canal near Glyndyris but Crawshay, as a principal shareholder in the canal, opposed this even removing plates on a tramway Robert was constructing. Nevertheless, Robert persevered and established a coal yard at the Iron Bridge at Merthyr which was for many years the whole source of supply for the inhabitants of Merthyr. The ledgers of the Glamorganshire Canal Company toll charges, the unknown writer explained, showed that Robert sent the first load of coal in July 1828 to Merthyr and the first supply of coal to Cardiff along the canal in February 1829. By 1831 trade had increased so much that Robert was applying to the Glamorganshire Canal Company for a special wharf for his coal on the eastern side of the Sea Lock pond.

Just as his business was booming, Robert died on 19 February 1833 when Lucy was 52–53 and she was left to take over the family business with their son William. Lucy had, according to the *Tarian Y Gweithiwr* writer 'especial business aptitude and amassed substantial profits by her colliery operations'.[2] Quite an achievement not just as a rare example of a woman running a coal mine, but she was also illiterate and business documents show she signed with an X. Although the 1841 census lists her simply as a 'coal merchant'.[3]

There are a number of stories that try to account for how Lucy became known as the Mother of the Welsh Steam Coal Trade. One of the first was by Charles Wilkins (1830–1913) from Merthyr a prolific writer of historical accounts of Wales and its industries, and the founder of *The Red Dragon: The National Magazine of Wales*. In his book, *The South Wales Coal Trade and Its Allied Industries* written in 1888 nearly forty years after Lucy had died, Wilkins outlines how George Lockett, a partner in Messrs. T. Wood and Co., came to Wales in the company of James Duke, afterwards Sir James Duke, Lord Mayor of London, and James Marychurch but Wilkins provides no date. The men stayed at the Angel Hotel, Cardiff and when a servant stoked the fire, they were amazed that it created no smoke – this was what they had come looking for.

During the early decades of the nineteenth century, the burning of coal had created enormous problems with air and light pollution, leaving towns and cities full of smog and grime and high death rates. The navy's ships were left billowing long trails of dirty smoke effectively advertising their position. There was a move therefore to find cleaner coal for industries powered by steam and the best on the market was Welsh. There had been previous attempts to widen the Welsh market in steam coal by selling to the London market but only isolated shipments had been made.

According to Watkins' story, the men were then directed by George Insole (1790–1851) an English entrepreneur who built an extensive coal mining and shipping business in South Wales, to visit Lucy Thomas at Waun Wyllt. 'That adventurous lady,' wrote Watkins, 'had by this time made her coal famous in London, and as her customers increased in business it was but natural that other Londoners should try and profit.'[4]

The *Evening Express* in 1909 describes Lucy as suspicious of the men's intent and so insisted the price be paid in gold at four shillings per ton after which the coal was taken on the back of mules to Cardiff where it was sold in London for eighteen shillings per ton.[5]

Another version of how Lucy struck up business with Lockett, Duke, and Marychurch appeared in 1917 in the *Pioneer* when it was reporting on the reopening of Waun Wyllt (it had closed in 1870). This story portrays Lucy travelling to London with a basket of Welsh coal to meet with Lockett and persuade him to come to Wales. He does so with Duke and Marychurch and at the mine, Lucy carried out lumps of coal in her apron for them to examine.[6] However, this is the only version where Lucy travels to London so probably can be discounted.

Once a deal was struck, Lucy did a roaring trade and in 1838 alone Lucy shipped 16,776 tons of coal.[7]

Five years after Robert's death, according to a 1910 *Cardiff Times* article, the Four Feet Seam at Waun Wyllt ran out and the Earl of Plymouth cancelled the lease in 1838. Lucy and her son William then took over a pit known as 'Pwll Widow' on the Graig Farm on 1 May the same year.[8] As the mine was so close to the Glamorgan canal, they made a large profit so much so that five years later in 1843, William took a lease of several coal properties in the Aberdare Valley.[9]

It was then that John Nixon, a man credited with enlarging the output of Welsh coal, visited Lucy.

John Nixon (1815–1899) was an English mining engineer and colliery proprietor and an influential figure in the development of the South Wales coalfield and export business. He was becoming aware of the importance of steam coal and sought to acquire a supply with little success so he was directed to the Graig pit, Waun-y-wyllt (sic), where he found Lucy sitting in her office, a wooden hut near the pit's mouth, and placing in a basket over her head the cash she received for her coal. 'Her cleverness, her witty tongue, her pleasant manner were known to all the countryside,' Nixon wrote. Females worked around her 'laughing girls', grimy with coal-dust were sorting coal by hand, picking out the lumps and placing them on boats, 'as carefully as if each lump was an egg'. Lucy was raising a considerable amount of coal in those days, around 150 tons a day but despite this, she did not have enough to spare for Nixon. She also mentioned the appalling quantity of coal she was extracting adding that, after supplying the wants of the town of Merthyr and its neighbourhood, she found a ready market with Mr Marychurch for the entire surplus. Finally, she informed Mr Nixon that she would not undertake to produce more coal or to spare to him any at all.[10]

Lucy died on 27 September 1847 aged 66 having suffered for two weeks of typhoid fever. According to the death notice in the *Monmouthshire Merlin* she died at Waun Wyllt and is described as the 'proprietor of the Waunyllt (sic) and Graig collieries'[11] despite the fact she had left the former in 1838. She was buried in the family plot in the cemetery of the Unitarian chapel at Cefn-coed-y-cymmer near Merthyr.

Of her eight children, little is known of three of her sons Thomas, Francis, or John and it is not known when they died; Margaret married, had children, and died in 1877. The eldest son Robert had died four months before Lucy and in her will, she left his children eight leasehold properties in Upper Abercanaid. William who had worked so closely with his mother died three years after her as did her other son David, also a coal proprietor, who died of tuberculosis. Catherine married William Rees who took over the Lletty Shenkin Colliery from his brother-in-law, William Thomas who died in 1850 the same year as William and David Thomas. Their daughter Ann married a coal mining magnate Sir William Thomas Lewis (1837–1914), the first baronet of Merthyr, arguably the most powerful figure in Welsh industry at the time but also said to be the most hated man in Wales due to his tyrannical rulings. He owned the Senghenydd Colliery which, due to a failure to implement safety measures, exploded on 14 October 1913 killing 440 miners, devastating the local community, and leaving 200 widows some of whom had lost entire families. Despite this being, and remaining, the worst UK mining accident in history Edward Shaw, the colliery manager, was fined £24 while Lewis' company was fined £10.

In 1906 Lewis and Ann erected a fountain in Merthyr to commemorate Robert and Lucy.

The story of how Lucy started the steam coal trade was to prove controversial and arguments would rumble on for years as to whether it was Lockett who first commissioned her or George Insole. Charles Wilkins contending that Insole was simply '*one of the first*' in the same year that Lockett had made the deal with Lucy. The *Tarian Y Gweithiwr* writer, who was apparently working from family documents, also stated that in those early days Insole was not doing business with the Thomas' and that he had no account with the Glamorganshire Canal Company for some three years after the Waun Wyllt coal was sent to Cardiff.

There were plenty of others, however, who claimed Insole was the first to commission Lucy. The *Cardiff Times* in 1899 claimed that when Insole sent his first cargo of coal the mine was 'owned by Mrs Lucy Thomas' and that he sent the coal in the *Mars* from Cardiff to London on 12 November 1830. It was this shipment that induced Lockett and James Duke to visit.[12]

On 18 March 1898, a letter appeared in *The Times* from G. C. Locket (sic) correcting an earlier report that Nixon was the 'pioneer of the Welsh coal trade' when in fact it was his grandfather George Lockett. According to the grandson, Lockett took to London a hogshead of coal from Lucy's Waun Wyllt and had it tested at the Eagle Brewery, Hampstead Road, and so satisfactory were the results that a consignment was commissioned. Later that year Insole also shipped a cargo but the test results were not satisfactory and so he did not follow up with an order. Lockett then opened a shipping office in Cardiff with Marychurch as his agent and manager. G. C. Lockett claimed it was from that hogshead of Lucy's coal that developed into 'the 23 million tons odd which make Cardiff the largest dead-weight port in the world'.[13]

Four days later F. H. Insole wrote from Llandaff disputing the grandson's claim and instead argued it was his grandfather that made the first shipment on 13 November 1830 in the *Mars* carrying 414 tons of Waun Wyllt coal. He added 'I can prove that Mrs. Lucy Thomas was not the owner of Wain Wylt (sic) Colliery in 1830.' But he did not provide the proof.[14]

This was countered five days later when the *Times* received letters from Howel Williams, Merthyr and T. Criswick, Bridgend, both affirming that Lucy was the owner early in the thirties. Williams wrote, 'Mr. Robert Thomas and his son William opened the Waen (sic) Wyllt Colliery by their daily labour, and, as I was a constant visitor at the farm, it is within my knowledge that in 1834 Mrs. Lucy Thomas was the owner of Waen Wyllt Colliery, Merthyr, therefore the pioneer of the Welsh coal trade.'[15] This does not however help with the date of 1830.

The *Tarian Y Gweithiwr* writer in 1901 had attempted to clear the confusion in an article entitled *Pioneers of the Industry* writing,

> it has often surprised me very much to observe such great discrepancies in the various accounts given by writers as to circumstances which might well have been within the memory of a number of persons living up to a few years ago. But, strange to say, very few writers on the subject

have given anything like the same account of those early days – the days literally of small things in the South Wales coalfields and in the development of the; South Wales coal trade.

R. J. Nevill in his paper *The Early Welsh Coal Trade* notes that Lucy could not have been responsible for the breakthrough which gave her the title of 'Mother of the Welsh Steam Coal Trade' because in 1830 Insole was still directing letters to Robert and it was not until 1835 that the account was transferred to Lucy's name, two years after Robert's death. In addition, the financial risk was taken by Insole indicating it was he who took the initiative.[16]

W. T Morgan in his *A Note on Lucy Thomas of Waunwyllt* (1958) concurs, stating that documents from the Llandaff Probate Registry in the National Library Wales show that Robert was still alive at the time of the 1830 contract with George Insole for 3,000 tons of coal a year to be shipped to London. It is Robert therefore who was the pioneer of the Welsh Steam Coal Trade.

However, what should be born in mind is that at the time of Robert's death, Lucy swore an affidavit (signed with an x) that her husband's effects were under £1,000 and her son Robert and George Insole were cosignatories[17] – but when Lucy died, she left just under £12,000 (about 1.3 million today). In the fourteen years since her husband's death this illiterate woman had prospered enormously and it is this success that is probably the origin of the legend.

A writer in the *Cardiff Times* described Lucy as 'an old Welsh lady with the commercial instincts of her race: prudent, enterprising, persevering. The story of her career has become part of the history of the coalfield; and it will be retold to succeeding generations as one of the stirring romances of industry. Mrs Thomas was essentially a pioneer; and it was her good fortune to acquire the first level in Glamorgan from which the sale of steam coal took place.'[18]

Eos Vach

The second individual who had a life outside the mine is Eos Vach (or Eos Fach). That she was a mine girl is first mentioned in an 1861 article for the *Merthyr Telegraph* entitled *Recollections and Records No. XVIII* where an unnamed writer provides a biography of Ieuan (or Iewan) Ddu, an Abergavenny schoolmaster. Ieuan organised and trained choirs, musical groups, and individuals for entry into competitive singing during the 1830–40s and, according to the article, Ieuan was 'emphatically' the first who used female singers at eisteddfodau – which is debatable. He was very successful in this respect but had difficulties persuading young women to appear at these gatherings.[19]

His first notable successes were with Morfydd Glantaf, Ddriw Vach, and Eos Vach and both Morfydd Glantaf and Eos Vach were to appear regularly competing against each other. One of the difficulties with bardic names is many people would use the same ones and so personal names can differ. In 1836 Eos Vach is identified as Ann Jones yet the name is changed in later articles to a variation of Ann Curnew, Cornow, Cernyw, or Cerniw. It is said that she was 14 when she started singing, which would seem to be in 1836, putting her birth year around 1823. No records can be found for Ann Curnew, Cernyw or Cerniw however there is a baptismal record for an Ann Cornow of Merthyr Tydfil on 2 June 1822. However, no further information can be found on her through the census and other records.

The *Merthyr Telegraph* article detailed how Eos Vach had been taken by her parents to sing for Ieuan when he, 'charmed by her voice' determined to provide musical training to the 'little mine tip girl' and taught her some Welsh airs 'as English was out of the question.' However, training girls 'so young, and so destitute of educations in everything' was a struggle as they:

> could not be taught properly, and it was all up-hill work ere they were fairly proficient. The fact is, at that time, females looked at a lesson in Sol Fa as they would at an algebraic series of its signs and quantities, and even when girls were willing to be taught parents blindly withheld their permission unless the sound of praise was heard and the jingling of prizes, girls fell back into their old habits in style, and forgot their master's teachings, and parents voted the whole useless and expensive.

The parents' attitudes are understandable. Competitive singing could generate a useful income for impoverished families as winning choirs would split the purse or individuals would keep most of the monetary prizes. Losing, however, often meant a loss of wages when attending competitions and travelling expenses so many competitors only appeared at local competitions – most of Eos Vach's appearances are limited to Abergavenny and Cardiff. Later in the nineteenth century when the eisteddfodau became so popular there were numerous choirs and singers drawn from the working classes with people commenting on how such rough, illiterate people could sing so well. Many of the singers learned the songs by ear which, when singing in other languages such as English or Latin, could produce very curious lyrics.

Almost as soon as Yr Eos Vach appeared, she became very popular. The first traceable appearance was in December 1836 at the Abergavenny Cymreigyddion (Welsh speakers) Society where the President, Sir Benjamin

Hall (1802–1867), 1st Baron Lord Llanover, near Abergavenny, (it is suggested the London clock tower Big Ben was named after him) was concerned that no prizes had been organised for the women. 'When he found that no one else had proposed any thing (sic) for the fair minstrels of his country, from whose lips they had heard such delightfully sweet strains of melody' he personally donated two medals one worth three guineas for the best female singer, and one worth two guineas for second place (a guinea was worth 21 shillings at a time when girls of Eos Vach's age were earning around 6–12s a week at the mines). However, a different version in the same article states that despite Morfydd Glantaf winning, the performance of Eos Vach, described as 'an extremely interesting young girl' was considered so excellent that the judges regretted they 'had not another medal to bestow as a reward for her taste and execution'. The Rev. T. Price volunteered to present her with a medal at his own expense. The Cambrian described her 'superior singing' which although eclipsed by Morfydd Glantaf was admired by all who heard it.[20] What was agreed on was that 'no competition, during the meeting, afforded greater pleasure to the assembly than this, and none was more calculated to give an idea of the richness and beauty of the Cambrian melodies'.[21]

It was at this, Ann Cornow's first appearance, that Sir Benjamin Hall gave her the bardic name of Eos Vach (Little Nightingale) because of her similarity to the famous soprano the Swedish Nightingale (Jenny Lind (1820–1887)).

The following year Eos Vach sang again at the Abergavenny Cymreigyddion Society where she impressed the audience with 'her thrilling tone' of a Welsh air and the audience demanded an encore. But once again Morfydd Glantaf won the best female singer with harp category despite the *Glamorgan Monmouth and Brecon Gazette* feeling Eos Fach 'displayed more purity and sweetness of voice than the successful candidate'.[22] She received a medal worth a guinea and a guinea in prize money (about two weeks' wages).

Later, she and others were invited to give a concert at the home of Lady Charlotte Elizabeth Guest (1812–1895) also of Llanover, wife of a leading Welsh ironmaster and best known as the first translator in modern print of *The Mabinogion* (the earliest prose literature of Britain). In her diary Lady Charlotte wrote, 'October 27 [1837] – in the evening we had a little concert. Little Eos Vach (a little girl from Merthyr) came to sing, and brought Davis, a Harper, to accompany her'. She goes on to note that Ioan Tegid (1792–1852), the Rev. John Jones, Lady Charlotte's Welsh teacher, was so pleased with Yr Eos Vach's singing that he composed an englyn (short poem) in her honour on the spot. At the current time, the englyn has not been traced.[23]

At Queen Victoria's (1819–1901) Coronation Festivities at Abergavenny in July 1838 Eos Vach sang the famous song *Jenny Jones*, and in October she was due to reappear at the Abergavenny Cymreigyddion Society but to her admirers' regret she did not turn up. She and colleagues had been travelling from Merthyr on the *Mountaineer* coach and she was sitting on a box on the roof with another singer, John Jones, when a sudden swerve at the turn near the bottom of the steep Llanelly Pitch, 'dashed' them to the ground with 'such violence that Eos Fach was rendered for some time after quite insensible, and still lies seriously ill at Abergavenny'. Jones was 'much bruised'.[24]

She recovered, and the following year was back singing first at Cheltenham for St. David's Day (1 March) and at the Cardiff Cymreigyddion Society in April 1839. These were her first appearances outside of Abergavenny and at Cardiff she received a more critical response. Morfydd Glantaf sang a few songs but did not compete due to an indisposition so Eos Vach was the only competitor for the best female singer with a harp. According to the *Cambrian*, she 'warbled' *Codiad yr Hedydd* and *Ffair y Wain* in 'her most melodious style. The first was warmly greeted, and the second ... appeared to excite a good deal of mirth'. Nevertheless, she was awarded the medal and Morfydd Glantaf was given 10 shillings and six pence (sic) as a token of respect.[25] The local newspaper, more supportive of their local girl wrote that she received 'loud plaudits and to please the crowd she repeated *Ffair y Waun*, unaccompanied'.[26]

It is possible Eos Vach married that year because as from this date she is often referred to as Mrs Ann Rees. Throughout the 1840s she appeared regularly winning prizes at various South Wales Cymreigyddion Societies, local eisteddfodau, and the Royal Eisteddfod (1840) in Caernarvon. By 1849 she was headlining as a lead attraction in concerts with words like 'celebrated' and 'famous' attached to her name. In 1845 there was a reminder of the singers' background when at the Abergavenny Cymreigyddion Society the audience 'hung with raptures on the "simple melody" which flowed from the "rude throats" of Morfydd glan Taff, Eos Vach, and others'.[27]

After this little appears in print with regard to Eos Vach although in 1858 *The Atlantic Monthly* in its article by an unnamed writer on *A Welsh Musical Festival* remembered Eos Vach Morganwg, the Little Nightingale of Glamorgan. 'Her rendition of some simple Welsh melodies were delicious; they as far excelled the outpourings of other singers as the compositions of Mendelssohn, or Bellini surpass a midnight feline concert. I have heard Chinese singing, and have come to the conclusion that, next to it, Welsh prize-vocalism is the most ear-distracting thing imaginable.'[28]

From the 1850s onwards the bardic name of Eos Vach/Fach was ascribed to a number of women but none seem to be of Ann Cornow.

Despite the 1861 article referring to her as a 'little mine tip girl', the phrase 'tip girl' does not appear until the 1850s when women and girls moved to the pit brow and without any further information it is not possible to say whether Eos Vach worked underground, overground, or both. However, with so little information available about tip women and girls, and women in general, it is pleasant to be able to get a small glimpse into the lives of Lucy Thomas sitting in her hut with her money in a basket above her head, and Eos Vach with her simple Welsh melodies flowing from her 'rude throat'.

Chapter 5

They are Murdered by the System

There was so much evidence collected for the 1842 Report that the Government issued a number of subsidiary publications including *The Condition and the Treatment of the Children employed in Mines and Collieries of the United Kingdom* also published in 1842 and in 1843 another report, *The Physical and Moral Conditions of Children and Young Persons Employed in Mines and Manufactures* was added. Much of the information replicated that of the 1842 Report but from both more details can be gleaned about the working conditions of the girls and women.

Hours

As well as the harsh conditions which had horrified the public, the long hours people were made to work also concerned them.

The hours varied little with the seasons – however, in summer when coal was used less, the working week could be a little shorter. When demand dropped off, people could suddenly be laid off work and find themselves without a wage for several weeks, even months.

In North Wales, the regular working day was twelve hours, from six in the morning to six in the evening but it was often extended to sixteen, or even eighteen hours. In South Wales the average was eight to ten hours, usually beginning at 6 am, but here too it was extended, often to eleven or twelve. Mary Day (11), a trammer, said she had worked eight to ten-hour shifts for two years and Elizabeth Lawrence (15) who wheeled coals at the Board-Moor Colliery had been working seven and eight hours daily for twelve months. Most children told the Commissioner they rarely worked less than twelve hours a day, some even went as far as eighteen.[1]

Reasons for extended hours varied from broken machinery; horses not behaving and so holding up work; being behind quota, or owners simply requiring more product and so more profit – usually for themselves. If work was held up by something outside the workers' control, they still had to fulfil their quota for the day, no matter how long it took, even if it extended work into the night. If work was incomplete, even if it was beyond the workers' control, they did not get paid.

In North Wales, workers had two or three days off a month, none of which they were paid for. In South Wales, there were few holidays.

Wages

Wages were usually paid monthly and varied according to hours, jobs, and places of work. Children's and women's wages were usually logged under the father/husband's name; but rather than being paid directly the money was credited at a 'tuck shop' – where families had to buy all their goods. These were shops that were run by mine owners for their own profit and often around 25% above ordinary shop prices. Due to the fact that families rarely had any cash, they would sometimes take tuck shop goods and trade them either between other families or at pubs and elsewhere, often at a disadvantage. In the Report, John Evans and David Edwards, both schoolmasters, admitted to taking goods from miners instead of money.[2]

According to the Report, on average children under ten seldom earned in excess of 3s a week (there were twenty shillings to the pound and £100 in 1842 is worth about £12,000 today, so three shillings would be worth about £6 today); from 10–13 they would get about 4–5s a week; and 13–18-year-olds from 6–12s a week. Some did pay these higher amounts such as at Rhymney where about eighty people were employed. Around thirty women and girls worked on the banks and twenty-seven of those were between thirteen and eighteen. George Evans, a collier overman, told the Report commissioners that the women's average wage was 6s a week.

However, females were often paid a lot less than males. Instead of the average four to five shillings a week for ten to thirteen-year-old boys, Mary Day (11) and Mary Davies (11), both trammers, earned three. Mary Jones (11) from Aberdare earned slightly more for carrying tools as she received three shillings and sixpence a week. Generally, jobs above ground were not as well paid and there was greater competition between those too invalided to work underground and older men and women.

Some were paid daily. Doorkeepers Elizabeth Williams (10) with Mary Enock (11) and Rachael Enock (12) at Dowlais were paid five and a half pence a day, just under three shillings a week. However, they and others who worked underground often had to pay for their own candles which for the three Dowlais girls came to sixpence a week which was effectively a day's wages; but the miner who employed Eliza Evans (19) at Aberdare gave her the candles. Elizabeth Lawrence (15) wheeled coals at the Board-Moor Colliery for 6d a day and Hannah Bowen (16) a windlass girl earned the same amount, both extremely arduous jobs.

For those aged thirteen to eighteen the average pay was supposed to be six to twelve shillings a week but girls rarely achieved the higher end. Those at the bottom end of the scale included Ann Bowcot at Dowlais (19) for oiling trams, Jane James (16) at Dowlais, for polling (cleaning the mine banks), and Eliza Evans (19) at Aberdare who worked for a miner.

Pay comparisons fluctuate between districts and jobs, Ann Thomas (16), a Pembroke windlass girl, earned between three and a half and four shillings whereas Eliza Prout (15), a trammer, earned four shillings, the same amount as her eighteen-year-old sister who worked on the windlass. Hester Callan (18), another windlass girl, received four shillings, about the same as Jane Evans (19) who filled trams at Dowlais.

Slightly higher wages were paid to Mary Clement (13), Aberdare, who took tools for sharpening. She received nine pence a month from thirty colliers each amounting to 5s 6d a week – interestingly, the girls who took tools for sharpening all earned higher wages possibly because they were getting money directly from the colliers, not the mine owners. Catherine Enock (15), Dowlais, received the same amount for oiling trams; and Mary Benjamin (16), Aberdare, who drove horses got about 5s per week.

In the early nineteenth century, women were paid significantly less than men but even so, the money paid in mining was often better than that in other occupations – and despite the laborious work in often harsh conditions, women often chose it over domestic service or the factories. At Merthyr, Charlotte Chiles (19) preferred drawing, landing, and weighing coal at the Graig colliery for 40s a month, to her former work as a kitchen maid at Lord Kensington's near Carmarthen for wages of 60s or 70s a year with keep. 'I prefer this work as it is not so confining and I get more money ... I cannot save money now: but I get more dress and more liberty, I work 12 hours daily ... the work, though very hard, I care nothing for as I have good health and strength.'[3] This was a familiar theme throughout the Report with women saying they had more pay and independence.

This was reflected in an article, *The Merthyr Iron Worker*, in the London-based nonconformist periodical *Good Words*, where the writer too believed pay was the main reason women in South Wales chose mining over more 'suitable employments':

> Perhaps the most painful features in the South Welsh mineral districts are the hardness of the work which the girls and women have to perform, and its unsexing nature. It is strange to see them so merry over it but if they threw it up, they could only take their choice between farm labour and domestic service, neither of which is remunerative in

Wales. A servant, in every respect as handy and as useful as many who are getting £10 or £12 a year in London, can be hired for 5s the lunar month in Merthyr.[4]

The article, which was hardly complimentary to the Merthyr workers, refers to the 'unsexing' of women and seems slightly puzzled that the women were 'merry' in their work.

Food

Workers would usually eat their breakfast before they left which could be five, or even four, in the morning depending on how far they had to walk to the mine. There was no set time for breaks or meals during the day so people would usually grab a few moments to eat their food which they would have taken with them or was brought to them. This often consisted of a small bag of bread and cheese; or bread and butter as Eliza Evans (19), Aberdare, had. Sometimes there were potatoes or a little bit of bacon and all this would have to sustain them until dinner. They ate whenever they wanted, children often ate everything very early in the day, but rats would also eat the food if they could get to it. On returning home people would have their supper, or dinner and lived chiefly on tea, milk, potatoes, bread, and cheese, but not a lot of meat.

Conversely, from the evidence collected by Jones in Monmouthshire, he claimed the diet was plain, nutritive, and plentiful with often one amount of 'animal food daily' and a liberal quantity of home-brewed beer. He reasoned that the good wages of the children enabled their parents to provide a more generous diet than the other labouring classes could afford.

However, the North Wales commissioner was not impressed by the food in Wales generally:

In respect to food, I must observe that the diet in Wales is of a lower order than that of England. Less of animal and more of milk and farinaceous food is used; but everywhere the Children have a sufficient quantity of nourishing diet, though in quality it may be esteemed inferior. Children at work in the pits and mines breakfast before they leave home; their dinner is brought to them by their friends, and consists of bread, butter, potatoes, a little bacon occasionally, with milk or broth. They have supper at home on their return from work; most of them have a piece of bread and butter to eat between breakfast and dinner, and between dinner and supper, which is eaten while at work.'[5]

Health

There was a rather lax attitude towards accidents and deaths. When someone died the coroner was notified but if it was not a suspicious death, he would issue a warrant for the police to appoint a jury and to bury the body without him. As juries would have been made of local people, whose livelihood depended on the mines, they would have rarely spoken out if death had been caused by any negligence of the owner.

In the Monmouthshire area, Commissioner Jones calculated that fatalities averaged around one per 1,000 and serious accidents, permanently maiming or crippling people, 1 per 500 per annum. Records of accidents, not including permanent maiming or crippling, were rarely kept.

Young children were particularly susceptible to accidents, not surprising given the long hours they worked. They could fall asleep when keeping doors and roll from their position into the tram road. Some were picked up by passing workers but others suffered broken limbs or were killed by the wagons. Rachael Enock (12) at Dowlais was a doorkeeper and suffered an accident when a tram ran over her and badly bruised her. She recuperated at home for a long time but eventually recovered.

Trying to manipulate the heavy trams caused numerous injuries and occasionally death such as Elizabeth Prothero (17) who was cleaning the sidings at Ty Trist colliery, Monmouthshire, when the overman told her to move out of the way for some wagons to be shunted. She didn't move fast enough and was crushed to death.[6]

The 1842 Report stated that the children of colliers and miners were in better health than in other occupations including agriculture. Their houses were better and clothes were equal to or superior to those elsewhere.

Lewis Redwood, the works surgeon at the Rhymney Iron Company which owned ironworks and coal mines, stated:

> I consider the physical condition of the children employed in these works to be generally good and unimpaired by their occupation or domestic circumstances. Those not so employed who have come under my notice are too few to enable me to compare the respective state of the two classes. They are for the most part rather robust, the girls more especially in consequence (no doubt) of their spending so much of their time in the open air. The young men brought up in the place and who have been employed from childhood in the works are in most instances a rather fine and athletic race but there certainly is to be observed some physical deterioration consequent on underground labour.

I believe that the children and adults can, with few exceptions, command good nutritious food. Their clothing is almost always sufficient and suitable. They are usually clean. I am not aware of the children employed being more subject to sickness than those who are unemployed. The surgical diseases enumerated by you seldom occur. There is nothing in the children's manner of life to induce them. Fever is a prevalent disease here but chiefly among adults. Chronic ailments such as those you allude to are not present themselves with peculiar frequency nor especially under circumstances leading to the supposition of their being directly or indirectly occasioned by the children's occupation in the works.[7]

However, this was not supported by others and Lewis would have been careful what he said in order not to lose his job. Jones, the commissioner to the report, stated 'that labour in the collieries of the counties of Glamorgan and Pembroke, in South Wales, and of Monmouth in England, is unwholesome, and productive of diseases which have a tendency either to shorten life or reduce the number of years of useful labour in the mechanic.' Indeed, many witnesses in the Report attested to the stunted growth of miners due to working early as children. Jonathan Isaacs, agent of the Top Hill Colliery, said, 'I have noticed that the children of miners, who are sent to work, do not grow as they ought to do; they get pale in their looks, are weak in their limbs, any one (sic) can distinguish a collier's child from the children of other working people.'

One woman, Ellspee Thompson (40), a coal-bearer from Scotland, complained that 'the oppression of coal-bearing is such as to injure women in after-life, and few exist whose legs are not injured, or haunches, before they are thirty years of age.'

The 1843 report, *The Physical and Moral Conditions of Children and Young Persons Employed in Mines and Manufactures*, by Jelinger Cookson Symons (1809–1860), one of the report commissioners in Yorkshire, looked at the physical stature of boys and girls in mining. He examined each district and commented on general conditions. According to his findings, North Wales colliers had better wages than agricultural and other labourers and it was claimed that their health and conditions were better. The commissioner for North Wales wrote that the physical appearance of those working at the mines suggested they had enough to eat and paints a rosy picture of boys bounding like 'young goats' after a full day's work. Although he adds, 'a little peculiarity may be observed in their gait, from the long-continued action and tension of some of the muscles and the relaxation of others, but it is scarcely observable.'[8]

Symons took ten collier boys and ten farm boys and found the average height for the collier boys was 4 foot 4 inches (132cm) while the farm boys were taller by an inch. The collier boys measured 27.4 inches (69cm) around the breast and the farm boys 27.2, so while the colliers were broader in the chest, probably from drawing the drams, they were shorter in stature than the farm boys.[9]

Of the girls from the collieries, the average height was just above 4 foot 6 inches (137cm) with a breast size of around 29.3 inches (74cm) and the farm girls were just over 5 feet with a breast size of nearly 28.7 inches.

The average difference in size was that all collier children were 8½% smaller than their farming counterparts.

Franks, the South Wales commissioner for the 1842 Report, described the girls and women employed in the collieries:

> Several of them are distorted in the spine and pelvis, and suffer considerable difficulty in consequence at the period of parturition [child birth]; but where this has not arisen from direct violence, it has been induced by general debility and bad habit of body, induced in infancy and childhood.

Working underground always brought with it difficulties in breathing from accumulated dust in the lungs leading to what would become known from the 1870s onwards as pneumoconiosis (or silicosis for short). Pembrokeshire women who worked the windlass underground had problems with shortness of breath, bronchitis, and asthma. Although the conditions were not as dirty, Franks commented on the cleanness of the windlass women.

Most of the children complained of fatigue, in some places so severe it damaged their ability to work safely. The *Morning Chronicle* noted it was not unusual for a 'girl of ten years old to wear her head bald by pushing the coal-car; or to carry above a hundred weight of coals along an inclined plane, too low-roofed for her to stand upright, and ankle deep in wet and mud. To do this, twenty times a day, a distance of two hundred fathoms ... a female collier is worked out or worked up, by the time she is forty years of age. If married, half of her children are still-born. They are murdered by the system.'[10]

Many of those working in the mines, no matter their age or sex, suffered from 'ruptions' (hernias) from carrying or pushing heavy loads. Often, they worked in soaking wet clothes which accelerated arthritis and other conditions as well as deformities of the body. The newspapers printed articles intended to generate sympathy as this in the *Cardiff and Merthyr Guardian*:

Who, indeed, with a heart in his bosom, could hear without a shudder of women crawling on their hands and knees, and dragging coals along passages scarcely larger than common sewers, through water, vapour, and almost perpetual darkness, in the midst of a poisoned atmosphere, and exposed to every vice and ferocity of natures rendered desperate by a life of toil scarcely human.[11]

One of the main concerns around women working in such laborious conditions was that of pregnant women who often continued in work right up to confinement. The Report contains several accounts of giving birth and suffering miscarriages. An unnamed witness said, 'three or four children born the same day that I have been at work, and have gone back to my work nine or ten days after: four out of eight were still-born.' Jane Watson, another Scotswoman, had two dead children and blamed oppressive work. 'A vast number of women have dead children, and false births,' she said:

> which is worse; they are not able to work after the latter. I have always been obliged to work below till forced to go home to bear the bairn, and so have all the other women. We return as soon as able—never longer than ten or twelve days; many less, if they are much needed. It is only horsework, and ruins the women; it crushes their haunches, bends their ankles, and makes them old women at forty.

Diseases of the spine were common and several of the women suffered considerable difficulty while giving birth probably adding to the number of miscarriages.

Clothing

From the evidence collected by Jones in Monmouthshire he surmised that the workers' clothing was of 'sufficient quantity and proper quality':

> In general the Welsh women are remarkable for attention to warm clothing, which they secure for themselves in woollens, flannels, etc; nor are they less anxious for their husbands and children; the men and children are always well defended against the general inclemency of the mountain country.

However, that image could not be supported by other evidence. Girls from five years onwards were employed in the same conditions as the boys and those who saw them remarked that it was almost impossible to tell them apart. They were often naked, or naked to the waist down, and wore ragged clothes. Many of those who worked underground did so because of the heat, the lower the shaft the higher the temperature. This would have been made worse by the smell of sweat from people and horses, urine, and defecation something which attracted enormous numbers of rats underground.

The 1843 report on *The Physical and Moral Conditions of Children* replicated the claim that women worked naked:

> That, in the districts in which females are taken down into the coal mines, both sexes are employed together in precisely the same kind of labour, and work for the same number of hours; that the girls and boys, and the young men and young women, and even married women and women with child, commonly work almost naked, and the men, in many mines, quite naked; and that all classes of witnesses bear testimony to the demoralizing influence of the employment of females underground.[12]

A woman identified only as 'E' described her work and wages noting that her clothes were her most expensive outlay:

> I am a coke-girl, aged 24, and have worked in Pen-y-darran three years and a half. My business is to stack the coal for coking in the pits ... I earn five shillings a week, but pay out of that a trifle for the doctor and 'fund' (provision for sickness). I have often to lift from the trains pieces of coal which weigh over a hundred weight, and carry them to the pit. I work eleven hours a day, taking the year through. I go often to my father's, though I live away from him. Without the assistance of my father and mother I could not live. My clothes cost me most, because I must have best and working clothes. My lodgings cost me ninepence a week. I cannot read or write, more shame for me, though I had the chance to learn. I work in all weathers—rain, snow, or frost. I stand the rain and wind often all day long, because we must work!'

Many of the girls and women bought their clothes as they simply did not have the time or skill to make them, something they were constantly criticised for. Jane Evans (19), Dowlais, said, 'I cannot make my own clothes because I cannot cut them out. If they were cut out I could sew them very well.' Hannah Bowen (16), a windlass girl, paid almost a week's wages for hers, 'The tailor charged me 2s. 6d. for the work and I paid 4s. for the cloth.'

The workers stayed in the same outfits all day. In the summer the dust particles in the clothes would chafe and in bad weather people often spent all day in wet clothes. They would have been heavy with coal dust and were sometimes beaten rather than washed, particularly in winter when drying times were longer. Shoes and boots wore out quickly and were expensive to replace so many children worked barefoot. Margaret Thomas (11) who worked at Ynyscedwyn Iron Works proudly told the Commissioner that she did not work barefoot and always had shoes.

Some girls occasionally wore trousers but this was socially unacceptable and for those girls and women seen in the streets in 'male attire' they risked arrest – it was assumed they were in disguise and up to no good. This social taboo had its roots in the Biblical passage Deuteronomy 22:5 'The woman shall not wear that which pertaineth unto a man, neither shall a man put on a woman's garment: for all that do so are an abomination unto the LORD thy God.' (King James Version). Evidence of trousers worn in the 1842 Report is mainly from Yorkshire and the Commissioner there wrote:

> One of the most disgusting sights I have ever seen was that of young females, dressed like boys in trousers, crawling on all fours, with belts round their waists and chains passing between their legs … In one near New Mills, the chain, passing high up between the legs of two of these girls, had worn large holes in their trousers; and any sight more disgustingly indecent or revolting can scarcely be imagined than these girls at work – no brothel can beat it.

None of the Welsh evidence mentions girls wearing trousers but it was a subject that was to cause controversy a decade later.

In a period when religion was very important it was expected of people to attend worship on Sundays; however, as many working-class people did not have Sunday best clothes they did not attend, adding to the negative attitude towards them.

Describing the Women

What is noticeable about the 1842 Report, and others produced at the time, is the language used to describe the women. Comparison with slavery crops up, Christianity was often invoked, and it was not uncommon to refer to working-class people as 'beasts' of burden, but for the women, it was much worse. They were described as 'repulsive objects', 'unsexed beings' or 'creatures'. Elijah Waring, supplying evidence on the Forest of Dean, wrote that the employment of females in mines and collieries was unknown in the Forest adding, 'I encountered no such repulsive objects there as the degraded and almost *unsexed* being I have often beheld, with mingled horror and compassion, among the iron and coal works of South Wales.'[13]

The *Cardiff and Merthyr Guardian* printed extracts from the Reports, and in their introduction wrote:

a more heart-sickening catalogue of heathenish ignorance, of vice, profligacy, indecency and cruel sufferings was never presented to the public eye than these reports furnish.[14]

The sensationalist language they and other commentators used implied a threat to public decency by the alleged immorality of the women and this was to receive far more attention than the gruelling work women were forced to endure.

It seems unfair to us today that women suffering from poverty should be described as such. Certainly, there seemed to be a correlation in the public's mind between simply being dirty, an unavoidable part of the job, and a disapproving attitude about the women's morals and behaviour. Something that was to dog them for another 150 years.

Houses

Living conditions for workers near the works were often cramped and unsanitary. In the Report Thomas Fellon of Blackwood described the dwellings in his neighbourhood:

> The interior of the cottages is small, comprising generally two rooms on the floor, one of them used as a bed-room: the rooms above are used as bed-rooms, and there is usually a pantry or scullery in the cottage. The district is particularly hilly, and the houses are for the most part scattered; some are built on elevated spots, while others are near the river, where the fog and damp exists to a much greater degree, in which places low and continued fevers, which frequently end in typhus, exist in a much greater degree than in more airy situations.

Drainage was a particular problem affecting whole villages. Toilets or privies were often absent; in Blackwood village, there were only ten. Jones, the Commissioner wrote:

> where houses are built by the proprietors themselves for the people employed in their collieries and mines that such arrangements are not made: but in a small cluster of houses, called the Land-level Houses, perhaps 25 altogether, which in themselves are well constructed and clean, inhabited by the colliers and other workmen of the Pentyrch Works, there was but one privy for the whole community. But perhaps the most miserable hovels inhabited by the working people are to be found in the neighbourhood of the Hirwain Works, and they derive a more comfortless appearance from the barren surface of the plain in

which they are situated. Many of these are nothing more than mud-cabins, in many instances a deserted cowshed converted into a human habitation; a rude thatch forms the roof, and, apparently to avoid the storms that sweep along that plain, they are built in every hollow that can be found, where of course they receive the drainage of the surrounding elevations. Hirwain itself, literally the long meadow, is bordered by a lofty range of hills, and is in many parts boggy and full of water. A more cheerless place could scarcely be found in South Wales: even, the school which I visited here more resembles a stable than a place for education, and is almost surrounded with a ditch of dirty water.[15]

Education

Before 1870 the chief responsibility for education lay with voluntary organisations, charities, or large companies.

> In South Wales during the nineteenth century the rapid development of heavy industries and coal-mining created centres of dense populations where voluntary efforts to provide education in many areas proved inadequate and ineffective.[16]

During the early part of the nineteenth century, few schools were made available for children, and where they did exist parents were expected to pay. The first colliery schools of the South Wales coalfield were established at Hirwaun in 1820 where there was one school for iron workers' children and one for colliery workers' children. The Colliers' School functioned 'in a room over a stable', was packed with fifty boys and girls, and confined itself to the teaching of the three R's. It was maintained by a 'stoppage' of a 1/2d in the £ weekly from the colliers' wages.[17]

In many cases, children could not go to school because their parents could not afford the weekly costs or the loss of wages. To combat this lack of attendance, provisions were made by religious bodies to educate children in Sunday schools where they would be taught to read and write but often the young people were too tired, stiff, and sore to go to school on their only day off.

Franks, speaking of the colliers in South Wales, wrote:

> Education is a subject to which the working people seem to attach little value. Ignorant themselves, and never having suffered severe distress, they note no distinction in the wages of the boy or the man who can read or write and those who do not; and they cannot appreciate the

value of that education of which they themselves never knew the want. The consequence is, that the children, if they go to Sunday-school, are sent rather as a mark of respect to those who recommend education, than from any esteem for the benefits to be derived from instruction.[18]

One of the difficulties with education in Wales at this time was that the official Sunday schools and public education were conducted in English when many of the local population spoke Welsh. It would have been hard for children to learn in a language they did not understand and nowhere in any of the reports do the commissioners attempt to understand the problem, or ask the people why their children were not going to school, they simply condemn them. Also, while it is acknowledged that many of the families sent their children into the mines very young due to a financial need and every member of the family needed to work, little of that is acknowledged when criticising the families for a lack of interest in education. A telling note in Franks' report is that:

> in a free-school opened for the instruction of the children of working people, copy-books, &c., were expected to be found for the children, and because they were not found, the children were withdrawn from the carelessness of parents.

If the school was not to supply the equipment it could hardly be expected for very poor families to use their hard-earned money to pay for books. Franks added that this problem was also found in Sunday schools, that children did not attend 'for the same cause', namely the lack of books before going on to condemn the 'large congregations' at the numerous chapels of 'the many denominations of Christians' that the 'spiritual education of the young seems to be grossly neglected'.

Franks' attitude was to be replicated in 1847 when a report into the *State of Education in Wales* unfairly maligned the Welsh so that the subsequent publications became known as the *Treachery of the Blue Books*.

Franks went on to recommend a 'little time and thought given to the welfare of the people, would not only tend to wean them from the gross habits in which they indulge, but would produce an abundance of kindly feeling between the employer and the employed.' He advocated establishing reading rooms for the men and 'small prizes' for the best cottage or garden. Having written of the long hours the people worked, and the affidavits of their exhaustion he expected them to spend their time off constructing pretty cottages or gardens. An interest in the welfare of the people he claimed 'would invite the labourer from the vulgar line he now treads in. As matters stand at the moment, in the largest manufacturing town (Merthyr Tydfil), the working man after labour has no resort but the beer-shop; his boy accompanies him, his daughter often passes the evening there.'

Sarah Davies (15), a trammer, who had started work aged eleven when she was taken down the pit by her father, said she attended Chapel and Sunday School and had been taught to read the Testament.

Mary Day (11), a trammer, said she always attended Sunday School and had learned 'a little reading there'. The three doorkeepers at Dowlais, Elizabeth Williams (10), Mary Enock (11), and Rachael Enock (12) all went to Sunday school; Rachael had been to day school but had been taken out to go to work. She could read a little but the other two girls could not. Many of the girls, including Catherine Enock (15) and Jane James (16) both from Dowlais said they did attend Sunday school but could only read a little. Mary Clement (13) and Mary Jones (11) from Aberdare had never been to a day school but both were learning to spell at Sunday school. Hester Callan (18), a Pembrokeshire windlass woman, learned to read but not to write. Eliza Prout (15), a trammer, Ann Bowcot (19) at Dowlais, Jane Dudlick (9), Eliza Evans (19), Aberdare, and Mary Benjamin (16), Aberdare, were unable to read or write.

Elizabeth Lawrence (15), a wheeler at Board-Moor Colliery, said, 'I seldom go to Church and have done so twice or thrice this year. I have never heard of Jesus Christ nor of the Lord's Prayer.' The commissioner added the note, 'very ignorant. The mother who was present, appeared equally as stupid as her daughter, for she could not assist in any reply to my questions.' It is not known what his questions were and if they were biased or not.

The evidence for the 1842 Report had been collected and published, the media reproduced huge chunks of it, and scandal ensued.

Chapter 6

Getting around the Act

What caught the public's attention almost immediately after the Report was published in May 1842 was that it contained illustrations – Samuel Scriven, the commissioner for Yorkshire, had included the sketch of the two topless teenagers, Ann Ambler and Will Dyson from Elland, sitting crotch to crotch being wound up a pit shaft, and two of his other sketches also appeared to show topless females.

These illustrations, which were not an accurate reflection of mining women in general, had a major impact. British economic and social historian Ivy Pinchbeck (1898–1982) pointed out, 'A wider interest was secured for the Report by the woodcuts since they captured the imagination of many who might not have been tempted to read an ordinary Blue Book. Almost more than by their heavy labour, Victorian England was shocked and horrified by accounts of the naked state of some of the workers.'[1]

The language of the Report also caused consternation as it highlighted what it saw as the immorality and indecency of employing women close to men. This horrified the public and placed in their consciousness that girls and women working in such degrading and intimate conditions could not fail to be corrupted and must therefore be bad wives and mothers.

Nevertheless, a number of writers did take up their pens in support of the women and children, including Benjamin Disraeli and Elizabeth Gaskell. Charles Dickens (1812–1870) was appalled by the Report and during a visit to a Cornish tin mine in 1843 was horrified to witness the appalling conditions the children worked under. He had for some time been alarmed about the lives of poor children and following the publication of the report he intended to put his feelings on the subject into a short publication *An Appeal to the People of England on behalf of the Poor Man's Child* but changed his mind and put them into *A Christmas Carol*, a story of a selfish man who controlled the lives of others but who through the help of a ghost changes his attitudes.

Poet Elizabeth Barrett Browning (1806–1861) wrote *The Cry of the Children* (1843) in which she laid the blame firmly at the feet of men.

> But the young, young children, O my brothers,
>   Do you ask them why they stand
> Weeping sore before the bosoms of their mothers,
>   In our happy Fatherland?

What is interesting about the poem is its gender-neutral tone, Browning talks throughout of 'the children' and only once mentions an individual, a girl:

> Little Alice died last year her grave is shapen
>   Like a snowball, in the rime.
> We looked into the pit prepared to take her —
>   Was no room for any work in the close clay:
> From the sleep wherein she lieth none will wake her,
>   Crying, 'Get up, little Alice! it is day.'
> If you listen by that grave, in sun and shower,
>   With your ear down, little Alice never cries;
> Could we see her face, be sure we should not know her,
>   For the smile has time for growing in her eyes, —
> And merry go her moments, lulled and stilled in
>   The shroud, by the kirk-chime!
> "It is good when it happens," say the children,
>   "That we die before our time!"[2]

Amid the backlash to the report, Lord Ashley hastily introduced a Bill into the House of Commons on 7 June seeking to regulate the age and sex of people working in mines and collieries. The Bill proposed that the employment of girls and women in any of these works should be prohibited and that no male child under the age of thirteen should be employed.

In his long introduction Ashley began by outlining where children were employed:

> Many ... are employed in North Durham and Northumberland at five, and between five and six: The instances in which children begin to work at seven, and between seven and eight, are so numerous, that it would be tedious to recite them. In the east of Scotland, it is more common for children to begin work at five and six than in any part of England. In the west of Scotland, children are taken down into the pits at a very early age, often when eight years old, and even earlier. In North Wales, the cases are rare of children being employed at five or six—they are very common at seven. In South Wales, more cases are recorded of the employment of children in the pits at very early ages than in any other district. It is not unusual to take them into the pits at four years. Many

are absolutely carried to the work. In South Gloucestershire, cases are recorded of children employed at six years, the general age is about nine. In North Somersetshire, many begin to work between six and seven. In the South of Ireland, no children at all are employed.[3]

Ashley then moved on 'with respect to sex' claiming that in many places women did not work underground with the exceptions of the West Riding of Yorkshire, where 'the practice of employing females underground is universal'; Halifax and its neighbourhood, where 'girls from five years old and upwards regularly perform the same work as boys'; at Bradford and Leeds, Lancashire and Cheshire it was 'the general custom for girls and women to be employed'; and in the east of Scotland, the 'employment of females is general, but in the west of Scotland extremely rare'; in North Wales 'some on the surface, none underground' but in South Wales, it was 'not uncommon'.

Throughout the century the word 'creature' was often used to dehumanise people and Ashley was no different. Referring to 'young creatures' he described their working environment and conditions but the blame was placed firmly on women. William Raynor Wood, a sub-commissioner who collected evidence for the Report had been invited to add his comments and replying to Ashley's speech, stated 'the wives are so little capable of rendering a house comfortable, that the husband is constantly driven to the alehouse, whence arise all the evils of drunkenness to themselves and to their families. From this source, a fearful deterioration of the moral and physical condition of our working population is rapidly taking place.' He continued:

> Women are allowed to work below, and because they are so, the evils here stated, continue without abatement; a man would complain and resist, but a woman is submissive. I feel confident that the exclusion of females will advantage the colliers in a physical point of view, inasmuch as the males will not work on bad roads (females are wrought only where no man can be induced to draw or work; they are mere beasts of burden). This will force the alteration of the economy of the mines.

By this logic, Wood argued, mine owners would be forced to improve working conditions for men if they got rid of women.

Henry Gibson from Wigan, one of the boys who gave evidence, echoed Wood's comments:

> Females submit to work in places where no man, or even lad, could be got to labour in; they work in bad roads, up to their knees in water, in a posture nearly double; they are below till the last hour of pregnancy;

they have swollen haunches and ankles, and are prematurely brought to the grave, or what is worse, a lingering existence.

In light of the evidence given, the House of Commons passed the Bill but the House of Lords stopped it dead. Many mine owners sat in the Lords.

Very few objected to the prevention of women working underground but they had a number of issues with the Report. Charles Vane, 3rd Marquess of Londonderry (1778–1854), an owner of several collieries, led the opposition and his main objection was the lowering of the age of children because, he complained, without them, many mines would have to shut. He believed eight was a suitable age, not 13 but he would accept ten. Lord Hatherton (1815–1888) complained of the Bill's 'hasty manner'[4] as the Report had only been published the month before and many had not had time to digest its 2,000 pages. Several members of the Lords objected to claims made which, by horrifying the public, had laid the blame firmly on mine owners, which they objected to; and the Duke of Wellington (1769–1852) went further and unfairly questioned the accuracy of those who collected the information. He wanted the nature of the commissioners and sub-commissioners to be investigated 'in what manner the evidence was taken' to see if it was taken 'according to the terms of the commission'.[5]

On 14 July the Marquess of Londonderry echoed Wellington's criticism of the accuracy and impartiality of the report stating in the House of Lords:

> It had been said in another place-, "Thank God, there is a House of Lords;" which implied an expectation that the bill would undergo careful consideration here. Time should be given to collect impartial evidence— not such as was contained in the 2,000 pages, before the House.

Londonderry claimed Franks, who had collected information for South Wales, had:

> kept two hat-shops, one in Regent-street, and the other in the city, and had failed, and that he had afterwards been imprisoned for a libel on the clerk of the Fishmongers' Company. He had other statements respecting the other commissioners, regarding their unfitness for their office, and he could not therefore place any faith in their report. They had got up the evidence by under-hand means, and had finished it with exhibiting upon their Lordships Table the most disgusting pictorial illustrations that ever were seen.[6]

On the whole, Londonderry supported banning women underground but he had received a letter from someone at Edinburgh saying it was impossible to use horses to bring up the coals so women were generally employed to carry the coal on their backs, ascending by ladders, and that they 'preferred this mode of gaining a livelihood, because by this work they could earn higher wages than by other employment'. The writer also stated, that if the women were debarred from gaining a livelihood by this means they would, in a majority of instances, be unable to obtain other employment. He added, that the collieries at present yielded little profit and if the owners had to employ men to do the work which was now performed by women, they must require higher prices for the coals, and he believed that eventually many of the collieries would be given up.

At the second reading of the Bill, William Courtenay, 10th Earl of Devon (1777–1859), pointed out that most people agreed that women should not be allowed to work underground, placing the blame on working-class men: 'it, would, indeed, be infinitely better if the husbands and fathers of these females would refuse to permit their wives and daughters to be placed in such circumstances.'[7]

Alexander Edward Murray, 6th Earl of Dunmore (1804–1845), moved a proviso, allowing females of twenty-one and upwards to continue working in the mines if unmarried. He considered, that the clause as it stood would be injurious to females who would be thrown out of employment.[8]

The *Economist* criticised the Act as 'the sickly sentimentality of the drawing-room presuming to regulate the world' and that banning women was a 'foolish, premature and cruel act which has arbitrarily deprived these women of their labour and driven them underground by stealth'.[9]

When the Bill came up for its third reading on 1 August Londonderry once again opposed it. The Bill, he admitted had 'been much altered and defaced' but 'it was hurried through in haste, and founded upon misrepresentation, and it would be far better to delay the matter,' and that the Report was filled with cases 'selected from the worst and most unfavourable mines, and though the favourable mines infinitely exceeded them in number, an impression unfavourable to the whole was thus excited in the public mind.'[10]

Nevertheless, despite the opposition of Londonderry and others, Ashley's Bill, *Mines and Collieries Act 1842*, was passed that same day, the first gender-specific act of parliament, and as of 1 March 1843 all women, no matter what age, were no longer allowed to work underground and no boys under ten – but as an Inspector of Mines was not appointed for another eight years it meant the law in many places was simply ignored.

Those who had objected to the Report on the employment of girls and women underground, had a point as all was not as it seemed. Their employment had already been on the wane for some time for a number of reasons, not least that boys were stronger than women and could do more of the work. Men also refused to work alongside women; these were predominantly small communities where everyone knew everyone else and society had strict rules about interactions between the sexes and men often worked naked so having women around was not acceptable.

Estimates from the census of 1841 show about 115,000 men, 41,000 boys under the age of 20, and 4,000 females employed in coal and iron mines.[11] Denise Bates in her article *The Scandal of Female Miners* notes that the investigators were hard pushed not only to find women workers but also those who were working topless.[12] Making it even more disingenuous that illustrations of topless women were included in the Report.

Part of the reason for the decline was due, not just to men's attitudes but those of the women. As Bates points out, many spoke of returning home exhausted and having to cater for the family, of the cuts and bruises which marred their bodies, cuts which could become infected, and feet and hands crushed. Many were too tired to wash but forced themselves to do so for the sake of decency. They spoke of having to try and do all the housework on the weekends (a familiar refrain even today) and would sleep for most of Sunday, or enjoy the fresh air as a change from being underground. By the time of the Report, many women had already made the move to the pit surface but for those who had continued to work underground, the new Act was not popular.

For women and working families the new law often meant a reduction in income. Throughout the nineteenth century, for women seeking work outside of domestic service, jobs were hard to come by. Women thrown out of work often had to find employment elsewhere and with so many suddenly out of work, they had to compete with each other. Some families were forced onto relief costing the county more by putting them out of work. In certain areas, such as the north of England and Scotland, families were badly hit so it is not surprising that girls and women ignored the law.

A year after the publication of the Report a 'South Wales Collier' from Abergavenny wrote to the *Mining Journal* in June 1843 about an article which had appeared in a recent issue entitled *Female Labour in Collieries?* Part of the letter writer's complaint was regarding comments made by MP and Alderman, William Thompson (1792–1854), a man who had interests in iron mining in Penydrarron and Tredegar. Thompson stated that in South Wales 'females in mines and collieries was utterly unknown' adding that he believed 'the people of that part of the country would submit to ten times the misery and distress they are suffering under, rather than permit their wives and daughters to engage in such degrading labour'. The letter-writing collier disagreed:

Now sir, I am no advocate for employing females in mines and collieries, but I am an advocate for the truth on all occasions. The worthy Alderman must possess a very imperfect knowledge of the district with which he is connected. In one of those works in this said district, it was my task to fill up the government of females and children employed therein, and in that work - and in one department of that work, viz., the mining, were nearly one hundred females employed, about sixty within the mine, and the others on the surface; within the last fortnight, it has been my painful duty, by order of my employers, to discharge a certain number of miners, amongst which were many robust females, performing some of the arduous duties of a miner, such as blasting the ground away with powder, to which I have frequently been an eye witness: one old miner, in particular, with a large family, all girls, told me if his three daughters, which he employed with him in the mine, were drawn out, the whole family must become inmates of the Union poor-house, as his own labour and exertions would not support them.[13]

Evidence to support the collier's letter can be seen in the 1841 census for St. Issells. The Thomas family consisted of a 57-year-old father and a 58-year-old mother both described as colliers. Their two daughters, Elizabeth (23) and Susanne (18) were also colliers with their 14-year-old brother William. If the three women were put out of work and could find nothing else, the family would be dependent on a 57- and an 14-year-old. Similarly, if Ann Morgan (50) was to become unemployed her sole support would be her 15-year-old collier son. Labourer Sophia Lewis (12) told the 1842 Report commissioner that she and her three siblings' wages were given to her widowed mother, 'who keeps house'.[14] For families with mainly daughters and the mother confined at home, young single women would have had to contribute to the family income.

And there are many more families like this.

Dressing as Men

In order to evade the law, women resorted to other methods, something which concerned Jacob Pleydell-Bouverie, 4th Earl of Radnor (1815–1889). In his protest again Lord Ashley's Bill he said preventing women from working would force them to dress as men in order to keep working[15] – something with a precedent as many women did crossdress, often for many years.

As thin children wearing similar clothes could rarely be told apart it made it easier for a girl to be mistaken for a boy. In Bolton, following a colliery explosion in 1846 three women killed had been 'taken into the pit dressed as boys'.[16]

In Wigan, which provides most of the information about women working in collieries, the *Northern Star* exposed a Mr Preston who, apparently, in an 'attempt to gull the public, by having the females dressed up in male attire!!'[17] They would also cut their hair short, in the manner of a man's.[18] A short line in *The Cornwall Chronicle*, a Tasmania newspaper, in their roundup 'from the latest English papers' noted under the title 'Necessity stronger than law' that 'the poor woman ejected by the recent law from the coal-pits have been numerously at work in them in men's clothes'.[19]

There are numerous other examples throughout the nineteenth century. Elizabeth Ann Holman was arrested in 1858 and in court was described as a short and very boyish-looking girl, so well disguised that it was almost difficult to believe that she belonged to the 'softer sex'. She had worked in Devon and Cornwall as a miner.[20] Josiah Charles Stephenson, originally believed to have come from Scotland, died in a quiet colliery village of Etherley, Durham in 1869. For fifty years Josiah had lived in the community and worked as a miner before getting married to a servant girl from the village inn. After the marriage, Josiah gave up mining and made besoms and pipe-clay rubbers, which the couple sold in surrounding villages but after twenty-three years together the wife died with journalists dismissing Josiah's grief, writing that he 'professed' to lament her loss. There was a second marriage but after several years together they parted. Prior to death, Josiah had lain in bed sick and 'strongly resisted' anyone coming close and 'persisted in wearing trousers in bed'.[21]

Sarah Madge's death in 1899, aged sixty-seven, appeared under the headline *A Masculine Lady*. Sal, as she was popularly known, had worked at the Whitehaven Collieries, and regularly wore a man's peaked cap; a jacket, and waistcoat; enjoyed a short clay pipe, and sat astride her wagon horse.[22] In Durham, an unnamed individual worked in the colliery for fifty years as a man, both in the pits and on the farm. When he died in 1895, he had been married for thirty years.[23] In Manchester, John Jones was prosecuted for creating a disturbance and threatening to beat his wife, Sarah. Prosecuted under the birth name of Ann M'Gaul, or Ann Hughes, she was accused of passing as a man for six years in order to earn 2s 6d a day as a banksman in a colliery, instead of 1s a day at 'women's work'.[24]

In Wales, Edith Philip who lived with her collier father and family in the engine house at the Glyndyrys Pit, Abercanaid, created a sensation in

1901 when she suddenly disappeared from her home. A large search was launched, including dredging the canals, but it turned out she had taken her brother's clothes and found work at the South pit, in the Plymouth mine as an assistant to collier Matthew Thomas as a pit boy underground.[25]

Cross-working and cross-living also gave freedom to those individuals we would today possibly regard as lesbian or trans, such as an individual described by Mary Louisa Gordon (1861–1941), a doctor who worked with women in a number of institutions, including prisons. In her book *Penal Discipline* (1922), Gordon wrote about an inmate who was frequently arrested for stealing men's clothes in the 1890s.

> I told her that there was no law against her wearing men's clothing decently, if she did not steal it. After she had two more convictions, I fitted her out with the clothes she wanted, and paid her fare to South Wales. She got work in a night shift, and lay on her back in a coal-pit hewing coal. All the year she did well, and wrote that she was living respectably. In her letter she said: "This is the first Easter for ten years that I have spent out of prison." She suffered many severe vicissitudes, including a mental attack, but came to prison very little in after years. To make useful citizens out of lost vagabonds cannot be done on prejudice of any kind.[26]

Those who did cross-dress locally to carry on working after the 1842 Act would most likely have been known in the neighbourhood and they seem to have suffered no adverse reaction despite the wearing of men's clothes being against public opinion. In many cases, however, it was not necessary as there was so little policing that women could continue to work illegally after the act – only one inspector was appointed for an entire county, and it was in the interest of coal mine owners to keep on low paid women. In Lord Ashley's speech to Parliament, he quoted a manager who stated, 'One reason why women are used so frequently in the coal-pits is, that a girl of twenty will work for 2s. a day, or less, and a man of that age would want 3s. 6d.'[27] The employment of women continued because they were cheaper than men and because they were illegal, owners could reduce the wages even lower. At a meeting of the Manchester Geological Society held in Wigan in 1871, a Mr E.W. Binney related a story of meeting a woman at the Ince pit who told him 'I have an old woman at home to support: I wish these chaps that got the women taken out of the pits would pay me the 3 shillings a week less wages which I get now.' She had been getting 11 shillings a week before, but after the Act passed, as she could only work 'on the sly' her wages were reduced to 8 shillings a week.'[28]

Getting around the Act

For some families, it meant having to move. A Mr Peace, an agent for Lord Balcarres, near Wigan, wrote in 1846:

> About a dozen men have left our Aberdeen Colliery and moved to Burgh Colliery near Chorley because there, their wives and daughters are allowed to work down the pit. I am reliably informed that upwards of 30 women are employed in one pit at that colliery. It is the property of Mr Hargreaves of Bolton. Our Aberdeen Pit is in consequence of this being carried on with about two thirds of its full complement which causes us great loss; the expense of keeping open, ventilated and drained the workings as well as engineers and other numerous attendants paid by day wages being nearly the same for a small produce of coal as for a large.[29]

Many mine owners were also local magistrates and when women were discovered working underground, owners were often fined a derisory amount which did nothing to prevent them from continuing to employ women and girls in dire conditions. Or the father/husband was fined as the woman's money was paid to the man he could therefore be seen as her 'employer'.

Joshua Richardson, a mining expert from Neath, in his 1848 book *On the prevention of accidents in mines*, noted that:

> it was anticipated by many persons interested in the subject, that the publication of these reports would induce such an improvement in the management of mines, as to supersede the necessity of legislative interference.[30]

It did not, and women continued to work underground.

Hugh Seymour Tremenheere (1804–1893), the first Commissioner of Mines, produced fifteen government reports between 1844 and 1858 researching the population of the mining districts, descriptions of strikes, education, housing, and other matters. Although biased towards mine owners he provided an insight into the lives of miners and their families.

In his 1846 report to the government, Tremenheere noted that convictions under the Act had been obtained at Wigan, Halifax, and in Monmouthshire.[31] On 3 December he visited the mining districts of Monmouthshire and Brecon but he notified the mine owners by letter of his visit, as all inspectors did. He found that the main provision of the Act had not been generally adhered to and that the employment of female underground 'was acknowledged to have been continued in eight of the works, and also of boys under ten years of age in several more.' He added a disapproving note that the 'payment of wages in public houses, by contractors, was very common'. In Glamorganshire, he stated 'female labour under ground was either never employed, or has been entirely given up'.

On his rounds through South Wales Tremenheere found that about 70 females and many boys under ten had been, according to mine managers, dismissed on the receipt of Tremenheere's letters – but how long would their employment have continued if he had not visited and how quickly would they have gone back? Three years later in 1849, according to a *Times* report, a manager in one South Wales company stated that he had turned out 70 women and girls, but 'that it was not until he had been there a month that he was able to discover their presence; and he had no doubt that since then many had from time to time gone back again.'[32]

Nevertheless, Tremenheere reassured readers, mine owners had promised they would see the Act was complied with in the future.

Visiting Pembrokeshire, where women working underground before the Act was common, he found that the practice had been 'pretty much abandoned', and in the few instances where women did work the managers pleaded justification in that the male collieries received low wages and there was little alternative work for the women. Of those that were employed the greater number were orphans or widows, or girls who had lost their fathers but when Tremenheere pointed out the managers were breaking the law they promised to find other ways of engaging the women either by work on the pit bank or other jobs. Tremenheere was confident in the manager's assurances, that the practice would stop adding, that the 'complaints of coal proprietors in other localities, that they are subject to undue competition from those who continue to use female labour, will suggest an additional reason to the latter for the necessity of its final abandonment within a short period.'

One of the reasons women continued to be employed was the need for labour. Richardson claimed that the increased consumption of coal and iron and the opening of new mines had driven up demand. Employers in Monmouth and Glamorgan told Tremenheere they were so desperate they had sent people to Pembrokeshire to attract those on low wages to move east. The 1851 census shows that of the 224 women identified 14% were born outside the county they were working in.

That women continued to work underground can often be found in records of deaths such as that of Martha John on 21 July 1847 in St. Issells when three 13-year-olds were killed underground.[33] However, where tragedies did occur female deaths were often covered up. In the Landshipping colliery disaster of 14 February 1844, about forty people lost their lives underground when the mine was flooded. Basil H.J. Hughes in *Pembrokeshire Parishes, Places & People* noted:

> There is also a suggestion that some, if not all, of the names listed "boy" were probably women, this shows that the exploitation of women and children working in the mines was still happening.[34]

Coflein, the online catalogue of archaeology, buildings, industrial and maritime heritage in Wales, also suggests that when a memorial to the Landshipping disaster was erected in 2002 by the villagers the first seven names were only given as 'miner' – these are believed to be women and children.[35]

Unfit for the Duties of Women

One of the notable features in the discussions around ending female employment at mines was that much of the blame was placed on the women. When Lord Ashley introduced the Bill into the House of Commons, in his long speech, he felt that women at work 'causes a total ignorance of all domestic duties; they know nothing that they ought to know; they are rendered unfit for the duties of women by overwork, and become utterly demoralized.' This detrimental effect, he believed would harm society and the country itself. 'It is bad enough if you corrupt the man, but if you corrupt the woman, you poison the waters of life at the very fountain,' because it made women unfit for the duties of a mother.

Tremenheere blamed 'overcrowded houses, or the dirt and discomfort around them, or both, had contributed to destroy the decencies of domestic life, and to drive old and young to the beer-shops and public-houses, which offered their temptations at every step.' He noted that wages were predominantly spent on eating and drinking and that women went with the men to pubs and beer shops or, if they remained at home would often 'send their daughters for spirits'. Once again, the blame is on women:

> With the participation of the female part of the population in these demoralizing habits the prospect of amendment in this particular seems remote.[36]

In 1847 the Reverend P.M. Richards argued mixing of the sexes in the workplace caused women to become 'bold, impudent, and wantonly vicious and sing the vilest songs and publicly behave in the most indecent manner.'[37]

The Treachery of the Blue Books

The nineteenth century was a period of social upheaval in Wales. The poverty of the working classes and the injustices and oppression by landowners led to public unrest and campaigns for social and political reform were held, often attended by large crowds. These events were widely covered in the press and as critics often cited the root cause was the lack of education in Wales, an inquiry into the state of education was commissioned, the *Reports of the Commissioners of Inquiry into the State of Education in Wales*. Three commissioners, R.R.W. Lingen, Jellynger C. Symons, and H.R. Vaughan Johnson, travelled throughout Wales to collect evidence, the work was completed by 3 April 1847 and published in three volumes in July that year.

In later years, the *Education in Wales* report became known as *Brad y Llyfrau Gleision* (Treachery of the Blue Books) due to the unjust way people in Wales were written about. Comments such as 'unfortunately they seldom apply the wages thus earned to any means of improvement, but solely to the fund for sensual and animal pleasure'. The piece went on to describe a 'promising young girl' who was removed from school to pick coal at the pit's mouth at one of the large ironworks where she could earn 2s 6d or 3s a week. A lady who tried to persuade the parents to change their mind went to the home and the father declared he could not afford to spare the girl's wages – 'and this he said whilst pouring rum into his tea'.[38]

Where children did go to school, most were from clergy and farmers' families, the working classes not being able to afford to keep their children in school as they would earn from 2s 6d to 10–12s a week. Although some mines did attempt to provide education such as the Colliers' and Miners' School in Aberdare.

The Rev. James William Morris, headmaster of Ystrad Meyric and Lledrod School blamed the mine owners:

> The working classes have a right to send their children to this school. About two years ago we had a good many, but the mine works have taken them off, so that only three or four are now in the school.[39]

A sentiment echoed by Thomas Francis, a shopkeeper in Wrexham:

> The children are employed in these mines at a very early age, some to carry food to their parents, others to clear the banks, and many work in the mines. The mines and quarries are for coal, lime, iron, &c. The

children are employed in the mines and pits to open the doors for ventilating the pits, to drive horses which are employed below, and to drag small carts on their hands and knees. The average age at which children are employed is 8. There are a great number of girls and young women employed, not in the pits but on the banks. Their employment is to carry coals on their heads to their own families, to remove obstructions from the mouths of the pits, to wind up materials from the bottom by the wheels, and in many cases to load coals. They acquire a taste for this employment at an early age, and will often leave good situations in respectable families, when they are grown to be young women, in order to return to their old occupation. Cases of this kind have occurred in Wrexham not a month ago. There is great want of instruction for girls in the neighbourhood of the works. The young women have no kind of industrial skill. When they marry, they are unable to make or mend any article of clothing, even a pair of stockings for their husbands. The husband's wages must be spent in buying in the towns an article which costs twice the money, and does not last half the time. In consequence of this, though the wages are high, the people are often in a miserable condition.[40]

Moving to the Pit Head

For decades after the passing of the 1842 Act women continued to work underground not just in the UK but around the world. The UK was the first European country to ban women and young children from working underground, although throughout 1817–25 Canada had been working towards a total ban. Some dates for other countries include:

1854 Austria/Hungary	1915 Norway, New Zealand (1915–26)
1874 France	1917 Bulgaria, Nigeria
1878 Germany	1919 Belgium
1901–29 Australia	1923 China
1906 the Netherlands	1924 Poland
1907 Italy	1928 Hungary, Romania and Japan
1910 Spain	1929 India
1911 South Africa	1931 Chile
1912 Sweden	1932 Brazil

For some of the later dates, this was because women did not generally work underground and it was merely a formality. Despite the 1878 legislation, French women were required to work underground in German mines during the First World War.[41]

Chapter 7

Unsexing Themselves

> Who saw the wrong? who brought the change about?
> 'Midst cavern'd earth, who found the sufferer out?
> There, with two worlds existing o'er her head,
> The female miner toil'd to earn her bread:
> Debarr'd the light, and shiv'ring with the cold,
> Is man a piteous object to behold:
> But in the tender sex, so frail and weak,
> Blush, tyrant, blush! the truth 'tis pain to speak, —
> Hard to believe! Doom'd to both toil and pain,
> Thy limbs deform'd, and gag'd by grinding chain;
> Thy growth all stinted, and thy beauty marr'd:
> Is woman's virtue worth no more regard?
> Is woman's love despised? —her peace, her all: —
> And man still unconcern'd to see her fall?
>
> Walter Kemp *Sketches of politicians, a poem* 1850

Following the condemnation of women during and after the 1842 Act, criticism had not abated and during the 1850s more voices were added not just about the coal mining industry, but other areas of women's work for the effect of the 1842 Act had:

> formalised and legitimised femininity as inherently dependent, and female morality as a valid basis for government intervention. Women and children became the same legal category, and recommendations for the latter category began to implicitly include the former.[1]

The impact of these attitudes focused others to consider legislation on regulating female employment. Throughout the nineteenth century efforts to ban females on pit banks resurfaced constantly and the referencing to the 'unsexing' of women and their alleged immorality was often cited as the reason. These efforts were presented as protecting the poor dears and despite doing laborious work in many areas of employment, including factory work and farming, women were infantilised as only capable of domestic work and child-rearing.

Unsexing

In October 1854 a local inspector, Edwin J. Roberts, published *A visit to Merthyr Tydfil* in the *Monmouthshire Merlin*. In Merthyr, women often worked with coal and coke at the ironworks and he wrote

> I had been struck with the number of girls that were employed around the kilns and furnaces. They were engaged in breaking up masses of coke, limestone, and "mine," with large and heavy hammers - operations which facilitated the labours of the men, and rendered the matter to be fused the more permeable to heat by exposure of a lesser surface. On the sloping mound, covered with coal dust, two or three had flung themselves down, either from weariness, or until the masses already broken had been carried away. They were tall well-grown girls, and clad in thick, warm, but dingy clothing; and, as their faces were as grimed as those of the men, it was not quite easy to obtain a correct idea of their features. Others were standing, hammer in hand, casting a half-curious look after us as we passed.

A feature of Robert's account is one that often came up when discussing the 'girls', that of lax moral judgements, and he describes an incident of a couple larking around:

> In one of the openings near the kilns, and opposite to the furnaces, a huge giant of a fellow had pulled a girl to the ground; or perhaps, finding her reclining there had, in his bearish play, cast himself beside her, and while she was half-laughing, half-screaming, and ineffectually struggling in his great grasp, he was stifling her with kisses and, though there were a dozen or twenty men and girls about, none seemed to pay the slightest attention to them. As his large limbs sprawled about, the whole suggested a grossness which did not exist, for it was only a "lark" – a piece of play – though coarse enough in all conscience.

Although Roberts acknowledged it was all a 'lark' he brought in another aspect of the criticism, their lack of femininity – the lark rendering 'these young girls unfeminine'. He blamed their work, 'while their irreconcilable labour taxed their strength, or else made them masculine in form as well as habit'.

As he watched two women working, he expressed an admiration, bordering on lasciviousness, and hints of language often used by those describing people such as the 'noble savage':

a portion of the machinery where a huge hammer was crushing masses of limestone into fragments, and which was attended by two girls, as fine-grown and elegantly-limbed young creatures as I had ever seen; proving, too, that their arduous work tended to the development of the frame, for handsomer arms and finer busts could not be met with. With heavy hammers they broke the large pieces, and with spades fed the trough in which the great hammer was at work. They scarcely left off their work as we passed; but all the grime and dust of their labour could not hide the pleasing lineaments of their young faces. Calm and modest as they were, with gentle eyes of a blueish tinge, their brown hair being only partly confined beneath their 'kerchiefs, I thought I had never seen anything so soft and charming in its retiring femininity, in contrast as it was with the rough accessories of the enormous mass of physical and machine labour around them the noise of hammers, the shoutings of the men, the roar of the blast-furnace, the sounding of the pistons, the hissing of the steam, and the almost infernal din and aspect of the whole. They retrieved the whole from whatever there was of the repulsive in its aspect.[2]

Roberts was not alone, and during the 1850s writers and travellers (a number referring to themselves as ramblers) featured women at mines. Most expressed pity, as the poem above by a little-known poet, Walter Kemp, whose extensive verse on politicians mourned the toil of the women and of their 'beauty marr'd' and her fall – a continuation of the 'unsexed' being.

An 1856 editorial, in the *Merthyr Telegraph*, entitled *Female Labourers* was also damming, 'how unnatural the word sounds in this English land of ours,' before imperialistically but falsely claiming 'where women are treated with more respect, and more deference is shown them, than in any country in the world'. Femininity, argued the writer with a flush of purple prose, is dependent on men, it 'is a synonym for gentleness, a meek confiding being; the ivy that twines around the oak, braving the storm with it, upheld by the vigorous tree, and dying but with its supporter'. However, his condemnation continued to the miners themselves:

> Do our readers recollect the time when females descended into the deep pits, and toiled in rude contact with too often dissolute men? That was a stain upon our civilization one, happily, that was not long suffered to exist, with all its hideous demoralizing results.[3]

Labour and the Poor

One of the most extensive examinations of working life in the 1850s was a series of articles written for the London newspaper the *Morning Chronicle*. These articles, entitled *Labour and the Poor* were inspired by the work of Henry Mayhew (1812–1887), a journalist, playwright, and advocate of reform and a co-founder of the satirical publication *Punch*. His article, *London and the Poor* (1849) caused a sensation when it was published so the paper commissioned a series of 'letters' investigating the working and living conditions of the poor throughout England and Wales. It was hoped these reports would bring about much-needed changes. The paper employed a number of 'special correspondents' who travelled around the two countries and the first of the letters was published in October 1849. At the time this work was unparalleled, its impact was huge, and its continuing historical importance is unquestionable. The series was to run for two years and consisted of 222 letters,[4] a selection of which appeared in book form by the publisher Ditto Books. Now the original articles can be accessed via the Gale Database found in any public library computer terminal or online through a library membership number.

The series proved to be extremely popular with the public and were widely read throughout the world but they caused particular consternation among the British middle classes who were horrified by what they were reading and donations flooded into the paper who set up a special fund for distribution.

The Special Correspondents for *Labour and the Poor* were recruited from well-known journalists and writers but the Correspondent from Wales is as yet unknown. His information appeared as a series of articles entitled *The Mining and Manufacturing Districts of Wales* (1850).

There were a number of issues that worried all these writers.

Immorality

The familiar refrain of immorality had not abated since the 1842 Report. Particularly, as the *Monmouthshire Merlin* complained, the law regarding females in mine and coal levels in Merthyr was being violated. 'It is bad enough,' they wrote, 'to employ them at the furnaces and on the tips, but it is infinitely worse to employ them in dark recesses, with persons of the opposite sex.'[5]

Irrespective of whether it was underground or overground, it was this close association with men that worried people.

Tremenheere, the Commissioner of Mines, was also highly critical of mining women:

while it is notorious that their association with the course description of men employed in that branch of labour, exposes them to every deteriorating influence of language, manners, and habits. It has been constantly asserted by every well-wisher of the improvement of the working classes in those districts, that the continuance of this mode of employing is most injurious to the progress of good morals, and to every domestic virtue and comfort, and that a general agreement among the employers to put an end to it is one of the steps now most urgently required to be adopted by them.[6]

However, the Welsh Correspondent for *Labour and the Poor*, having spoken to 'a gentleman of observant mind' was informed that the mining women were 'superior in manners, deportment, and conduct, to those who work in the cotton and other factories, and that 'their morals are even better than, surrounded continually as they are by temptations, could be expected.' Once again came the familiar refrain, 'circumstances have unsexed them' and 'their sympathies and ideas are like those of men more than those properly belonging to women'.

Having ideas like those of men and being ignorant of 'every domestic virtue and comfort' made them, most writers claimed, bad wives and mothers. This was something the Correspondent featured heavily. While he was sceptical of their supposed immorality, he did conform to a general sentiment that female mineworkers were bad wives and mothers but allowed that, having spent so much time from youth working at the mines, it was impossible for them to 'acquire the virtues which beautify the female character, when it is developed and formed at home'. As this affected most women it meant that when young girls were growing up, they had nobody in the home to teach them how to keep house.

While he did not blame the women for these failings, the Correspondent did feel their children were growing up exposed to bad habits and vice and because of this, husbands turned to drink[7] – so in the end, it was still all the woman's fault.

The writer believed, as did others, that the type of work at mines made women unsuitable for domestic service where they could have learnt how to take care of a home. Their masculine attitudes and lack of understanding of basic domestic tasks meant they were totally unfit as servants and could not apply for these types of jobs, making them even more dependent on mine work or general labouring.

In light of this, there had been a growing public call to educate girls and the Correspondent approved of the suggestion but reminded his readers that domestic duties could not be taught in school.

Meanwhile, Tremenheere was investigating if the 1842 Act was being adhered to, and in his 1856 report he echoed the Correspondent's comments, listing the women's failings as:

1. She does not know how to keep a house clean and tidy.
2. She cannot cook.
3. She knows nothing of the management required to make her husband's earnings go as far as possible.
4. She is ignorant of the proper management of children.

Tremenheere added, 'so sensible are the men of the value of these qualifications in a wife, that according to the observation of a gentleman who has been conversant with these districts for many years, they look out for wives among the girls who have been in domestic service. These are sure to find husbands, and nearly every tidy house is that wherein resides a woman who has been in service. These facts and suggestions are particularly applicable to this town, where, to any thoughtful observer, the evil is ever perceptible.'[8]

This attitude was in no way restricted to mining women, all those doing heavy laborious work received the same type of criticism. Agricultural workers, fisherwomen, factory women, were all treated as a 'race apart' and were subject to the same claim of poor mothers and wives, bad housekeepers, immorality, and crossing gender lines.

Education

Education was seen as the means to end all this criticism. Despite schools existing for some thirty years attendance was still low. In addition to the schools set up by the collieries, the National Society for Promoting Religious Education had been set up in 1811 to provide a number of schools in England and Wales for the poor – but they were based on the teachings of the Church of England despite much of Wales being nonconformist and they were in English while most local people spoke only Welsh.

A Rector, interviewed by the Correspondent, told him, 'the National Schools … are not half attended. The good old dame schools are unknown. Troops of children, who should be at school, are literally infesting the streets, acquiring those habits we see matured in the Sabbath breaker and the drunkard. The mortality amongst children is exceedingly high!'

The fault, of course, was with the women as the Correspondent explained 'Women! they are at the bottom of everything, for good or evil; they sway our thoughts, and rule our actions' and went on to suggest that it:

should be particularly requested that female children be sent to the various schools in the neighbourhood. Parents who violate the act by sending their children to work before they are ten years of age should be punished. Gradually, the assistance of females in the iron works and on the tips may be dispensed with and if some means could be found to employ them in a more feminine capacity, a priceless bono would be granted.

He urgently recommended that night schools be opened

> St. David's National Schools could be opened in the evening twice or thrice in the week. Females, from 13 or 14 to 20 years of age would, we doubt not, attend in great numbers when they know the ladies of Merthyr will undertake the pleasing duty of training them up to be good and gentle help-mates for the ruder portion of humanity. Great results must not be immediately expected. "Our civilization," said Disraeli, "is as slow in growth as our oaks." All- wise, and great, and valuable movements are slow in their operation. Some years may pass away, but not many, before the influence of these remedies will be felt; then we may perceive a higher moral tone amongst the people; comfort and happiness existing where neither had ever been before and trace with pleasure amongst the rising generation, signs of a high and hopeful character.

The Correspondent seemed to expect girls and women who were working long hours and still had to cook and clean at home (no matter how badly), to find time to attend evening schools. Once again, all of society's ills are laid on women and once they are educated to be 'good and gentle help-mates' to men there would be a 'higher moral tone amongst the people; comfort and happiness'.

A surprising attitude, given elsewhere the Correspondent, and others, wrote and sympathised with the harsh conditions the girls and women were working under. A Rector from the Merthyr and Dowlais area, where a number of schools had been established said that the local women's intelligence and quickness were beyond praise, that they learnt to read in an astonishingly brief time. But these opinions were drowned out by the criticism.

In addition, the cost of education could be difficult for families. In an editorial piece for the *Merthyr Telegraph* in 1858 discussing the cut in wages, they noted in the ironworks at Dowlais the poorest male labourers were receiving 12s a week, while the tip girls received 5s a week.[9] Hardly enough to live on, let alone pay for education.

Harsh Working Conditions

In 1853 Herbert Francis Mackworth (1823–1858), Inspector of Mines gave a lecture in which he claimed mining had advanced very little since the end of the sixteenth century when George Owen of Henllys (quoted in chapter one) had 'so graphically described it'. Speaking of a mine he had visited that year in Pembroke, Mackworth described the harsh conditions, adding, 'Women, as is usual in Pembrokeshire, perform part of the severest labour, and land the coal at the pit's mouth'[10] showing that windlass women were still working.

The Correspondent made similar comments:

> The pitiful conditions of these girls once very forcibly struck me, when, on a day of heavy rain and high wind, I saw them at work on the mountain-side, with the rain literally running off their coal-bedaubed petticoats over their boots, in black streams, to the ground.[11]

He went on to describe meeting an old Irish woman who was wheeling coal to the kilns:

> Living in an atmosphere of smoke she was necessarily dirty, but her clothes were thick and warm. She told me she had followed that occupations in the same place for two years. I asked her to show me her dinner, and went with her to a hole in the wall where she had placed it. She pulled out a bag from which she drew a large piece of fair wheaten bread. "What no cheese?" said I. "Devil a bit do I have," replied she, with a smile. "It's five and sixpence a week I gits, and out of it my rent is a shilling. My boots costs me most, because the fire burns them. Since I have been at this work I have suffered much from the sulphur it makes me cough, and I cannot sleep at night. I had no cough before."[12]

He later added that when he examined other meals of both men and women, they contained no meat and in their tins were only bread and butter and tea.

Another woman referred to as E_ (24) was a coke-girl at Pen-y-Darren ironworks where she had been for three years. It was her job to prepare the coal for coking, a job noted the Correspondent, 'that requires considerable skill, or the mass will not burn evenly and make good coke.' She earned five shillings a week and paid out of it a 'trifle' for the doctor and a fund for provision for sickness. She had to lift from the trams pieces of coal which weighed over a hundredweight and carry them to the pit for eleven hours a day throughout the year. She did not live with her parents but lodged with an old couple in a well-furnished house who treated her almost like a daughter, but she visited her father regularly adding, 'without the assistance of my father and mother I could not live. My clothes cost the most, because I must have the best and working clothes'. Her lodgings cost ninepence a week. She could not read or write, 'more shame for me, although I had the chance to learn'. She worked in all weathers and would 'stand the rain and wind often all day long, because we must work'. The Correspondent added that she 'seemed a very thoughtful girl'[13] yet after writing all this he still thought it a good idea for her to attend, and pay for, an education.

The Correspondent also wrote of 'tippers' those individuals, men included, who emptied the trams of coal, and he described one perilous position at the 'balance pits'. Full trams ascended as empty ones, weighted with water, descended. As the loaded tram reached the pit mouth the women dragged it away but to do so they had to step onto the platform which had raised the tram; they then hauled at a line overhead via a pulley which opened a valve letting water out from the bottom tram but to do this one woman had to suspend a foot over the platform to release the valve. The Correspondent was not sure if this was a common method as he only saw it at one pit but when he later referenced the 1842 Act he found it was illegal for everyone except males over 15 to have charge of any engine including windlasses. If found guilty the mine owner could be fined between £20–50 half of which went to the informer and the other half to the poor of the parish. The Correspondent notified the owners of the pit where he had witnessed the infringement but generously suspected they were 'unaware'[14] and so they were not fined.

Evasions of the Law

It was precisely these kinds of accidents and infringements of the law that Tremenheere was determined to stop. He set out to ensure the laws outlined in the 1842 Act were adhered to and set up a system of inspectors around the country – marred by the fact that owners were notified of a visit. He also employed policemen to watch the shaft mouth and paid local professional gentlemen 25 shillings per week to produce evidence leading to a conviction.[15] However, many cases were overlooked when owners simply promised to change. Nevertheless, prosecutions for women working underground continued until the late 1850s.

For those working above ground, Tremenheere, in his 1850 annual report, estimated that '200 women and girls were still working in collieries in South Wales, many of whom were only eleven or twelve years of age'.[16]

In 1850 Tremenheere specified one regional characteristic of South Wales where many of the mines did not have a pit-mouth but were 'accessed by a number of corridors cut into the hillside'. These, it was claimed, made it more difficult to detect women working underground and 'provided the potential for deviancy and subverting the authority of the Law'. Aberdare employed women and one particularly notorious area, he continued, was at Nantyglo where the practice had 'never been entirely eradicated'.[17]

To address the problem of a lack of compliance with the 1842 Act, Tremenheere had been influential in setting up the Coal Mines Inspection Act (1850) introduced due to the growing public concern over the high number of accidents in mines. The number of coal mine inspectors was increased to four – still not enough to prevent owners from breaking the law in regard to the employment of children and women underground. By 1952 there were eight inspectors. However, an underground inspection was still difficult and even Lord Ashley admitted it was 'altogether impossible, and, indeed, if it were possible it would not be safe... I for one, should be very loath to go down the shaft for the purpose of doing some act that was likely to be distasteful to the colliers below.' In his 1854 report, Tremenheere noted on two occasions 'persons attempted inspection of their own accord, were maltreated, and very nearly lost their lives'.[18]

In 1858, *The Times* reported on an inquiry that was to take place regarding the illegal employment of women underground in Wales, stating: 'It is understood that in the district of Merthyr the law is daily violated in regard to the employment of girls and young women in the mines and coal levels.'[19]

In the same year, the *Cardiff Times* reported that the local inspector claimed Tremenheere was particularly critical of these female mine workers.

> very little progress can be made in the moral improvement of the population generally. The employment of the females upon the pit banks and cinder tips has long been pointed out as one degrading to the female character.[20]

One particularly degrading aspect that worried many people, was the women's appearance.

Appearance

The Correspondent for *Labour and the Poor* wrote a long description of the 'class' of females in the iron works and collieries of Wales 'they are below the middle stature, small, and delicately formed,' he wrote, 'and the stranger, when he sees them clustered at their dinner in the works, or returning home at the close of the day, congregated as is their fashion together, can scarcely fail to be struck by their prettiness, and by the clear tone of their voices when they chatter or sing.'

Not all his accounts were flattering, however, such as when he describes women on their way to work at 5.45 am, noting they were interchangeable with male coal workers:

> girls clad in a rather tightly-fitting canvas dress, with sleeves, reaching from the bosom to below the knees, gathered in around the waist, and worn over a woollen petticoat, are also on their way to the works, where twelve hours of heavy labour, lifting and piling iron, loading and unloading trams, stacking coal at the coking pits, or making fire-bricks, are before them. A small bonnet of small coarse black straw (flattened at the crown from the habit of carrying home coal for firing, and other burdens on the head), beneath which, and with a corner pendant over the back, is worn a handkerchief of some bright colour, black woollen stockings, and thick quarter boots, complete the costume of these hard-working females. Can I say they are cheerful? No doubt many are light-hearted, and many resigned to their hard lot. But the instinct of the woman's heart for home duties, for that which is gentle, benign, and good, must revolt at the life of masculine toil and long-tasked physical endurance which they are compelled to undergo.[21]

Many writers had a low opinion of collier families. An unknown writer in the *Merthyr Telegraph* in a piece entitled *Our Welsh Cole Pits* (1857) wrote:

> a little village of white-washed cottages; and here a labouring community lived, loved, and died like the rest of humanity. Colliers dwelt in this village, men, generally speaking, of rude habits and little forethought; living up to, and in many cases far beyond, their small means; yet managing by some ingenuity on their wives' part to make both ends meet once a month.

He continued that the village 'in a dingle amongst the Welsh hills' was rarely visited by travelling salesmen with their stores of 'cheap knives and candlesticks, Hodge's razors and little fineries for the aspiring collier youth or tip girl' and presented them as something 'other':

> some of our Welsh women are rude and untrained, the heart of a tip girl, or a collier's wife beats as lovingly, feels as acutely, as those of more polished women – more so perhaps; for to the uncultivated there is no recourse no harbour of consolation into which the shattered hulk may drift.[22]

This lack of consolation was highlighted by another unnamed writer in *Notes by a Rambler No V.: A run through the hill* for the *Merthyr Telegraph* (1858) who drew attention to the longing of the tip girl for nice things:

> Glimpses now and then we had of well-built houses, gay shops too came in sight, with such *"dears"* of things; looking *so* enticing, and such loves of bonnets; with ribbons – ah! many a tip girl gets the heart-ache before those windows and those ribbons![23]

A similar lack of consolation appears in 1856 in a piece on the Cwm Rhondda tragedy:

> The tip girl and the collier's wife can love as fondly, and mourn as bitterly, as those whose feelings have been refined by education. Perhaps more so. The educated person falls back for consolation on his or her mind – the other is cast as a wreck upon the sea – the sea roars madly, the clouds lour, *and there is no haven*. Picture reader, the sad calamity, its dire results, and then unhesitatingly gather relief for the unfortunate.[24]

References to women working in men's clothes also came up in Tremenheere's report – 'Where the females themselves are so degraded as to work in men's clothes for the purpose of avoiding discovery'. However, he was equally damming about the women on the pit brow whose attire 'rendered necessary by the masculine nature of the employment, and the blackness and dirt with which these females cannot avoid being covered, can scarcely fail to undermine their modesty and self-respect.'[25]

Yet according to another rambler's piece, *The Welsh Collier* (1857) relating the life of an average male collier, up to the age of 10 children wore neutral clothing:

> At the present time, from the period when the exchange of neutral garments, equally adapted for both sexes ... In his 10th year, and we fear often before, work is found for him, in the coal pit or on the surface, either driving empty and laden trams to and fro, taking care of airways, or with loaded trams of shale ministering to the wants of tip girls.[26]

Given that the majority of tip girls were teenagers it may not have been considered unusual for them to wear neutral clothing.

Death

As with previous decades, one way of locating women in coal mining is through deaths; and two of the most common causes were falling down the shaft and being run over by trams.

As shown above, working on the balance pits was precarious. Hannah Rees (17) of the Tredegar Iron and Coal Company, fell from the top to the bottom of the deep pit at which she worked – she was pulling a loaded tram away from the pit edge when a mistake either from signals or a 'reduction in power' moved the cage she was standing on and as a result she was 'dashed to pieces'.[27]

Sarah Read (16), a banks woman, died on 5 December 1855 at the Plas Isa colliery in Ruabon, Denbighshire when she fell down No 2 pit.[28] She was employed on the coal pit bank and was in the process of removing the covering usually placed over the pit mouth but feeling herself overbalance tried to jump over the pit mouth. She made the leap, but then fell backwards into the pit and was killed instantaneously.[29]

Margaret Atkins (16), a banker at the Hope Colliery, Bedwelly, was landing a water barrel one night when her skirt caught in part of the machinery and she was crushed to death.[30]

Working with and around the heavy trams caused many accidents and deaths. An unnamed woman from 1851 was employed at Dowlais and was crossing the tramlines while full trams were ascending (taking down empty trucks on the other line). Seeing the trams approaching, she 'lost her self-possession' and the empty trucks passed over her, completely severing her body.[31]

Sometimes women's names appear not as victims of accidents but as witnesses. Elizabeth James worked at the Glyndyrus Pit with Mary Owens both as landers and they were called as witnesses in the inquest in the death of a man. They described part of their job:

> we remove the trams as they arrive at the top, and push them on to the parting, where the horse is hitched on to them to take them away. It is a balance pit, and Elizabeth James, myself and John Jones, are the only parties working at the top. On Saturday, at two o'clock, while we were at work, a full tram of mine had just come up

The tram then got stuck and an accident occurred resulting in the man's death.[32]

Ann Davies, a tipper in 1857, was tipping the last tram of rubbish when she too witnessed a fatal accident.[33]

Newspapers

One of the other ways to try and locate female coal workers is to look in the newspapers where it is possible to pick up some names, particularly from court proceedings.

In 1855 Eliza Price (21), described as a tip girl of Trevethin, was in court for obtaining beer by false pretences.[34] Ruth Watkins, a tip girl, in the Rhymney works in 1858, had given birth to an illegitimate baby and they were going to court so the father could officially adopt the child. However, the case was adjourned and they returned to Rhymney by wagon, but as they were alighting Ruth noticed something was wrong and so she took the child to a neighbour's where it died shortly afterwards. At the inquest, a jury decided it had died from a fit. The *Merthyr Telegraph* added an editorial footnote, 'It is lamentable to observe in a class of women, the strongest and healthiest in the world, how great a number of children are cut off in the first 6 months of their existence.'[35]

Instances of assault appear such as Mary Williams who worked at the Varteg as a mine-filler. When William Jones was charged with assaulting her, he was found guilty and fined 15s.[36] Rachel Davies and Sarah Morris, both patch girls of Pendarren, had fallen out and Mary sued Sarah for assaulting her – she was duly fined 2s 6d and costs.[37]

One brave woman decided to challenge her employer. Mary Efferin, a mine filler, sued Tomas Guliford for refusing to pay her for work. She had agreed to work for him for 10s 6d a week but when he tried to claim she was a bad worker the magistrates argued if he was unsatisfied with her, he should have discharged her and ordered him to pay her and the costs.[38]

Chapter 8

The 1851 Census

As women moved out of the pit and onto the pit bank, they did so mainly in concentrated areas such as West Lancashire, Shropshire, South Staffordshire, South Wales, Cumberland and Scotland. They were also known around the country by different names, although not exclusively. In South Staffordshire, they were generally referred to as Pit Bank Women and in Scotland Pit Head Women, and patch girls or women was used intermittently throughout the country. Only in Greater Manchester and South Wales were names affiliated predominantly to those areas, Pit Brow Lasses and Tip Girls respectively. Lancashire women were often given the male title of banksman but this rarely applies to Welsh women until the 1911 census when women are called both bankswomen and banksmen.

1851 Occupation Tables

In order to ascertain some idea of numbers in the following decades after the 1842 Report it was decided to return to the censuses as, despite the growing numbers of women at the mines, few contemporary records include them despite a large number of publications on the coal and iron industries.

By 1851 the census had expanded enormously reflecting not only the growing population but the growing number of job descriptions around Great Britain. From the supplementary publication to the census *Occupation Abstracts of Great Britain*,[1] published by government three years later, 332 different occupations are listed and those employed in the coal industry accounted for 4,284 women with 2,649 defined as a *miner* – however, the term must again be taken as a generic one.

Under the heading of coal, the term *coal miner* has been added with a total of 2,649 females of whom an almost equal number were under twenty (1,295) as those over twenty (1,354) confirming that most female work in coal mines was by young women.[2]

Other mining was split into individual categories and women were involved in six of these, dropping from eight in the 1841 census. Once again, the term *miner* is ambiguous, as it does not indicate what work was being done, and it is applied to both men and women. The largest number recorded for women is as a copper miner (3,918), followed by coal miners (2,649) and tin miners (2,138). Tables, such as those for the 1841 census which split the results into countries is not available for the 1851 census.

Compared to women working in other mines, the coal women are only superseded by those defined as *copper miners* (3,918) but somewhat higher than *tin miners* (2,138).

Robert Hunt (1807–1887) was a British mineralogist, among other things, and his principal work was the collection and editing of the *Mineral Statistics of the United Kingdom* from 1860–1881. He used the same census data and broke the figures down even further by county although he records 2,642 women not 2,649.[3] According to Hunt's figures, South Wales had the largest concentration of women working in coal in Great Britain for 1854.

1851 Census

When examining the census returns for this book, many women listed under the term *labourer* were not included because even when these women existed within a family of coal miners it cannot be said with certainty that they were labouring at coal pits. Other equally vague terms have been discounted.

Prior to searching the censuses manually, keyword searches had been undertaken and for the terms *mine filler, mine cleaner,* and *labouring in the mine*, seventeen individuals were recovered. However, these all appeared as 'census samples', an index of approximately 10% of the individuals enumerated in the 1851 census, but no accompanying original files are included so data is restricted.

Attempts to recover women from the 1851 census were undertaken in the same manner as that for the 1841 census and have resulted in 310 named women. However, these figures can be misleading for the reasons given above and because women were often employed on a casual basis therefore the 310 number can only be taken as a guide.

The census was taken on Sunday 30 March 1851 and contained a number of significant changes. Familial relationships were recorded for the first time such as 'daughter' or 'wife' but whereas before only those females with an occupation were listed, now they were identified as 'coal miner's wife' or 'coal miner's daughter' making it a long job to examine the records manually. Due to the fact the 1851 census contained more information, it means instead of the 1841 double-page spread it had become single-paged, doubling the pages for each district to be examined.

There was no more rounding down of ages but errors were still common. The average age of the 206 women from the 1841 census was 26, for the 310 women from 1851 it was 25. The youngest age had gone up from nine to ten and the oldest age had increased from 77 to 86 but on the whole, the ages were reasonably consistent in the decade that had passed.

Tracing girls and women from the 1841 census into the 1851 census proved difficult. Most began work in their teens so by 1851 were often married with different names, and a younger generation had taken their place, making it difficult to trace families who remained within the same location.

The recording of the birthplace in the census also changed. Before, one simply answered yes or no to being born in the county, now the actual town of birth was recorded making it easier to track emigration. In 1841, 45 females had been born outside the county but we cannot know from where they came, by 1851 that figure had grown to 57. Apart from 7 women who moved to Breconshire, 1 to Monmouthshire, and 1 to Pembroke, 48 moved to Glamorgan in keeping with what we know about the rise in industry in that county.

Without chasing each individual through other genealogical records, which would be a very long job, we cannot know when these women moved or with whom. All that can be said is that in 1851 the majority of women in this study who had emigrated from their birth county, were single, 22 out of the 57, with an average age of 24. About half, 22, were daughters living with their own family so some probably moved as a family unit and had established themselves enough for one of their parents to be the head of a house. However, 19 were lodgers either with other family members or alone, possibly because they had recently moved, were not economically stable enough to afford the rent of a house, or were living with extended families. Rachel Griffiths (26), who had been born in Carmarthenshire, and Rachel Watkins (18), from Glamorgan, both working as mine fillers, were single and lodging at 36 Howell Road, Lower Merthyr the head of which was a widow on parish relief.

Occupations were also more detailed, but as iron and coal works are often conflated it can sometimes be difficult to know where the women worked. Some enumerators helpfully added coal or iron, such as 'coal mine filler', in other cases it is a case of looking at the family makeup and if it is not clear the female is in the coal industry they have not been recorded.

One aspect that is noticeable from the 1851 census is that the 1842 Act was not being adhered to in places. When inspectors visited mines, they would often provide notice giving owners and managers time to move people from areas of work. In the census, however, some people are more open about their work. In Merthyr, Mary Evans (12) is recorded as a 'door keeper in mine works' along with her brother Philip (10), both working illegally, Mary for being a female underground and Philip for being under 11 years of age. Ann (27) and Mary Morgan (24) both mine cleaners had a brother Evan (9) who was a doorkeeper as was Rees Knie (9). Mary Griffiths (42) was an oiling woman and her daughter Elizabeth (17) was *filling mines,* Mary's son Rees (9) was a doorkeeper. Also, in the household was a seven-year-old boy and a one-year-old daughter so if Mary and Elizabeth had their employment terminated as many wanted to do, they would have been reliant on the wages of an illegally employed nine-year-old doorkeeper. This precarious situation can be seen regularly in the census.

Elizabeth Evans (42) was a widow cleaning mines at Merthyr with her two daughters Jane (24) and Mary (16) with a 12-year-old boy with no occupation listed. If they lost their jobs the whole family would have no income.

David James, a retired coal miner was living in Lower Merthyr with Margaret Lannes described as his wife but who has a different surname. Mary Lannes (43) described as a daughter of the head was unmarried and a five-year-old, described as a granddaughter to the head was also called Mary Lannes. Mary senior, a tip shipper, supported the whole family.

There were many more.

Pembrokeshire

The four Pembroke areas of the 1841 census were revisited and ninety-nine females were recovered in total, one more than the previous decade.

One of the difficulties with comparing areas is that many of the districts are still missing, for example, in 1841 the Amroth districts only included 1 & 2 but for 1851 only districts 7a, b, and c are available; and only one district was available for Begelly (5) whereas there had been eight previously (4–7 & 9). A similar situation occurred with Jeffreston and St. Issells where districts did not match. These are all relatively small areas, emphasising once again that census returns can only be taken as a guide and not as exact figures of females working in coal.

The number of girls and women recovered included Amroth (10), Begelly (24), Jeffreston (6), and St. Issells (58) compared to 1841 when it was Amroth (20), Begelly (13), Jeffreston (18), and St. Issells (48). Nothing can be read into these figures because so much of the data is missing. Only one woman was born outside the county – she lived in Amroth but was born in Marros, Carmarthenshire just four miles away.

The ninety-nine females lived in seventy-nine households and of these eighteen had female siblings working in coal. Seventeen had just one sister, while the John family from Begelly included Elizabeth (21), Rachel (19), Ann

(17), and Hannah (11) who were all described as a *labourer at colliery*. There were seven in the family including their mother, a ten-year-old brother, with only their 56-year-old father working (as a coal miner) – meaning most of the family income would have come from the four unmarried sisters.

As familial relationships were included for the first time in a census it is easier to see who is related to whom. Daughters of the head of household accounted for 55%; lodgers were 6%; wives 6%; granddaughters 2%, mothers-in-law 2%, sisters of the head 2%, and 2% were nieces. One, Elizabeth Rees (44) from Amroth was described as a housekeeper to a pauper widower who used to be a coal miner, however, Elizabeth was also *employed at a coal mine*. The only other occupant was an 11-year-old boy described as a *collier* – given that the 1842 Act banned those under 11 from working underground he must have been right on the margin if he was indeed working underground given how flexible the word *collier* is in the census.

The remaining 24% were heads of the house which is a great reduction from the 1841 figure of 61% – the forms had been filled in on Sunday 30 March which is a busy time in the agricultural calendar for calving and lambing but working on a Sunday was normally prohibited so it is not known why there was such a large drop within the ten years. One of the difficulties with the earlier census is that it was unknown if the women heads of households were married or not, making it difficult to know if they were on their own, but in the 1851 census, those relationships were included.

The average occupancy of a house was five people with an average age of 32, ranging from the youngest being ten and the oldest a 59-year-old widow who lived with her daughter and son, all three described as colliers. Paupers are included more often and eleven women were described as such, most with an additional comment that they were formerly a collier or worked at a coal pit. Their ages ranged mostly from the 60s, with the exception of Ann Rees (79) who lived with her daughter Rebecca (27) in Jeffreston, both unmarried paupers but included in their household was a nine-month old child with a different surname and described as *nursing*, so they may have been earning money doing some child care.

Breconshire

In the 1841 Breconshire area of Llanelly, thirty females were recovered from the Gellifelen and Darenfelen areas associated with the Clydach Iron Works and the 1851 area shows a similar pattern but this time sixty-eight females were recovered.

The picture that can be built up is that most of the females, 90%, were born within the county with 63% from Llanelly itself; the average worker was aged 19 with the youngest at 11 and the oldest at 65. Most, 87%, were daughters still living at home, 66% were unmarried, with only one married woman, two widows, and the rest unknown. Very few women, just two, were heads of the household and two were lodgers. Mary Whittney (13) was described as a lodging as a servant for Marchery Walters (71), a widow confectioner, but Mary also worked as a mine filler at Blanafon (Blaenafon). Next door is a family with the same surname as Mary, the head of which is Ann Whittney with three small children and although stated as married the husband is not present so it would seem her daughter moved next door to look after Marchery.

With regard to occupations, whereas in 1841 Breconshire mine cleaners were the highest (27%) in 1851 *mine fillers* accounted for 48 females (71%) with five *tippers*, six *labourers*, and cleaners being reduced to two. Other single mentions include a *banker in coal mine, haulier,* coal *weigher, hitcher,* and a *picker.* Due to the small numbers recovered, the results should be seen as approximations.

Glamorganshire

In the Glamorgan areas, 18 women came from Aberdare, 20 from Upper Merthyr, and 97 from Lower Merthyr showing the split in industrial areas. Both the Aberdare and the Upper results have little to add to the narrative other than the term 'patch' appears as part of a job description. A patch was an area on the pit head where people worked and later the term *patch girls* was to become an alternative name describing women working in the coal and iron industries, however, in 1851 it only applied to men such as Rees Jones (40) a *patch man (coal)* and Thomas Jones (53) *patchman coal* both from Upper Merthyr.

Lower Merthyr

Ninety-seven women were recovered from the Lower Merthyr area. They lived in 82 households in which 20 had female siblings working in coal, the greatest number being three sisters.

The domination of daughters as the largest group of women continues from the 1841 census – 69% of Lower Merthyr workers compared to 55% in Pembrokeshire and 87% in Breconshire and roughly a quarter of those households had women as heads of the household (with the exception of

A—Long table. B—Tray. C—Tub.

Women sorting ore, from De Re Metallica (On the Nature of Metals) by Georgius Agricola, 1556. (*Public domain*)

Women sorting ore, from Münz- und Mineralienbuch (Coin and Mineral Book) by Andreas Ryff, 1594. (*Public domain*)

Welsh lady carrying coal, 1859 by Francis Elizabeth Wynne. National Library Wales. (*Public domain*)

One of the images from the 1842 Report that shocked the nation. (*Public domain*)

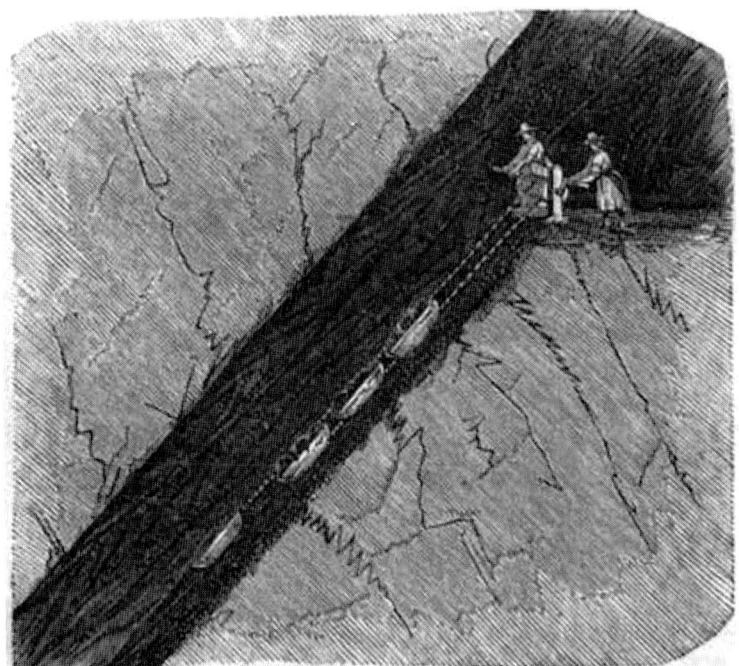

Windlass women working underground in Pembrokeshire from the 1842 Report. (*Public domain*)

Dowlais pit woman, 1860. (*By kind permission of Glamorgan Archives*)

Pit Hands from Merthyr from The Art-Journal, 1860. (*Public domain*)

Wigan women photo in the Clayton collection. By kind permission of Manchester Art Gallery. (*Manchester Art Gallery*)

A Clayton woman by kind permission of Manchester Art Gallery. (*Manchester Art Gallery*)

A Clayton woman by kind permission of Manchester Art Gallery. (*Manchester Art Gallery*)

Clayton woman. Note the posing stand behind their feet. By kind permission of Manchester Art Gallery. (*Manchester Art Gallery*)

A Clayton woman by kind permission of Manchester Art Gallery. (*Manchester Art Gallery*)

Clayton women. Note the ornate hats. By kind permission of Manchester Art Gallery. (*Manchester Art Gallery*)

A Clayton woman by kind permission of Manchester Art Gallery. (*Manchester Art Gallery*)

The only cheerful looking Clayton woman. By kind permission of Manchester Art Gallery. (*Manchester Art Gallery*)

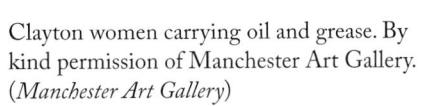

Clayton women carrying oil and grease. By kind permission of Manchester Art Gallery. (*Manchester Art Gallery*)

An extra Clayton. She is wearing trousers and this may be why she was not included in the Crisp collection. (*Courtesy of Big Pit: National Coal Museum Wales*)

A tip girl at Merthyr Iron Works from Good Words, 1869. (*Public domain*)

Woman and young miner, Pontypool, from Underground Life (1869). (*Public domain*)

Pochin Pit Head, Tredegar, date unknown (postcard). (*Public domain*)

Workers at Blaennant Pit (Mountain Colliery). (*Reproduced by kind permission Rhondda Cynon Taf Libraries*)

Women workers at Bwllfa Colliery, ci1870. (*Reproduced by kind permission Rhondda Cynon Taf Libraries*)

1873 Colliers Strike in S Wales. Wikimedia Commons. (*Public domain*)

Sackcloth and Ashes: Tip Girls Leaving Work. Engraving of the painting held at Cyfartha Castle, 1879. (*Public domain*)

Female surface hauliers, c1880, Treorchy. (*Public domain*)

A Pitwoman at Work.

Working in a wagon, from the Weekly Mail, 1897 redrawn by Eve Morgan for the Tip Girls Exhibition at Big Pit National Coal Museum. (*Weekly Mail, 1897*)

"Women miners by Vincent van Gogh, 1882." (*Public domain*)

Women on War Work, Coal Workers. Black Cat cigarette card. (*Author's collection*)

External steel board, part of Tip Girls of Wales, exhibition at Big Pit National Coal Museum. (© *Norena Shopland*)

Tip girl costume, part of Tip Girls of Wales, exhibition at Big Pit National Coal Museum. (© *Norena Shopland*)

Breconshire who had just two women). Of these heads, just under a quarter were widows; 14% were lodgers; 3% wives; 3% sisters or sisters-in-law, and the average occupancy of a house was six with the highest number being thirteen.

The average age of the workers was 23 with the oldest Mary Jeffries (55) a mine cleaner, and the youngest Elizabeth Davis (11) 'filling coals' and Ellen Griffyths (11) a 'tip shipper'. Margaret and Susan Rees were both 18 so maybe twins. Another illegal worker, Mary Davies (13) was *working underground at a colliery* at the Dan-y-deri Colliery; and several brothers were working illegally, one aged eight, three aged nine, and a ten-year-old boy. The details of these boys were only collected in relation to the women in this study, there were many others – which shows how the employment of underage boys working underground had continued nine years after it had been made illegal.

The occupations of the women and girls in the Lower Merthyr area consisted mainly of cleaners (22%), most described as *cleaning mine* or *mine cleaner* with only one specified as *cleaning coal road* and one woman *clearing on top of coal pit*. 6% were weighing coal, 12% were either *working* or *labouring* at the coal mine/pit; 11% were *landing* or *unloading* coal from the trams; 3% were oiling trams; 17% were *fillers* presumably filling trams with coal. The only additional term, *coal picker*, is from Aberdare; and a Mary Thomas (37), a widow, is described as the proprietor of a coal mine.

The word *tipping* was used extensively in both the 1841 and 1851 censuses and covered a number of descriptions but in 1851 a new term appears, that of *tip shippers*, a term not fully understood and it is exclusive to Lower Merthyr. Also, the term *tip girl* which was to become so synonymous with the Welsh women in later decades, appears for the first time. Jane Sullivan (24), originally from Ireland and a visitor when the census was taken in Lower Merthyr, was called a *tip girl*. Unfortunately, we do not know where Jane was visiting from. A similar phrase appears in the Breconshire results for Charlotte Richards (20), a married woman from Llanelly, who is described as a *tipper girl*.

The 1841 census research revealed 206 women working with coal, and by 1851 this figure had risen to 310. Not a huge increase in ten years, but the high level of negative publicity gave the public a false image, that the industry was swamped with dirty and immoral women. Whipped on by zealous social reformers who sought to ban their employment, the public demanded an end to the tip girl.

Chapter 9

Should Female Labour be Employed?

Changes in female labour at coal works began to alter as a result of higher demands for coal. Initially, coal supply was primarily local, particularly to feed the ironworks and other manufacturing industries, but from the mid-nineteenth century, demand increased, particularly in personal and transport use as the railways grew. Industries, like the ironworks which had been operating their own mines, also stepped-up production.

William Menelaus (1818–1882), manager of the Dowlais Ironworks from 1855 onwards, was instrumental in changing the coal industry not only by introducing a system of management methods, which included weekly reports from all departments but also by proposing a revolution in the way coal was sold. In his landmark report of 1861, Menelaus suggested that Dowlais improve sales by utilising small coal, normally considered a waste product because it was too small to sell, in the furnaces thereby releasing large coal for sale to other industries. He wrote, 'while the coal owner finds difficulty in getting rid of the small from his screens at 1s per ton, we can use it in the works where it is worth upwards of 2s. 6d. a ton.'[1]

This idea was widely adopted, meaning the coal had to be sorted into sizes, a job done mainly by women and girls and it was a job essential to the economy of the mines.

However, as the work increased, concerns about women's employment grew.

Women at work on the surface never made up a large proportion and their numbers steadily declined as the image of them being immoral persisted. In the whole of the UK, their numbers were only four to five thousand, about 7% of the colliery workforce, and centred principally in West Lancashire, Scotland, South Staffordshire and South Wales. There were also small numbers in North Wales and Cumberland.[2]

Economic necessity meant many women had to work and most remained in areas where other family members lived and worked. General female employment offered few choices; in the 1841 and 1851 censuses there are few mentions of factory work in the areas where tip girls were recovered and the largest area of employment was in domestic service followed by work in industrial areas, such as coal mining and ironworks, but it was the latter that social improvers wanted to address.

Attempting to locate these women working with coal in the census becomes harder from the 1860s due to changes in the compilation of the census. Returns had become much more extensive with a greater number of districts and a greater number of pages making the sort of manual searching used for the 1841 and 1851 censuses too time-consuming. Nonetheless, a number of women's names have been recovered from a few cursory studies.

One curious entry is for Martha Harris (24) living as a border with her husband, a bailer in the ironworks in Merthyr who is described as a 'haulier underground' but as this would have been illegal in 1861 it may well be a mistake as the male person next on the list has exactly the same description. In addition, Hannah Jones (36) is listed as a 'collier' which may have been a mistake as her husband is listed as a collier and four male lodgers indicated by *do* mean the same. It may simply be the enumerator forgot to leave out Hannah as women in Glamorgan were not usually identified with this description.

Some in Pembrokeshire were, however, still being described in this way. Six women were described as 'colliers' but this may have been more habit than fact because working underground was illegal and the census *Population Tables* published by HMSO records no women coal miners in England and Wales in 1861. Under the vaguer employment of 'coal labourers' the *Population Tables* recorded 3,763 women with 1,828 under 20 and 1,935 over 20 and there were 35 female coal mine owners over the age of 20.[3]

Something else that starts to appear more frequently in the 1861 census are children born on the mine premises, many families, particularly in management, would have had accommodation at the mine. Four women were shown to have been born at Dinas Colliery, Llantrisant. Some women remained at the mines and began their own families there such as Mary Richards, wife of coal miner Jenkins Richards, who had been born at Dinas Colliery c.1836 and she also gave birth to her daughter Anne Richards there in c.1860. This is something that continues in later censuses, in 1911 Any Snook (nee Dorman) was born in Morfa Colliery, Glamorgan c.1872 and was still at the same colliery living at 5 Overmans Row, Morfa Colliery, as a married woman with a four-year-old daughter Jane, also born at Morfa Colliery, thirty-nine years later.

These birth details can sometimes show how some people moved around the country. Margaret Reed (15) had been born at Morton Colliery, Derbyshire c.1856 and became a domestic servant to Taylor Swainson, an underground manager, in Mold, Flintshire so remained within the coal industry; Jane Jenkins was born at the Bry Colliery, Glamorgan c.1876 but the family had moved to Cardiff by the time of the 1881 census where her father Morgan Jenkins was a police constable; Hannah Evans was born c.1831 at Newdigate Colliery, Carmarthenshire but by the 1851 census was living in Blaenavon; and Catherine James, born at Old Colliery, Monmouth c.1875, was living in Newport where her husband was a hewer in the mines in the 1911 census.

The Leeds Conference

At a Leeds mining conference on 12 October 1863 a large congress of miners' delegates, from all parts of Great Britain, assembled for the purpose of stating their grievances, and to discuss the best means of remedying them. Those men representing their local areas consisted of forty-two from England, three from Scotland, four from South Wales (Blaenavon, Rhondda Valley, Abertillery, and Blaina), with just one from North Wales (Pentrefelin).

The report was published the following year with, on the front page, four drawings of Wigan women adapted from photographs. Women workers were not discussed extensively in the report but it must have been decided that an image could conjure up more than just text.

In the introduction, under the heading 'Females Working' the writer praised the legislation that had banned females from working underground and that those remaining were only in certain areas in Scotland, Lancashire, Staffordshire, and in Wales. All members of the conference, readers were reassured, were 'strongly of the opinion that the withdrawing of females from pit labour would be a benefit to all concerned'. Nobody asked the women what they thought.

The conference Chairman mentioned that he had seen females on pit banks in every district of Scotland and that they were as 'clean and tidy as the nature of their work would allow; still there was something abhorrent in seeing them begrimed with dust, and placed in the way of temptations that might lead to immorality.'

One of the difficulties, it was argued, was the lack of inspectors. Bryan Smith, of North Wales, said there were many men there who did not know what a mine inspector was, never having seen one; 'there were men who had been at a colliery for thirteen years, and had not seen one during the whole of that time'. The Vice-Chairman noted that in the Wigan area females were still employed underground but added that 'refined ladies did not seem to think that females working on the pit back was unbecoming' and gave as proof at a local bazaar raising funds for a chapel in Wigan, the ladies sold photographs of 'females dressed as they worked on the pit banks'. The reference to 'ladies' and 'females' enforced the class distinction.

Reuben Price, (Blaenavon), complained of 'a great evil in Wales was young girls being employed about the pit banks and mines. Instances of gross depravity, through the girls coming in contact with the male sex at their work, were frequent.' Accusations of depravity were rarely applied to the men.

'It is a most sickening sight,' the report concluded in its few references to women in the 174-page report:

> to see girls and women, created and designed for a much nobler sphere of action, clad in men's attire on the pit's banks; but it is a much sadder sight to see them, day by day, losing everything modest and womanly – those noble characteristics ever desirable to be manifested in the gentler sex. In fact, many of them very soon, as may be expected sink into the deepest depths of moral degradation. The miners themselves, as a class, abhor and detest those *scenes of demoralization* and ruin, which are common on and around the pit's banks where females are employed.'[4]

The conference had not been widely covered in the press and when it was, little was mentioned about women, although letter writers used the opportunity to air their opinions on the subject. Most complained about wearing 'male attire', of being indistinguishable from the other sex, their dirtiness and immorality, although few offered any examples to support their claims.

In 1864 the journal *Once a Week* produced a piece by political author and poet John Plummer (1831–1914) part of which was reproduced in the *Merthyr Telegraph*. His piece, entitled *A Real Social Evil* concerned women labour in the coalfields and stated:

> Incredible as the fact may appear to some, it is nevertheless true that hundreds of females, habited as men, are to be found at the present day working on the pit banks in Wales, Scotland, Lancashire, and Staffordshire. In Wales it is stated by competent witnesses, that "instances of gross depravity, through the girls coming in contact with the male sex at their work, were frequent".

In another edition reproduced in the *Aberystwyth Observer* Plummer writes of a Wigan woman:

> It was difficult to believe that the unwomanly looking being who passed before me was actually a female, yet such was the case. Clad in coarse, greasy, and patched fustian unmentionables and jacket, thick canvass shirt, great heavy hob-nailed boots, her features completely begrimed

with coal dust, her hard and horny hands carrying the spade, drinking tin, sieve, and other paraphernalia of her occupation, her not irregular features wearing a bold defiant expression, and with nothing womanly about her except two or three latent evidences of feminine weakness, in the shape of a coral necklace, a pair of glittering ear-rings, and a bonnet which as regard shape, size, and colour, strongly resembled the fantail hat of a London coal-heaver; she proceeded unabashed through the crowded street, no one appearing to regard the degrading spectacle as being anything unusual.[5]

Plummer then relates how often women in the Wigan district were mistaken for men, in one case a witness only accepted the fact when someone called out, 'Betty, how is your husband?' Having visited a Wigan coal mine himself, he recounts how 'I beheld a spectacle utterly repugnant to my feelings ... in various directions might be witnessed women with bared arms, one or two with short pipes in their mouths.' After berating the women for their appearance and behaviour he concluded, that the 'more intelligent and thoughtful of the miners themselves have repeatedly protested against it, but their protests are of no avail'. This was not strictly true as many families had no options but for women and children to work or they would be penniless.

Employers put the blame squarely on husbands whom they claimed should stop their wives and children working and so 'the evil will be checked at once'. While Plummer agreed he argued 'does the misconduct, folly, or what we will, of the men justify the employers in thus permitting or tolerating the misuse of female labour? The truth is, female labour is plentiful and cheaper, far cheaper than that of men, and unscrupulous employers will be found very slow in encouraging a change which may tend to diminish their profits.' Plummer claimed there were many collieries where no female labourers were allowed and he had not heard of any losses to the proprietor as a result. If employers did have to pay more for male labour then 'they had that labour far better and more effectively performed than if it had been done by females, while they were exempt from the frightful amount of demoralisation entailed by the toleration of a pernicious and utterly unjustifiable system.'[6]

Should Female Labour be Employed?

On 7 January 1865 a letter appeared in the *Merthyr Telegraph* under the title *Should female labour be employed in the iron works* and signed by 'W'. In the piece, W considers if female employment benefits the employed or the employer in both the iron works and coal pits. 'A woman's place,' W stresses, 'is at home – under cover – unexposed to rude and demoralising companions,' before compiling a familiar list of grievances about the immorality of employing women to work alongside men. Even adding, 'the petty gaffer, it is rumoured, often keeps a seraglio of black and dirty sultanas!' Whether this is true or not, it is the only occasion so far uncovered that such an accusation appears in print. W did not believe the abolition of female labour could be left to the masters and rather generously allows that 'their hands are tied, and they are powerless to do it. They cannot afford to sacrifice a portion of their profits for the sake of an idea.' W's final suggestion was to set aside a column to discuss the matter and the editor agreed.[7]

The first reply, by an unnamed writer, was printed a week later and complained mainly about the paucity of domestic servants. The writer did acknowledge the reasons why women preferred working at the iron works and coal mines:

> a female servant is the most tied of all being. Not only is she frequently in the same building from morning to night, and throughout the night, but also like this from one month's end to another ... the girls employed in the iron works have their liberty after the work is done. They have three or four hours every night after six o'clock to do as they please, and if working at night, have a few hours in the early morning for a stroll and a gossip. But the domestic servant is forbidden this privilege.'[8]

The idea of exhausted women having time for the 'privilege' of 'a stroll and a gossip' suggests the unnamed writer had not met many working women.

Philanthropy, whose letter appeared the same day, worried about females employed in the iron works and on the tips 'exposed to all weathers from an early age' growing into 'beings in too many cases but one remove from semi-civilised savages, barely distinguishing between right and wrong'. Philanthropy, like W, advocated getting women into domestic service and promised to outline plans in another letter. That plan duly appeared a week later when Philanthropy suggested establishing a Female Protection Society. These types of societies had been in existence since the 1830s but this particular name is mainly associated with unwed mothers although this does not seem to be Philanthropy's aim, which was to form a committee detailing the cruelty of employing women and how it might be remedied by the aid of a subscription to found a training home for female children for domestic service. They could also prepare a Bill for an Act of Parliament prohibiting the employment of females in iron and coal works. Philanthropy invited, 'the ladies to ply their needles and their talents in preparing pretty little articles and ornaments' and start bazaars. To start the ball rolling perhaps 'two thousand men of Merthyr to give a shilling each'. What Philanthropy did not cover was how the 'pretty little articles and ornaments' made by 'ladies' were going to compensate those 'females' who had lost their jobs. Both the unnamed writer and Philanthropy may well have been 'ladies' as this was at a time when women were often writing on female suffrage, but at no point, it seems, had either of them actually talked to the 'females' they were proposing to 'save'.

The next writer to weigh in was Medicus, the name implying some sort of medical connection and in their long letter, they did outline how hard physical work made women's bodies weak. 'They are physically weaker than males, yet they are subjected to a degree of physical tension that many hard-worked males would fail under.' This weakening of women's bodies, Medicus argued, gave birth to weak children responsible for a large number of infantile deaths in Merthyr 'beyond the average of other places'. If the children did survive, they died younger than elsewhere, 'some ten or twenty years of many workmen's lives are sacrificed for the sake of securing female labour'. Merthyr, Medicus believed, had been overlooked by the wider world:

> There are no scribes with long quills about Merthyr to draw up a picture of woe in the *Times* newspaper ... our remoteness from the centralizing influences of modern government gives a sort of impunity to a disregard of a statute. Those who have the power to establish legal proceedings against the individuals who break or infringe any Parliamentary statute, are too hardly worked to allow them to discover but a portion of the instances in which regulations are broken. And even if it were not so they are too mixed up with the society of the district, are so related by marriage or friendships, that it is pardonable in them not to press the law too rigorously.

Medicus did have a point, with so few inspectors visiting and so few fines against infractions it would have been easy for local managers and overseers to turn a blind eye when it came to people they knew. 'We are too far removed from the seat of Government to attract much attention. We have no philanthropists travelling our way; no vacation tourists to write us up in any of the magazines.'[9] The only tourists who had written about Merthyr tended towards the negative.

A week later Philanthropy endorsed Medicus' views, and repeated calls to form a society in Merthyr to save females from the evils of work, and called on local men to protect the women, 'Who will go into the works, or on the "Tips," and see young girls following their laborious occupation, and say it is not a grievance? To the young men of Merthyr I would say, come forward and be champions of the sex to which your mothers belong – rescue the race from further degeneracy. Come forward as Christians and men in defence of the helpless, and oppressed.'[10]

A fifth writer only identified as 'Q' suggested rules should be introduced to get masters to keep a strict watch over these 'poor girls' while they were employed, something that would have been almost impossible to do, and to 'deal as severely as they can with every instance where a gaffer has abused his position and influence over females, to effect his own base designs.' Female conveniences Q argued, should be erected to prevent them using the same facilities as men, or to expose themselves publicly. 'Such things as these are a disgrace to a civilized community; but then we in Merthyr are only semi-civilized, we make no pretension to being a go-ahead district, except in the matter of making money.' Q wanted the Factory Act that restricted children and women working, to be extended to Merthyr in line with a proposed extension for the Birmingham area. 'It is no use,' Q lamented, 'sitting with our hands folded and deploring the sad condition of those around us. We must work and work hard, and work long.'[11]

Philanthropy returned to point out that societies for the Protection of Females had long been in existence, and frequent reports in the newspapers 'fully testify the great good arising from them'. 'Will Merthyr – the great metropolis of the iron districts – stand back in the march of progress ... there are many intelligence and good men in Merthyr, and surely among them a few will come forward and form, in the way I have already suggested, a Society for the Protection of Females.'[12]

Of the six writers, only one who went by the name of 'A Reflected Ray' (possibly a woman's name) defended the women:

> I find by my intercourse with them that they are nature's gems; rough, yet capable of a very fine polish. Very many of them accept their condition without a murmur or complaint, the idea of their being fit for anything better never having once crossed their imaginations. Satisfied and patient they are achieving successes –
>
> > "Not scorned in Heaven,
> > Though little noticed here."
>
> Finding that these females were treated so hardly, and yet not because they are of the criminal class, I imagined that it was only the rougher kinds of men, men of no sympathy, no fellow feeling, brutish men, who were the cause of the incessant labour and hard lot of these poor females.

Despite the rather patronising defence and reference to their apparel as 'criminal's clothes' A Reflected Ray was critical of the owners and complained that the 'pecuniary benefit' of women's employment went to the 'coffers of an imaginary god called "Capital"'.

> I cannot bring myself to believe that any kindly feeling exists between your employers, and the poor beings who are employed by them, when no efforts are made by the masters to mitigate the evils, which all confessedly agree to be inherent to the employment of females in the iron works. Do these millionaires discuss in their quarterly meetings any plans to amelioration of the condition of the female labourer?

If such a discussion happened, A Reflected Ray concluded, they would be sent to Bethlehem Hospital (a London psychiatric hospital).[13]

On 4 March the editor of the *Merthyr Telegraph* brought the correspondence to a close with his own views echoing that of A Reflected Ray in noting that Acts passed in Parliament were essentially useless as they were framed in the interest of the master, and not in the interest of the working-man. In a final bitter accusation, he added, 'But we cannot expect it otherwise from our present aristocratic House of Commons, which does not embody what its name would lead us to suppose – the opinions of the common people of Britain.' Only when the working man is represented, the editor concluded, would things change and:

> we would prefer waiting for a more convenient season before attempting to carry a law for the abolition or restriction of female labour in connection with our iron and coal works. For a law passed having no *"executory principle"* would be of little service.[14]

Nevertheless, calls for new Acts to ban women working in the iron and coal industries continued.

The Third Children's Employment Report

In 1863 the Children's Employment Commission which had been responsible for the report of 1842, produced their third report (the second had also been in 1842). Assistant Commissioner Mr Longe conducted enquiries the previous year and in the introduction to his evidence, he noted that young girls and women were still being employed in Staffordshire and in South Wales on the pit banks and on the coke heaps, not only by day, but also by night. Despite the 1866 *Select Committee on Regulation and Inspection of Mines* report that had shown women workers were not immoral, Longe perpetrated that image:

> This practice has been often noticed in Reports presented to Parliament, as being attended with great and notorious evils. These females, employed with the men, hardly distinguishable from them in their dress, and begrimed with dirt and smoke, are exposed to the deterioration of character arising from the loss of self-respect which can hardly fail to follow from their unfeminine occupation.

Longe, part of the growing band of people trying to prevent females working on the pit banks and on coke heaps, called for their employment to be banned.

While in South Wales, Longe visited the Dowlais, Plymouth, Cyfarthfa, Ebbw Vale, and Rhymney Iron Works. He found no girls or women working at Dowlais but at the Plymouth the manager, Mr Roberts, confirmed that girls were employed at the tops of the furnaces unloading coal from the barrows, making coke heaps, breaking limestone, and filling the barrows with different materials for the furnaces. Most of the girls only worked during the day although there were three who worked during the night filling barrows with coal. At Cyfarthfa Mr Tracey Rees, the manager, gave evidence that girls were employed in piling, sweeping, breaking limestone, and in unloading coal; a few women were employed in putting coals on the furnace. Mr Adams, the manager at Ebbw Vale, stated they only had girls employed in unloading coal at the furnaces, and in the brickmaking and none worked at night and was very keen to stress that the work was very healthy as it was in the open air.

These types of reports are sometimes the only time we hear directly from the women. Ann Williams (20) at Ebbw Vale gave evidence:

> I unload coal. I was 12 when I began. I used to work in a mine (open). I wheeled mine. I got 5s. a week then. I never went to school. Mother was a widow when I went to work. I have been three years here altogether. Some girls begin to work at 10 years of age. I generally begin to work about 7 in the morning. We come here at 6, and wait for the trucks. I give up at 6 at night. We sometimes begin at 4 o'clock. When we begin at 4, we give up at 4 in the afternoon. We all go home to dinner. We get our breakfast before we come. Some girls don't go home to dinner when they live a way off. None of the working girls can make their own dresses, can mend them ourselves. The dressmaker comes to the house to make our things. It costs more than 2s 6d. to make a dress. The dressmakers seem to make a good trade, I find I am more healthy when I am working out than when I am in the house.

Another who gave evidence was Margaret Daniel (17) also from Ebbw Vale:

I unload coal. I don't work at night. I have worked at night. I worked for three months during the night as well as the day time. I don't like working at night. I get 6s. a week. I have been to school. I can't make my own things. I can sew some. I can knit a little. I can't read. My sister works with me. She is going 14. She has worked two years. She throws coal the same as I do. I have four sisters and three brothers. Father works.[15]

The Peculiar Dress

As demands to prevent women from working increased, so did the criticism of their clothes. Although, when it came to Welsh women wearing trousers, there is very little evidence. Photos from this time can be ambiguous but it should be borne in mind that when the photographer arrived the women may have ensured they had respectable attire that could have been different from other workdays. Or they may have tucked the hems of their dresses into the trouser waistband as others had done, and let them down again after the photographer left. Most women in Welsh images wear a long dress of flannel or a coarse material like sacking tightly closed at the neck, with aprons of cloth or leather scarves, plaid shawls, woollen or worsted (closely twisted wool) stockings, and lace-up hob-nailed boots. Some tip girls wore leather or cloth shields over the back of their hands to protect them, and to give themselves a sense of individual identity they wore personalised items such as imitation flowers in their hats or brightly coloured scarfs, head coverings or belt buckles.

It is not surprising, given how often working women were written about, that they also became tourist attractions generating yet more articles which on the whole, were detrimental.

In 1866 a London writer signing himself 'a Saunterer' was encouraged by a friend to see the industrial works of South Wales and Saunterer wrote up his experiences in *A vacation at Merthyr* for the *Merthyr Telegraph*. The friend had listed some of the places he should visit, 'go down,' he had said, 'into the "lower regions" of a coal pit; then take a trip over the hill to Aberdare':

> pay a visit into the solitary public hour on the top of the hill, and have a chat with the fat old landlady; ... look at the peculiar dress of the "tip" girls there, and remark their big brawny arms and blackened faces, so very different from our pale-faced little ladies up here; listen to some of them singing a song in the guttural Welsh language; see them then at some other time, suddenly falling into a passion with one of their

neighbours, and engaging in a bit of a face-scratching hair-tearing scrimmage – remark all those things, and, I bet you my life you will return better satisfied with the way in which you spent your time, than if you went down to any of those monotonous fashionable places where so many go to spend their summer months.[16]

Occasionally the tip girls fought back. Angela V. John notes in her paper, *A Miner Struggle: Women's Protests in Welsh Mining History* that in 1867 a Dowlais pit girl wrote a letter to the Welsh language newspaper *Y Glorian*. They had stated that the publication wanted to hear frequently from 'the black collier, the red-faced puddler, the happy tip-girls, the determined quarryman,' and others including women copper workers of North Wales who were referred to as 'ladies' a description not afforded to the tip girls. The letter writer was stung by this omission and wrote:

> I saw in an issue of your papers that someone was talking about me and other girls who work out in the open and calling us tip girls. Why are we treated like this? If we like going out to work, instead of staying at home and isn't that proof that we want to earn an honest living instead of going from house to house like some around the works? If I could get hold of the person who made use of our names, he would be sure to feel what he would get. We are not any worse than the 'girls' who stay at home, and if you want a readership for your paper you had better shut up about the colliers, the furnace men and about us, the tip girls.[17]

Given that many of the young women were illiterate this feisty lady was determined to present tip girls as honest and equally ladylike.

A couple of years later in 1869, *Good Words* commissioned an article from an unnamed writer entitled *The Merthyr iron worker* at the Plymouth Iron Works. The writer sees a 'girl in semi-masculine costume, and with a most unfeminine face. Seven or eight young women in coarse, sleeved pinafores, handkerchiefs tightly bound over their heads, battered hats, bristling with frayed feathers, blue stockings, and in some instances, masculine overalls – some helping to unload the trucks that come up the shaft, and others pottering with shovels about the "tip;" ... at the foot of the tip, where more girls and a boy or two are shovelling coal.' The writer is given clothes to go down the mine and then shown for inspection to the tip girls whose response was 'fuller of fun than flattery'. Despite the article appearing three years after the parliamentary report of 1866 women's work had not changed much and he contradicts the idea that women did not use shovels:

pinafored girls – very dirty, very bold-eyed, and yet squalidly picturesque, with their cheap ear-rings and their coloured kerchiefs, now and then giving a hint of a concealed mild chignon. They ply their shovels like navvies, and lift blocks of stone and coal that make your arms ache as you fancy yourself lifting them ... Perhaps the most painful features in the South Welsh mineral districts are the hardness of the work which the girls and women have to perform, and its unsexing nature. It is strange to see them so merry over it.[18]

Despite this 'merry' attitude one of the most significant collections of photographs of Welsh tip girls appeared during the 1860s showing the women as nervous and uncomfortable – and these photographs are steeped in mystery.

Chapter 10

The Clayton Images

During the mid-to-late nineteenth century, a type of photograph became extremely popular, the carte de visite (CDV). The format was developed by Frenchman André Adolphe Eugène Disdéri (1819–89) in 1854 and consisted of a photograph mounted on a card about the size of a formal visiting card, hence the name. They first appeared in the UK in 1857 and after Queen Victoria posed for such a photograph demand for these cards soared, and despite declining in popularity in later decades they remained in production until the twentieth century.

Early photographic portraits closely followed conventions of paintings including props used as a language indicating aspects about a persons' class or occupation, but as the craze for mass-produced images grew, working-class people began to be included. Women working in the coal industries were popular, the most famous being those of the Wigan Pit Brow Lasses. Hundreds of these images were produced in the Manchester area and sold as CDVs portraits or as postcards often showing the women in work clothes, or as side-by-side comparisons of work clothes and 'proper' Sunday best. The aim was to amuse or shock, to present the women as something 'other', something alien to societal expectations of what women were expected to look like for the edification of the armchair tourist.

Much has been written about the Wigan photographs but less research has taken place with regard to a similar set of images from Wales.

The Photographer

William Clayton was a photographer about whom little is known. His first appearance in the census at Tredegar is 1871 when he is recorded as a photographer living at 31 East Lane, aged 51, making his birth year c.1820 and he was born at Milford, Hampshire. He seems to be missing from the 1881 census but by 1891 he is still at East Lane but now his age is given as 76 making his year of birth c.1815 and the place of birth is changed to Blackburn, Lancashire. His wife Eliza was born in Symor (possibly the Seymor Estate), Hampshire in 1822 and they had an 11-year-old daughter

Georgiana born at Lymington, Hampshire. This means they were still living in that county in 1860 when the daughter was born.

Outside the census, the earliest reference to Clayton at Tredegar is in 1865 when he is described as an 'artist' in the *Merthyr Telegraph* for taking photographs of the choir of Saron Chapel, Tredegar.[1] Meaning the date of the move from Hampshire must be between 1860–1865. He had definitely moved on to a shop in 1870 because an advertisement for the purchase of shares for the Art Union of Great Britain states tickets could be bought from Clayton's premises. In 1884 he is on the jury of a coroner's inquest into a colliery explosion at the Pochin Pit, Tredegar, in which two men were killed.[2]

Clayton died on 5 October 1894 at 'his residence, Iron Street' and a public funeral was held on 9 October at 3 pm.[3] The reference to his 'residence' is curious because his residence was always listed in the census at East Lane although he did have a studio at 19 Iron Street however no advertisements can be found for his business in the local newspapers. Gail Baylis in *Tredegar Patch Girls*, states his name appears in directories between 1868 and 1895[4] but due to lockdown restrictions it was not possible to identify these directories at the time of writing.

There is no record for Clayton at the Royal Photographic Society and he does not appear to have exhibited his work, meaning he was simply a high street photographer.

The Album

The originals of what was to become known as Clayton's Tip Girl photos are in Manchester Art Galleries in a bound album. The name 'C.B. Crisp' appears three times in the album, on a scrappy cover, underneath a newspaper cutting, and on the back of one of the photographs. The identity of C.B. Crisp is currently unknown and the only other references that have been found is a short notice in the *Merthyr Telegraph* about a letter to a C.B. Crisp concerning postal arrangements from Bristol to Tredegar in February 1865.[5] The only other references to someone of the same name is an individual from Oldham (just outside Manchester) who in 1899 joined the board of Thomas Sowler and Sons – Thomas Sowler was a Manchester newspaper proprietor. In 1900 a person of the same name stood as a Unionist candidate in the general election for Oldham. While the last two may not be the same person as the one who signed the Clayton album it would seem there is a connection by name alone.

The date for the album is consistently quoted as 29 April 1865 because that is what Crisp has written underneath a newspaper cutting pasted into the album. The text is an extract describing a visit to Tredegar iron works:

Travellers see strange sights, and strangers coming into the iron districts of South Wales often make strange remarks. It is, however, a fine sight at night to see the blaze issuing from the numberless fires of the Tredegar iron works, illuminating the sky far over the distant hills. These immense works occupy a large area of ground and employ several thousand hands, and continually send forth flames from furnaces burning some hundred tons of coal. Surrounding the town and the works are what strangers call the "Black Mountains" which are the refuse and burnt coal tipped and heaped together from the works, and being accumulated, forms in the course of time a range of semi-mountains, until these tips consolidate and get covered with verdure; and on part of some of the old tips, George-town, Vale-terrace, and rows of houses have lately been built. On top of these tips, rails are laid down for trams to carry away the useless mass of cinder from the fires and furnaces, and on arriving at the extremity the trams are tipped, and by this means the black mountains or tips are everlastingly on the increase in length and height. To do this work women and girls are employed and wear a peculiar style of dress, consisting of a short frock and apron, tight to the neck, made of a material resembling hop cloth or fine sacking and red worsted stockings, and lace-up boots heavy with hobnails, tips and toecaps that would pull the legs off some of the ploughmen in the Middle Counties [or Midland Counties]. The bonnet or hat, for it is difficult to discern to which of the classes this headdress belongs, is bedecked with beads, brooches, and feathers, the latter addition in a small way imitating the Prince of Wales plume. In this dress, with faces black with dust and smoke, it is difficult, when elevated fifty or a hundred yards, to discern the sex to which these objects belong; and a gentleman, who evidently had never witnessed such a sight before, on visiting the town of Tredegar repeatedly expressed his astonishment at making mountains on mountains, and inquired what animals those were he saw moving about on top! In the tempest and the storm, in rain and in snow, in the sun and heat, exposed to all weathers, women and young girls are employed on the tips in South Wales.

Above the cutting, the words *Bristol Mercury* have been written and underneath the signature C.B. Crisp and the date 29th April 1865. From this almost all writers have extrapolated that the cutting must be, as indicated, from the *Bristol Mercury* on the date inscribed by Crisp and this date has been used for the album itself. However, there are problems with this.

No digitalised version of the *Bristol Mercury* contains this text. No other newspaper contains this text, in fact, it cannot be located anywhere. The digitalisation of newspapers is a very time-consuming and expensive job and nineteenth-century papers could have several issues a day with content changing according to incoming news so it may be that this text appears in a later/earlier issue than that available online. Also, the words *Bristol Mercury* along with Crisp's signature and date are handwritten yet another newspaper cutting pasted into the album, the name of the paper and the date are cut straight from the publication. If Crisp had cut the *Bristol Mercury* piece why not include the other details? The letter concerning postal arrangements from Bristol to Tredegar in February possibly suggests Crisp was in Bristol that month, so perhaps someone sent the cutting in April knowing of Crisp's interest in the subject but neglected to cut the name and date of the publication.

The other newspaper cutting pasted into the album is from the *Should Female Labour be Employed* series of letters from the *Merthyr Telegraph* discussed in the previous chapter. Of the ten letters only one is included, that from Philanthropy suggesting work should be found for working women in domestic service and that she/he would shortly be publishing a plan to that effect. This short letter is the least informative of the ten and one wonders why it is included. Perhaps it was the only one Crisp had. It was dated 14 January three months before the inscription in the album and about a month before the letter about postal arrangements to Bristol. The *Merthyr Telegraph* letters ran from January to March, and only in that publication and the cutting in the Crisp album was the third in the series, so if Crisp was in Tredegar during January and February why not include some of the more interesting letters? Even if the letter was sent to Crisp the same question can be applied, why not send more interesting ones.

Some writers have suggested Crisp commissioned the photographs in association with work on Female Protection Societies because this was Philanthropy's plan but no link can be found and the letter discussing the societies does not appear in the album so we cannot be sure Crisp even saw those letters and was aware of Philanthropy's proposal. Another writer has suggested Crisp was Philanthropy but that seems unlikely, if a point was being made why not actually include more informative letters?

Simply because Crisp wrote a date in the album does not mean that is the date of the album, it could have been compiled years later. However, there is another possibility.

A photo of two Wigan women is included in the album. This was by local photographer John Cooper (?-1894) who worked as both a pub landlord and a photographer. He took a number of photos of the Wigan pit brow lasses but as with many of these images, dates are difficult to pin down. One of the difficulties of the Crisp album is there is no way of knowing if the album was constructed in one instance or was collated using images collected over a period of time, but it seems once constructed it remained as a whole. If Crisp's inscription of a date is merely in relation to a newspaper article then we have no evidence on which to place a date for the album or Cooper's image.

We do have to ask why Cooper's image has been included in what is otherwise an exclusively Welsh collection by another photographer. The possible link may be in relation to an album of photos submitted to the *Select Committee on Regulation and Inspection of Mines* that sat in 1866 but the inquiry, and collection of evidence, had begun in 1865. Images of coal women had been dominated by the Wigan women and it is not unreasonable to suggest that Clayton was given Cooper's image as a template for a sister volume to the album submitted to the *Select Committee*. Unlike Cooper and others who sold their photographs as CDVs or postcards Clayton appears not to have sold any copies of the Tredegar women, adding to the argument that they were possibly commissioned.

Currently, there is no evidence the album was ever used in an inquiry or elsewhere and it slid into obscurity until acquired by Drs Cecil (1878–1961) and Phillis (1887–1974) Cunnington, authorities on historic costumes and clothes, accessories and photographers. It is not known how Crisp's album came into their possession but in 1947 the Cunnington collection was bought by Manchester Art Gallery where Crisp's album remains to this day.

Munby

Another suggestion put forward by some writers is that the photos may have been commissioned by Arthur Joseph Munby (1828–1910). The rather eccentric Munby was a diarist, poet, portrait photographer, barrister and solicitor – a few of his poems were republished in the Welsh press. When he died in 1910 it was revealed he had married his servant Hannah Cullwick, a Shropshire-born maid.

Munby was fascinated by working-class women, particularly those engaged in hard physical labour such as female coal miners and would often walk through city streets talking to working women about their lives and work. He would keep a record of them, their conversations with him, clothes, and other details in his diaries and it is from these diaries we know that he visited South Wales in 1861, 1865, 1869, and 1870.

In 1865, Munby was in the area during September and October, five months after the date in Crisp's album. He went to Nantyglo and described women lifting large lumps of coal; Blaenavon where he observed women unloading and loading coal and ironstone; and the Dowlais Iron Company when sketched an image of Jane Matthews (20) during 'a quiet moment' while she was 'mending her stocking, seated on a heap of ironstone. Pencilled on spot, 26 September, 1865'.

Munby had been collecting hundreds of mass-produced photographic images of working-class women but he does not seem to have acquired any Welsh images or knew of any because in 1869 he was in Swansea seeking images of 'minetip girls' to be told there were none:

> Sunday 10 October 1869. Got to Swansea by 12.30. I walked down the High Street to find Andrews the photographer, and found his house, with no one in it but his servant, a strong Welsh lass from H'arfordwest, with a kindly face and large broad hands. She showed me the stock of photographs, but we found no minetip girls among them. She had seen these girls: has a brother a pitman: but thinks they 'work like slaves', and that 'Government ought to stop em'. How would you like it, said I, if Government was to stop your being a servant? 'Well Sir' said she naïvely 'I should be glad! I wouldn't be a servant, not if I'd the means to live without it.'[6]

If Munby had been aware of the Clayton images, he would surely have mentioned them, but neither Clayton's name nor that of Tredegar appears in his diaries making it unlikely it was he who commissioned the images.

The Images

In the album, there are 43 images of Tredegar women, two of men, and the Wigan picture. The background in the pictures of men conforms to those of the women suggesting they were taken at the same time and consist of a single man and a group of men.

The number of individuals in an image range from single portraits to groups of five giving a total of 72 females, however, four appear more than once making it 68 individual women. In addition, there is an extra picture at Amgueddfa Cymru – National Museum Wales that is not in the Manchester collection, increasing the number to 69.[7] It is not known why this image was excluded from the Crisp album or who Mrs Williams was who donated this, and six other Claytons, to the museum in 1928. These prints are also on paper, not CDVs.

Mrs Williams' collection consists of three images of men, two copies of the single man from the Crisp album, and two new single shots of men that appear nowhere else; as well as three of tip girls, one copy from the Crisp album, one additional shot of a woman from the album, and the new woman mentioned above.

All the Clayton women have been staged, posed for examination for whatever reason, so they become unified as a category. Four of the images have been partially coloured but only on the shawls and headscarf's perhaps to emphasise that the women would often use highly coloured accessories to add individuality.

Some of the girls look so young it tugs at the heart strings and they are unsmiling and nervous with the exception of one woman who sits on stones, relaxed, and smiling and about to eat what looks like a boiled egg from her billy can. Some writers have suggested that the Tredegar women were more uncertain of being photographed, it was after all a relatively young profession and outside the price of most working women. However, this does not explain why most of them look so uncomfortable, surely a few would have enjoyed the novelty.

Several theories have been put forward as to why the pictures were taken and then not sold. One is that many of the Wigan women wore trousers which may have been their unique selling point resulting in a larger trade. Women wearing trousers was an erotic lure to men, something that is covered in detail in my book *A History of Women in Men's Clothes*.[8] That the Welsh women did wear trousers is a frequent theme in articles about them and when Munby visited ironworks in the Blaenavon valley he noted 'some of the girls wore short cotton trousers, and some woollen stockings only'.[9]

There was also a growing trend in tourist photos of the archetypical Welsh woman with the tall black hat and the Clayton's did not fit in with this idealised vision. The bad publicity of women as immoral beings may have influenced the public's reluctance to buy, along with a negative image of the industrial works as demonic-looking, full of blackness and fires, an underworld of 'other' which may have played a part in people not wanting the photos. There are a number of images of Welsh women in industry from the second half of the nineteenth century but few appear as commercial postcards or CDVs in the same way as the Wigan women.

In fact, there is no record that Clayton's photos were ever intended to be sold. Most CDVs have on the reverse an advertising notice by the photographer and Clayton is no exception, his commercial pictures have on the back 'Photographed by W. Clayton. Iron Street Tredegar. Copies can be had at any time' yet only two of his tip girl images carry his advert. Both of these are of a different design and there is no information to be able to date which notice preceded the other. It is possible he used some old cards and saved his best ones for commissioned work but also, he may have wanted some acknowledgement in the collection that he was the photographer because his name appears nowhere else and were it not for these two examples Clayton's name would have been unknown.

The Women in the Photos

There are 69 individual women in the Clayton collection and these were examined in detail to see if any further light could be shed on what type of work they were doing. The largest employer in the district was the Tredegar Iron Works which also owned coal mines such as Pochin Pit and a postcard does exist of mines workers at that pit with two women, dressed in a similar fashion to the Clayton women. One of the difficulties in attempting to define the women in the images is that both iron and coal workers dressed alike.

Nevertheless, it has been possible to divide the women into roughly two groups by an analysis of their clothes.

In 1869 the journal *Good Words* included a piece on the *Merthyr iron worker* in which there was a description of women workers that included the line, they had 'handkerchiefs tightly bound over their heads, battered hats, bristling with frayed feathers'. The latter is certainly true of the Clayton women. and over half (37) wear straw hats or bonnets, some worn at jaunty angles, often with intricate designs and they are indeed, bristling with feathers. In an 1874 newspaper article describing two 'tip' women who got into a fight, the writer described their hats as 'something prodigious'.[10]

One particularly stylish woman in the Clayton collection has an ornate hat with feathers, a brooch that appears to be a pearl-like cluster, a necklace of dark and light-coloured beads, earrings, and a circular scarf around her neck. She appears in two separate pictures but in almost the same pose suggesting they were taken at the same time, although one has her holding a small hammer and the other does not. A third picture of this woman, not in the Manchester collection but one of those Mrs Williams donated to Amgueddfa Cymru, differs from the other two in that it is a wider shot and the background wall has a very ornate vertical strip.[11]

Another woman also uses pearl-like objects in four rows on the front of the hat to create an eye-catching design and one has some light-coloured stitching creating a pattern on the peak. Many of the decorations include light-coloured items, particularly circles, contrasting against black, or dark-coloured feathers or material, and one hat has a selection of round bright objects reminiscent of a 1960s cap covered in button badges. On one hat is a single white disc placed directly in front that immediately draws the eye. Several have what appears to be imitation flowers, including one woman photographed outside who has a hat full of what looks like pale-coloured flowers, it is too difficult to say if they are real or imitation, and another has several perched on the top of her hat. One very young-looking girl has a series of what look like four small metal rings hanging from the brim and these same rings appear on another woman's hat stretched across the brim and onto her forehead. In the 1861 census occupation tables there were 109 female straw hat/bonnet makers in Monmouthshire under the age of 20, and 374 over 20. In Tredegar, Ellen Hinton (29) of 30 Market Street, is listed as a straw bonnet maker, and her husband Frederick (28) is a hairdresser. It would be nice to indulge in a flight of fancy and think that Ellen made some of the bonnets for the Clayton women.

Just under half (28) of the women wear what appears to be 'handkerchiefs tightly bound over their heads', perhaps not handkerchiefs as such but thin material stretched tightly over the hair and tied at the back. These types of head scarfs range from short pieces to those with long wings often draped down the shoulders or tied under the chin so they can be 'muffled about the head, and tied, bandaged, strapped, and so arranged from her neck downwards as to defy, so far as possible, the defilement of the hated coal-dust'.[12]

Most of the hat wearers have similar scarfs, either under the hat and draping downwards, or around the neck but the scarf wearers rarely wear hats. In fact, there is a distinct division between the women who wear hats and those who wear scarfs – of the 37 hat wearers, three wear shawls, but of the 28 with scarfs 18 wear shawls.

Many, irrespective of what they wear, are holding billy cans ('Tommy Box' is the modern colliery name), water bottles or leather holders. Other accompaniments include a 'bottom mandrel', a heavy form of the coal face 'cutting mandrel', which was used for heavy work in the collieries, and eight images have women posed with this tool. However, six of these are in the same external location and look as though the mandrel has remained there as a prop throughout the shoot. Only two internal images include women with a similar tool. Six of the mandrel holders wear hats, the only one with a scarf is a group of three women with it lying across their laps as if it's simply been propped there. The last photo is of both a hat and scarf wearer and one holds the mandrel while another holds a brick maker's wooden frame. Given that the mandrel appears predominantly in the same position nothing conclusive can be concluded about its use but it does appear more frequently with the hat wearers. In the extra picture at Amgueddfa Cymru a smaller, crossed mandrel lies on the floor at the woman's feet.

Other tools included with the women is a shovel held by a hat wearer; and three women, two hat and one scarf wearer, are holding a small pointed hammer for breaking up materials on the 'picking belts'. Little can be drawn from this other than that more hat wearers have the hammer. A brick maker's wooden frame is held by two women both scarf wearers. One image that has generated an enormous amount of discussion is of two women, one holding a pick mandrel and an oiling can, the other holding an oiling can with a cloth and a ledger of some sort. The latter has on her head, cushioned by the straw hat, a cylindrical metal container with a spout so is obviously for pouring something, probably the oil. The other woman has on her head and cushioned by a hat, a rectangular box with what appears to be cloths on top and staining down the sides of the box. This probably contained some sort of grease and we know from the census returns that women were employed in oiling the trams and rails. No other image of women in the coal or iron industry is similar to this, and the only other items on heads is from 1875 of two Dowlais women with baskets of coal. However, an article, *Among the Miners in Dowlais*, from 1872 by an unnamed writer noted the women, 'hardly less brawny and masculine-looking than the men, accoutred for work with pads on top of their heads, short petticoats, and strong heavy boots'.[13] They may have mistaken the 'pads' for the straw hats but it could also be possible they were for carrying items on the head.

Ten of the images feature women wearing woollen plaid or paisley shawls that were widely worn in rural Wales, even becoming accepted as part of a 'Welsh' woman's costume, although there is nothing traditionally Welsh about it at all. In the Clayton's most of the shawls are associated with scarf wearers and five of the women are posed alongside a rather poor effort at making an external-looking scene with a few wooden pallets, straw, and branches of trees propped up.

Apart from the highly decorative hats, accessories are limited. A few wear earrings. The only other option for individuality is belt buckles. Many of the belts are simply cords tied around the waist in single or double strands, some have buttons, some have plain metal buckles. One has a round buckle similar to a military design, and one young girl has a very ornate buckle of a pale-coloured metal. Enlargements have indicated quite a vibrant scene but sadly it is impossible to distinguish any details. Most of the scarfs are simply tied at the neck but some of the shawls have small round fastening pins or buttons.

As to the women's dresses, they can be divided into three categories, those who wear dark-coloured, heavy dresses often tatty with patches and holes; those who wear a similar dress but of a lighter colour; and those who wear pinafores. Of the latter, there are only seven women in four images, and one holds what looks like a milk pail, but could be a large tin plate container for oil as her stains look a bit too black and 'oily' for working with food stuffs.

With the exception of a group of three who appear very clean in an external setting, the fronts of the pinafores are dirty and all of the women's arms are bare.

Twenty-eight women wear the dark material dress, none have bare arms, all bar three wear hats, and only two have shawls.

The third set of clothing is similar to that of the dark dresses but of a lighter coloured material, and there are 35 of these. Some dresses are clean and unmarked while others are pitted with holes and have patches in a similar fashion to the dark-coloured dresses. Eighteen women have bare arms and most of these have less damaged clothing. Twenty wear shawls. One woman is extremely grimy with highly damaged clothes and wears a type of glove that covers the back of her hands which Angela V. John identified as 'clappers' (loose cloth shields) over the back of their hands to protect them implying the job required those areas to be protected.

In the 1862 *Children's Commission Report* Ann Williams (20) who unloaded coal at the Ebbw Vale Ironworks, Monmouthshire, gave evidence that she arrived at the mine at 6 am to wait for the coal trucks to come to the surface around 7 am. She told them, 'none of the working girls can make their own dresses. We can mend them ourselves. The dressmaker comes to the house to make our things. It costs more than 2s, 6d. to make a dress. The dressmakers seem to make a good trade.'[14]

Only one woman appears to be wearing trousers under her skirts and that is the extra image at Amgueddfa Cymru, and that may be the reason she was not included in the Crisp album.

The final part of the women's dress was the stockings and boots. Unlike many of the Wigan women who wore clogs, almost all of them wear the same type of dark-coloured lace-up boots, although two women wear boots with no laces. The woman photographed outside eating a boiled egg sits on some stones with a foot raised and the hobnails can be clearly seen on the soles. As noted in the *Bristol Mercury* cutting in Crisp's album, describing 'lace-up boots heavy with hobnails, tips and toecaps that would pull the legs off some of the ploughmen'.

Above the boots can often be seen stockings, some plain some striped, and it is clear from those images that no trousers were being worn.

Very few of the women and girls have dirty hands and faces implying the pictures were taken at a time when they had not been working. One woman has a distinct line across her face with the lower part mottled with dirt implying she wore some sort of covering over her upper face, and the mottling looks as though she has touched her face several times. Another's face is mildly dirty; the woman who is very begrimed has a black nose as if she has been touching it with dirty hands and the lower part of her face is also dirty.

Identities

None of the women are named and there are few clues for us to be able to track them. The Blaenau Gwent Access to Heritage Facebook group has suggested identities for those in one photo. It features three women and those on the left and right bear a striking resemblance, as if they were twins – there are a few examples from censuses of sisters with an exact age who may be twins. The suggestion is that the two in the Clayton image may be Ann and Mary Morgan (both 18) who according to the 1861 census lived at 1 Plummer's Row, Tredegar, in a household of six people, headed by their father, an iron miner. With their sister Elizabeth (23), who may be the woman standing between the two in the photograph, all are listed as *unloading iron mine* namely unloading iron ore probably from the trams.[15]

Despite not being able to identify the women, it seems they can be divided into two groups. The hat wearers tend to be those women wearing the heavy, soiled and tatty dresses, regardless of whether they are dark or light-coloured dresses and possibly they worked with materials and conditions that damaged their clothes such as unloading and handling heavy coal. The dresses of the two women with the oil and grease containers on their heads are not torn or patched, nor are the pinafores despite being dirty, implying a less damaging work environment but it is difficult to speculate what that would be. Two women hold a wooden brick-making frame but given the mandrel appears to be a prop we cannot make any definitive statements about the frame; women did work in the colliery or ironworks brickworks and Ceri Thompson knows of a woman who lost an arm in the Cambrian Colliery brickworks.

In the 1861 census the returns for Tredegar were examined and while there are several mentions of *iron mine fillers,* working at the *iron mines,* or *tipping* the majority of the women are cleaners, one even being specified as *cleaning the rails.*

Locations

Most of the women were photographed indoors but the rooms have a shabby unkempt look with stained walls and tatty carpeting or tiling, it is often too difficult to tell which is which. Little attempt has been made to place the women in any kind of context, most simply stand against a wall unsmiling and nervous. When a 'well-known photographer' Mr Eastman took over

Clayton's studio in 1895 it was described as 'well-appointed'[16] indicating a more professional-looking premises but this could have been improved in the intervening thirty years. Some have suggested the shabbiness of the backgrounds suggested Clayton was catering for the 'lower end of the market'[17] but there is the possibility this is not his studio.

There are nine external photographs covering four locations, some sitting on stone steps, some just on stones, next to a plastered wall and a shed, and one in a sort of shed with a cobbled pavement. One image has a group of three women in pinafore dresses and scarf, one with both a hat and scarf wearer, all the rest wearing hats.

Of the internal rooms, there are six locations but all have the same shabby look. Only occasionally has an effort been made to include some sort of background, a tatty tree and pallet with either hay or sacking on the floor and for one woman a pile of stones was placed next to her. All the images are full length and well-lit, highlighting all the folds and creases in their dresses but there seems to be no specific locations associated with hats/scarfs or dresses.

If the images had been taken in Clayton's studio in Iron Street the question arises as to when they were taken.

The distance from the Tredegar Iron and Coal works to Clayton's studio is about two miles. At a normal pace, it takes on average fifteen minutes to walk one mile so a round trip would take an hour, plus about half an hour to take the images. For the 69 women, this would account for 102 hours or about ten days work and it seems unlikely, even if the pictures were taken over an extended time period, that employers would want to lose so much work time and the women themselves would not be paid. As Sunday was the only day off and it was not permitted to work on the holy day it seems unlikely the pictures were taken then, and unlikely they were shot after work as the women would have been dirtier and the light darker. In addition, 69 women traipsing back and forth to the mine would surely have raised interest in the local newspapers but nothing appears in the press.

If the pictures were taken at the works, allowing for half an hour per individual, then the time lost would be about 34 hours or three days work. While this seems much more likely it still raises the question of why the employer would allow this and why the newspapers were not aware of the exercise?

In addition, an 1870 photo of Bwllfa tip women shows all of the women with a clear dividing line across their faces showing they must have worn some sort of covering over their upper face to protect their eyes, and their hands are dirty indicating they were pulled away from their work for the picture to be taken. Only one Clayton woman has this line across her face and few of them have dirty hands indicating the pictures were probably taken in the morning before they started work.

Posing Stands

Despite a number of accounts which talk of laughter and fun among the women, the Clayton images, with the exception of one, show the woman looking nervous and ill at ease. Benjamin Price from Amgueddfa Cymru — National Museum Wales provided a suggestion that might explain this – in a number of the pictures it is possible to make out just behind the women's feet a dark horizontal shape, the base of a posing stand. These helped people keep still during exposure time, which at this time could take between 10–20 seconds or longer, long enough for the slightest movement to blur the image. Usually made of cast iron they consisted of a single pole on a base with a moveable arm at the top and a u-shaped attachment that fitted around the neck. More extensive ones would have a bar in the middle for the waist. They were not particularly strong, in that they could not be leaned against, so the individual would have to stand with their neck in the brace for as long as the photographer needed.

Six of the images have either all or some of the women sitting, or leaning against pallets; one stands holding a shovel and two hold picks. Some online commentators have stated the women would not have used picks, however, breaking up large blocks of coal (or stone) would have needed a tool similar to a pick and essential if they were employed in road making. A pick is not always swung from above but can be used for levering stones at a low angle. While the inclusion of these tools enhances the masculinity of the portraits, given they are in the minority it is possible they were given to the women as an aid to steady themselves. This leaves 35 free-standing women who had to hold still and balance, and smiling was not encouraged because it is difficult to hold a smile for the long exposures – being held in a brace and ordered not to smile may possibly explain the stressed looks on the women's faces.

Where women appear in groups they are often touching, holding hands or have their arms around their shoulders or waists. This could be a method of stabilising each other during the long exposure times, or they might be a tight community of women.

Why the Clayton images were taken remains a mystery, as are the women's identities, but they are an important and unique collection of working women in Wales in the 1860s.

Chapter 11

Sackcloth and Ashes

The *Select Committee on Regulation and Inspection of Mines* had exonerated mining women of immorality and decided to leave them alone but social reformers would not rest in their determination to have the women sacked and six years later they began again.

At the Amalgamated Association of Miners conference held in Merthyr Tydfil in October 1871, a delegate from Lancashire outlined a conversation between himself and a Welsh delegate who told him that several women had made enquiries about joining the association. The audience laughed. One man, a Mr Picard, was sorry to say that they had about 600 women working, but he would never recognise females being connected with the association, to which members of the audience shouted 'hear, hear.' He added that some years ago they had made a strong move 'with a view to getting the evil abandoned' and had even had photographs taken of a gang of women in their working apparel, and forwarded them to Queen Victoria [the Royal Collection has been unable to locate this album] and other influential people, seeking sympathy for 'the poor women'. It was moved by John Davies, and seconded by Mr Dodd of North Wales, 'that this conference condemns the employment of female labour at the pit banks of the various mines in the country' and it was carried unanimously.[1]

One reason for the continued concern was that numbers were difficult to assess. Women were not generally recorded in the wages books as they tended to appear under a man's name and their work was more intermittent than the men's. In 1866 the estimation had been 3,763 women at mines in England and Wales while the 1871 census *Population Abstracts* cites 3,251 women working as *Coal heaver, Labourer*, 1,511 under 20 and 1,740 over 20.[2] However, three years later, in 1874, according to a table compiled by Angela V. John, that number had risen to 6,776 – South Wales being the largest area with 1,603 compared to 1,312 for West Lancashire and 1,363 for South Staffordshire.[3]

In 1879 the *Cardigan Observer* in a piece entitled *Female Employment in Mines* cited the figure as 5,000:

> it is a somewhat startling fact to find that there are still nearly 5,000 women and girls employed about the coal mines of the United Kingdom.

In the official summary of persons employed in and about the mines under the Coal Mines Act, it is stated that 21 females under the age of 13 years are employed—Glamorgan employing 10 of these; East Scotland, 2; Yorkshire, 5; and the remainder being distributed in ones and twos amongst other districts. Of girls between the ages of 13 and 16 there are 433 employed—129 in West Lancashire, 94 in Shropshire, 71 in East Scotland, 14 in the Liverpool district, 25 in Glamorgan, and the remainder in smaller numbers. Of young women above the age of 16 there are no less than 4,502 employed- West Lancashire, Glamorganshire, East Scotland, Shropshire, South Staffordshire, and Cumberland being the chief offenders, and the midland district being entirely free from this employment; whilst in South Durham-the largest of the coal-fields, if production be the test—only 8 women are employed. In the mines registered under the Metalliferous Mines Act, there is a larger proportionate employment of females. At the tender age of between 8 and 13 years, there are 96 girls employed, chiefly in the Cornwall district between the ages of 13 and 18, there are 931 girls employed about these mines, Cornwall and the North Wales district employing the bulk; and there are also 1,741 females above the age of 18 employed—Cornwall, North Wales, and Ireland employing all these except 20; and of this score, somewhat singularly, the chief part are employed in the North of England, which has been remarkably free from women's work in the unfit employment of mining. The proportion of women employed, it is satisfactory to notice, is decreasing; but the fact that girls of such tender ages are put to mining operations—or to work above ground at the mines, rather—is a sign that the unsatisfactory symptom is not likely to entirely die out.[4]

All showing how unreliable figures for women in mines can be.

In some places, however, employers were actively reducing their women. Munby in his diary for 1870 noted that women at Nantyglo were replaced by men who were paid double the women's wages.[5] In March the same year the *Cardiff & Merthyr Guardian* claimed discussions of a new Factory Act (which came into being in 1874) caused the Dowlais Works to dismiss upwards of a hundred girls and that boys and men who replaced them would be paid at a higher rate.[6] This, the paper claimed, would be better for families ignoring the fact that many poor families were dependent on women's wages. While marriage was considered by society to be the ideal situation for both women and men, it was not always possible. In a society where only men are supposed to work, and often in difficult circumstances with little health and safety rules, it meant they died quicker than women. This was becoming apparent in the 1850s when it was recognised nearly a million women were single, and in 1870 *The Times* wrote of its concern that one in three women had no 'natural protector' or 'natural sphere of duty' and that 'women with nobody to work for them must work for themselves'.[7] Few considered these statistics when they tried to ban women from working.

Whatever the exact number of women employed, they continued to be treated as curiosities. In *The Travelling Menagerie*, author/poet Charles Camden (1817–1912), describes a journey through Wales noting a description of the women similar to the Clayton images, 'Some bold tip-girls with their leather buskins still on, their dusty handkerchiefs still bound tightly over their hair, and carrying shovels on the shoulders of their dirty long-sleeved pinafores.'[8]

The Graphic produced a stylised image of Welsh women on the pit bank and the accompanying text describing their work was reasonably positive, this too conforms with the pictures of the women in the Clayton collection:

> Her costume is a canvas frock, reaching a little below the knees, displaying well-shaped legs and feet, clothed in hob-nailed shoes or half-boots. On her head she wears a light coloured handkerchief tied closely over the hair to protect it from the black dust. On top of the handkerchief is a hat, often ornamented with large blue beads. Her skirts are, of course, short, and all the rest of her costume is durable and consistent with her work. The Tip-Girl works in all weathers on the exposed tips, or rubbish heaps, brought from the mine. She picks out with a hammer the bits of ore left along them. She stacks the ore thus found in oblong beds, and also empties the tram-waggons. Besides this, she works on the patches, which is that part of an iron mine where the ore is near enough to the surface to be dug out without the aid of machinery or the sinking of deep pits; often, too, she stands at the mouth of the shaft to receive the loads of ore or rubbish. Her hours of work are from six to six, with intervals for meals, and her average earnings are about 9s a week. She usually begins at fourteen years of age. She is herself a healthy, happy, sturdy woman, not without her share of good looks, and more than her share of freedom, ease and grace. She is, moreoever, honest, frank, fearless, independent, and virtuous, the exceptions to the last good quality being rare.[9]

Needless to say, criticism of the women's dress continued throughout the decade and those in Wales still attempted to deny that their women wore trousers. An inspector for South Wales mines, Thomas Evans, stated that Welsh pit girls did not wear trousers and were 'respectably dressed'.[10] However, at the Bwllfa colliery, Aberdare, in the 1870s, some women did dress in trousers although unlike the Wigan women they kept their skirts low down the leg – at least in a photograph they did. In this image, the women's dress is similar to the Clayton's although each of their faces has a line delineating between the clean area around their eyes and their dirt-grimed mouths showing they were at work when the picture was taken.

Some commentators tried to play down women wearing 'trousers' by linking them to the bloomer, a new type of clothing from America that divided a skirt into separate legs.

1872 Act

Henry Austin Bruce (1815–1895), 1st Baron Aberdare, was a Liberal MP, a senior trustee of the Dowlais Iron Works, and Home Secretary from 1869 to 1873. In 1870 he introduced proposals for a new Mines' Regulation Bill intended to tighten up legislation regarding the work of children and women. The term 'child' was defined as one under 13, 'young person' 13–18, and 'woman' as a female of 18 and upwards. The Bill barred any child under ten, and any boy 10–13 from working more than six days a week underground. No child under eight was to be employed above ground. No woman, young person, or child was to be employed between 9 pm and 5 am, after 2 pm on a Saturday, and not at all on a Sunday.

This would equate to a monetary loss for families and was not popular. Crawshay Bailey (1789–1872), Ironmaster of Nantyglo Ironworks prohibited women fillers to work at night in 1870 and their wages dropped from 8–11 shillings to 6 a week.[11] In 1887 an Irish priest, Father Bede, came to Swansea at St Joseph's Church and recalled that a number of tip girls would go to church in bare feet.[12]

Menelaus, the General Manager at the Dowlais Iron Company, had previously written a detailed memorandum defending night and Sunday employment for females and young people. In 1866, 781 females had been employed at the farms, quarries, mine works and collieries at Dowlais[13] working day and night shifts but if night work was stopped the women would have nothing to do during the day and would have to be sacked.

Lady Charlotte Guest (1812–1895), wife of ironmaster John Josiah Guest, had objected to women working nights alongside men and for a time it was stopped but soon resumed due to necessity. Menelaus pointed out that there was little alternative labour for the women and that keeping them on saved the country from having to pay poor relief.

Another clause in the Bill stated that everyone should have intervals amounting to an hour and a half for shifts that exceeded six hours. While intending to be well-meaning it simply meant people had to work longer hours to maintain the same wage. A similar result came with regard to a reduction in the time women could work, not more than fifty-four hours in a week or more than ten hours in a day. As many women worked in excess of ten hours a day this meant another loss of income.

By June the rights of women had seeped into the argument, namely whether women had the right to be steam-engine drivers. Richard Fothergill (1822–1903), an English Liberal ironmaster with iron works in South Wales, was in favour and suggested an amendment to that effect but, the *Cardiff Times* complained, 'the House appears to have been in that illogical, but practical, frame of mind involving a disposition to draw the line somewhere'. Conservative MP Henry Liddell (1821–1903) argued the dress women wore was a sufficient reason why they should not be in charge of engines and Henry Bruce said charge of an engine required firmness, courage, and presence of mind and ought not to be trusted to a woman. 'We can easily imagine,' the *Cardiff Times* interrupted its coverage to note, 'the burning wrath with which many energetic ladies engaged in the emancipation of their sex' read the cruel remarks. If she was allowed to wear 'a bloomer costume or trousers,' they continued, that would that not be acceptable and:

> here is an example of the injustice of man! He forces women to swaddle her naturally free limbs in a petticoat, and then says you shall not be allowed to do what you want because you are not dressed properly for the purpose? Women shall not manage engines because they have not firmness and courage. Why, there is a female colonel just elected to command a regiment of volunteers in New York. Shade of Grace Darling, have women no courage? Henpecked husbands of Britain, are women destitute of firmness? We can imagine Messrs. Liddel and Bruce morally annihilated at a female discussion society.[14]

Richard Fothergill (1822–1903), an Englishman who had inherited the Aberdare Iron Works before buying up industries across South Wales in the iron and coal trades, had become an MP for Merthyr Tydfil in 1868. He said he did not wish to compel women to be drivers but 'if they liked the occupation he did not see why they should not follow it'.[15] Fothergill took the opportunity to defend the women:

> Against the doctrine which evidently obtains in the minds of certain honourable gentlemen, that if a woman wears a dirty dress she must

necessarily be of immoral character. Now, I have passed my life among the mining community of South Wales, and I can truly say that the wives and daughters of the working classes there are as modest and as well able to guard their honour as any woman in the land. (Cheers.) Dirty clothes! why: sir, in my opinion it is too often smart clothes which indicate a loss of innocence, and Parliament should take care that, in prohibiting honest women from gaining an honest livelihood, they do not change their dirty clothes to smart ones upon the public streets— (cheers)—It was said that they wore men's clothes, but the fact was that, as a matter of propriety, their trousers were lengthened to their ankles and occasionally throwing a man's coat over their shoulders during severe weather, or where is the degradation he refers to in their lengthening their trousers through simple decency in their labour. (Cheers and laughter) I think, sir, the committee is much obliged to the honourable member for South West Lancashire (Mr Cross) for his manly outspoken views on the subject of women gaining their own livelihood, and I am glad to have an opportunity of publicly expressing my contempt for the nonsensical sentimentality, if not worse, which associates dirty clothes with immorality and degradation.[16]

The clause was modified allowing women to be drivers of horses but rendered it illegal for them to be in charge of engines.

Before long the old argument of banning women from working came back into the argument. Conservative MP, William St James Wheelhouse (1821–1886) wanted an amendment to prohibit all employment of women above ground. 'The labour,' he told the House of Commons, 'is undoubtedly debasing; the women so employed are surrounded by demoralising associations; the character of the labour itself has a tendency to unsex them employed in it.' He was aware that a contrary opinion had been expressed by the Select Committee and also aware it would have a detrimental effect on wages but hoped it would not sway people's resolve to see the ban through.

While several agreed, many disagreed with Wheelhouse. Henry Richard (1812–1888), the Merthyr Tydfil MP known as the Apostle of Peace, claimed the miners 'very strongly object to the employment of women and their reasons are fairly stated by themselves'. If women were excluded more men would have to be employed at higher rates. Parliament interfering with the freedom of adult labour meant a source of income would be closed to a large class of women in the colliery districts. Richards also added a defence of the women:

the women who work on the pit banks of South Wales – the tip-girls of Dowlais – the tram-girls in the iron mines of Cyfartha (*sic*) – the screen-girls in the Aberdare valley – are as virtuous a class as any other in which women are engaged in conjunction with men; and these hard-working Welsh women are certainly less famed for immorality than the straw-weavers of Luton, the glove-makers of Yeovil, or the girls in the cloth mills of Stroud. That their virtue triumphs over associations and circumstances antagonistic to its welfare, we are not disposed to deny; but admit that there is a moral power at work which makes women superior to the degrading influences and frequent temptations of their avocation, and the case against female labour is reduced to one of abstract principle alone – a principle unquestionably good, but, because abstract, difficult of application.

However, a number of MPs rose to bitterly condemn the women, simply repeating the unfounded claims of immorality and 'unsexing' and provided no supporting evidence. A. J. Mundella (1825–1897) claimed women needed rescuing because they were nothing more than slaves of their husbands 'his horse, his ass, his anything' – language that shocked some members of the House.

Isaac Fletcher (1827–1879) agreed that in some parts of Wales and South Staffordshire some women were not 'properly dressed' but thought the work was relatively easy. Sorting out the refuse from the coal was neither hard nor degrading, and it was performed under cover. He claimed the women who picked out this refuse were better adapted to the work than men, and 'they earned 9s. a-week by their labour. If the Amendment were adopted, a large number of deserving women would be deprived of the means of support which was now open to them.'

Jacob Bright (1821–1899) was the only MP to suggest speaking to the very women whose livelihood they proposed to take away.

In the end, it was agreed that the best option was to leave the employment of women to 'be regulated by the improved feeling of our countrymen' and the amendment was negatived[17] although the rest of the Bill was enacted in 1872.

Pay Dispute

In August of the same year, all the women, around 120, employed at the coal pit banks, and unloading coal at the forges and mills of the works in Rhymney went on strike over wages. They were receiving 7s 6d per week and wanted a rather large rise amounting to 12 shillings. Two pits in the area had stopped due to the women going on strike and a number of labourers, it is not known if they were male or female, were temporarily employed to keep the works going. However, due to intimidation, of a sort seen during the strike of 1868 when the women had been violent towards blacklegs, the police had to guard the labourers throughout the day.[18] By early September the owners had given in and paid the women which immediately set the piling women at the mills on strike making a similar claim.[19]

The following year most of the miners of South Wales went out on strike. They had asked for a 20% increase in wages citing the high price of coal as justification, after all when coal prices fell owners cut their wages, but the owners argued the prices were illusionary and they could not afford a wage rise. The miners reduced their claim to 10% and asked for the matter to go to arbitration so the owner's figures could be examined independently, but that was refused and some sixty thousand men went on strike, no figures were given for the women. It was a bitter strike for the miners and their families who suffered dreadfully from starvation. The *Illustrated London News*, *The Graphic* and other publications printed numerous articles to illustrate the suffering and often it is difficult to tell if the women are tip girls or housewives, they wear similar dresses, hats and handkerchiefs tied over their heads. Some did specific pieces on the tip girls, such as that in *The Graphic* featuring a Welsh pit girl with a skirt over trousers scavenging coal from the slag heaps, another of the 'tip girls leaving Dowlais' at the start of the strike. Only one publication included the women in their text when they described, 'a more pitiable picture of utter desolation and abject misery cannot be conceived than that presented today by the once thriving town of Dowlais'. They took the opportunity to describe the women's work:

> tip-girls scattered all over the immense yard – on the colliery bank above the furnaces there; below, where more trams are bringing ironstone to the great kilns that are ever being fed; and here, where sulphurous fumes arise from an artificial hill of broken bricklike cinder, these strong-bodies, brawny-armed, yet withal comely lasses, are working, with head enwrapped in a check cloth that hides only to emphasise the bulky chignon protruding behind; with bodies enveloped in a tight sack or a man's jacket; with dress of coarse texture, which, short as the skirts of the *corps de ballet* that provoked the Lord Chamberlain's censure, reveals the fact that this generic type of the strong-minded hard-working Welsh woman has adopted the Bloomer costume so far as to wear the garment which is generally considered the prerogative of man to monopolise –

these all, nailman and railmaker, haulier and girl of the tips, added the animation of real life to the stir of mechanical activity.[20]

The strike lasted about three months and the miners returned with a small pay rise.

The output of coal was increasing, in South Wales it rose from 4.5 million tons in 1840 to 16.5 in 1874[21] and in 1875 the miners planned another strike over wages but the owners pre-empted them and in January locked the workers out in what became known as 'the lockout of colliers and ironworkers'. The effects were 'calamitous' and it was impossible, wrote an unnamed journalist for the *Monmouthshire Merlin*, 'to exaggerate the gravity of the catastrophe':

> With the exception of the purely agricultural districts, almost the entire population of the two counties of Glamorgan and Monmouth are reduced to idleness, for the suspension of the staple industries of coal and iron involves the great copper and tin-plate works, patent fuel manufactories, and hundreds of smaller concerns dependent upon the coal supply, which this lock-out cuts off from the continuance of their own activity. As to the numbers of men idle, the colliers and pit labourers alone number about 70,000, the ironworkers 40,000, and the men whose employment is contingent upon the employment of these, are certainly 10,000, so that we have a host of 120,000 workmen in enforced idleness.

The number of women out of work was not given.

Once again, various publications produced images from the Merthyr area including an *Illustrated London News* illustration of four tip women talking in a street. One woman is wearing an ornate hat and scarf in a style draped down her back reminiscent of the Clayton images, two are wearing kerchiefs over their heads, tied at the back, and an elderly woman has a check shawl over a peaked hat.

The pressure on the poor rates in the districts became exceedingly heavy, particularly in Merthyr and Tredegar. Many of the men went to break up stones for roads to earn money but the women struggled to find alternative employment, something discussed during consideration of the high number of applications for relief from the Merthyr Tydfil Poor Law Union. A Rev. William Davies 'gravely' asked how they were 'going to deal with those young women, who have been in the habit of working on the tips?' Mr Kirkhouse replied there were jobs going in the workhouse but the Rev. said he knew of 35 women who, since the stoppage, had needed relief and food and the numbers were rising, too many for the workhouse to employ. One unnamed member suggested, 'they can try for places as servants,' but that too was impractical as there had been a glut of servants and people had been discharging them, adding, 'they are all about Penydarren'. When the Chairman asked if Rev. Davies had come on the women's behalf, he said he had but the Chairman insisted the women came themselves on the Saturday to ask for relief and if in the meantime they were destitute they would be relieved with food. The Chairman added a final note that 'the tip girls at Cyfarthfa are all at work I know'.[22]

The months dragged on with the insistence that the men return to work on 15% reduced wages because the owners' profits were falling and, in the meantime, the *Western Mail* mourned the 'one numerous class' at a 'sad loss for employment':

> I refer to the tip girls, that semi-masculine class; who used to haunt tips in bloomer costume, and indulge in rough horse play with haulier lads on every possible occasion. Merthyr streets have lost one of its most novel and picturesque class of frequenters by their disappearance ... These constituted the novelties, with their half male dress, and heads bound round with showy handkerchiefs to keep the coal dust from that glory of woman, as Solomon has it - her hair. "Where are they gone? strangers exclaim. I cannot answer the question, but fear they are starving in the obscure corners. If they could be polished, something might be done with them, but for servant-girldom they are of little use. When the tinworks start I shall expect to see them re-appear from obscurity, and figure again, but then at an occupation more suitable for them.[23]

When the pay reduction was reduced to 12½% for three months the miners had little option but to return to work and they did so in May – after the three months, of course, the owners could increase it again.

Newspapers

Newspaper accounts of tip women for the 1870s do seem to concentrate more on the sensational, highlighting immorality and crimes in the courts, however for the period of ten years only fifteen stories of tip women have been so far located.

Men's assaults on women accounted for four of those stories.

In 1873 Gwen Thomas, a tip girl in the Aberdare, Rhondda Cynon Taf area had a bakestone (a type of griddle often used to cook Welsh cakes on) which another woman took and hid. Joseph Hopkins an ex-policeman, accused Gwen of taking it but when she denied it, he told her unless she gave it back, he would strangle her. In self-defence, Gwen picked up a sprag (a prop used in coal mines) but Joseph took it from her, struck her on the head, and she fell, bleeding from a cut. Ever since then she had been in pain. The magistrate gave Joseph the choice of settling with Gwen or going to trial. He returned shortly afterwards and said they had settled.[24]

Two years later two lads, Evans and Welsh, were charged with an indecent assault on Jane Lewis, a coal filler in Sirhowy Ironworks Works, Glamorgan. The boys caught hold of her and got her down, one held her hand and mouth while the other behaved indecently. Fortunately Jane's mother, Ann Lewis happened to come along, and the boys ran away. Evans was sent to prison for six weeks with hard labour and Welsh for one month.[25]

That same year, in a rare story from North Wales, Ellis Valentine, from Trefechan, was summoned for assaulting Catherine Owen as they worked at the Groes pit, Rhos. Catherine was working on the coal bank with Mary Jane Morris when Ellis came up the shaft and started to playfully scuffle with Mary, but the pair fell onto Catherine causing her an injury. He claimed he was 'obliged' to strike her because she then slapped his face, and threatened to hit him with a quart can. Catherine denied she slapped him and called Sarah Roberts, another tip girl, as a witness who said after the three got up, Ellis struck Catherine twice in the face because he had lost his temper. Mary gave a different version saying she and Catherine were playing around when Ellis caught her around the waist but her friend had been sitting on the cabin bench with her foot out which Ellis tripped over, she had slapped him and then dared him to hit her back. Unable to find a verdict the case was dismissed.[26]

A more serious case occurred in May 1877 when Thomas Holloway (21) of Penydarren, Merthyr, quarrelled with his sweetheart, Sarah Ann Evans (23), a tip girl, as they were breakfasting together at 9 am at the Colly Colliery at Bedlinog near Garnddulais belonging to Dowlais Iron Company. Both were employed as shunters (although elsewhere Sarah was described as a tipper) at No 5 pit. Thomas had been toasting some meat on a pocket knife and offered her some but she refused. 'I suppose' he said, 'that other people's meat is better than mine?' as she had previously taken some from other men. Sarah resented the remark and so he stabbed her in the left side with the knife which went through her clothing and into her breast just under the heart, then he casually wiped the blood off the blade with his finger and thumb. Given the toughness of their clothing, he must have stabbed her with some force. In order to examine the wound unseen, they went to woods just below the pit bank and found that the blood was clotting around the clothes, but they both agreed to keep quiet and Sarah carried on working. Shortly afterwards, she began to fail and had to be taken to her father's house at Garnddulais. P.C. Hunt was called and arrested Thomas just as he was about to leave on one of the Taff Bargoed Railway engines which was taking a train of coal from the colliery; he was taken to Caerphilly and locked up. 'The excitement in the district is at a high pitch,' wrote a journalist in the *Western Mail*.

At the first hearing, Sarah was very reluctant to give evidence against her 'sweetheart'. 'My father and mother,' she told the court, 'were not willing for us to keep company, and I told the prisoner I did not want to have anything to say to him. He had a knife toasting bacon in the lodge, and I do not know whether he stabbed me when I was trying to turn around or not. I did not see a knife in the prisoner's hand when I was stabbed. When I was taken home he wanted to go with me. When I went into the lodge he asked me why I did not go when he called me.' Ann Williams, who also worked at the colliery, had examined Sarah's wound afterwards and said Thomas had been jealous and wanted to carry Sarah home, threatening to kill Sarah and then himself. As Sarah collapsed against a tram Thomas said 'I've broken her heart,' and distraught he confessed to a colleague John Richards that he had stabbed Sarah. Thomas was found guilty and as he had already been in prison for three months before the trial, he would do another nine with hard labour. As he was being taken down, he told the magistrate, 'I beg pardon, my lord, I could not help it; indeed, I couldn't.'[27]

Another case of falling out with a sweetheart was in 1877. Dinah Pugh (18) living at 20 Solomon Street, Penydarran, who worked at the coal-washing machine, Dowlais was found drowned in Goitre Pond. The couple had rowed and so she had taken her life.[28]

Not all the cases of violence were about men, women were also brought up for assaults on other women.

In 1874 three 'ladies of the "tips"', had a fight. Sisters Margaret Sullivan and Mary Ann Sullivan were charged with assaulting Mary Ann Lyons at Abersychan, Monmouthshire. The defendants 'who were got up in the height of fashion, and whose hats were something prodigious,' were "tip girls," – the use of the inverted commas around tip girls shows this phrase was only just gaining popularity and so had to be highlighted. The few lines in the paper were there to gender interest in the women and there were few details about the fight other than it was something about a truck. They were all found guilty and ordered to pay 5s each and a third of the 15s court costs.[29]

Two years later in another rare story from north Wales, Sarah Hussey was charged by Martha Trevor with assaulting her on Nerquis (or Nercwys Colliery, Mold), Flintshire coal-bank. They were picking coal and had quarrelled, Sarah kicked Martha and assaulted her but Martha argued that Sarah had knocked her with a stick on the shins. She was fined 5s and costs.[30]

In 1878 the *Aberdare Times* ran a piece entitled *Tip Girls*, beginning, 'as a rule we are rather proud of the moral character of our "trousered tip girls," as a contemporary calls them for we very seldom hear of anything like utter loss of sexual individuality which always marks the true woman.' Once again, we see the unfamiliarity with the term and the denial that Welsh women wore trousers. The story concerned 'an occurrence' in the Rhondda Valley 'which will long be remembered in the locality if the ill odour thereof does not attack the Welsh tip girls in general, and those of the Rhondda in particular.'. The girls in question were employed in sorting coal on the screens at Abergorki pit, and one dinner time they began to 'lark, when John Lloyd joined in the "spree"'. Two of the girls threw Hannah Evans on the ground and did 'that which well deserved a sound thrashing from the hands of every decent woman in the valley'. It must have been quite a serious sexual assault because Hannah went to the police and the court case excited 'so much interest in the neighbourhood that every approach to the Pentre police office was crowded'. John was fined 20s and costs, Elizabeth Davies 40s and costs, and Ann Jones £4 including costs, or in default imprisonment in each case. 'We hope,' concluded the *Aberdare Times*, 'this sudden repression of the indecent amongst those "tip women" will have a salutary effect. If Hannah Evans had allowed her modesty to keep her out of court her name would have been a by-word in the valley, and goodness knows where else besides. As it is she has vindicated her virtue and offered a warning to others.'[31]

One very sad case took place in 1872 when an inquest was held at the Greyhouse (probably the Greyhound) Hotel, Tredegar, into the death of a child found on a coal tip. Margaret Price, a widow, worked as a mine cleaner on the tips near the Globe pit, said 'some of the tip girls called on her ... and on going to them she saw certain signs which showed that a birth had taken place'. On searching a few yards off, she found the body of a newly-born boy buried among the mine rubbish. Another tip girl, Sarah Thomas and two men went to inform the police. The inquest showed the baby had been born alive but died from bleeding, the umbilical cord having not been tied, and exposure. Death was put as 'wilful murder against some person or persons unknown'. Nothing more was heard on the subject.[32]

There are a number of minor cases involving tip girls discovered during the 1870s. The *Merthyr Express* titled one piece 'Colliers in Petticoats' about women stealing coal in Merthyr in September 1871.[33] It is unlikely the journalist meant they were working underground and used the phrase for sensational purposes only.

Mary Thomas, single, a tip girl 'apparently', was drunk in Upper Union Street, Dowlais in 1872 and was sent to prison with hard labour for seven days in default of paying a fine of 10s and costs.[34] There were three cases that same year involving thefts. Jane Jones, a tip girl, was charged by Elizabeth Jenkins, of Rhymney with stealing boots. She had taken them to a pawn shop run by Tobias Fine and police believed she was 'wanted' for other offences.[35] Kezia Williams, 'evidently by her appearance' was a tip girl charged with stealing a straw hat valued at 1s 8½d the property of Edward Lee Lewis a draper in High Street, Merthyr. She had purchased a hat for 3s 8d at his shop but half an hour later he saw her again leaning on the counter with something under her apron, later found to be the hat. She claimed she was going to buy it and when caught she offered to pay for it but Lewis declined and called the police. As it was his word against hers, she was discharged.[36] Margaret Connor (18) a tip girl was charged with the theft of a pocket handkerchief and 7d from the pocket of another tip girl, Margaret Daley in 1879. They had been walking to a cinder-tip at Cwmbwria, Swansea and later the handkerchief, a sixpenny piece, and a penny were found to be missing. Margaret asked for them back but was told she could have the handkerchief as she had taken it for fun, but she had not taken the money.[37] She too was discharged.

Two years later seven young women aged 17–20 'dressed in the most elaborate style of "fashion," as prevailing among "tip girls"' were charged with stealing 269lbs of coal valued at 2s 4d from Rhymney Iron Company. Due to the number of thefts two police sergeants had disguised themselves as workers to keep watch on the coal trams at Nantllech, Brithdir.[38] A year later, Louisa Cray and Ann Donovian, tip girls from Merthyr, were charged with stealing a quantity of rope from the same works at Rhymney. Louisa received fourteen days and Ann seven.[39]

There were undoubtedly other stories involving tip girls and women that do not mention occupations. Also, many newspapers have yet to be digitalised, for example, the whole of the 1870s for the *Merthyr Express* is missing, showing that more information is still to be discovered.

Only two deaths in the 1870s that mention occupations have been recovered. Hannah Jennings (22), a mine filler, died at Abersychan in 1872[40] and Elizabeth Protheroe (16), a tip girl at Tyler's Pit, Tredegar, was killed in 1878.[41] In 1881 W. Simons of Gwaunfarren, Merthyr wrote to the *South Wales Daily News* tabling the 324 fatalities in South Wales collieries for 1878 to draw attention to the dangerous working conditions for miners. He lists the age, occupation and cause of death including that of Elizabeth Protheroe:

At No 29 is a tip-girl of 17 who was cleaning sidings on the surface, and just before the accident was told by the man in charge to move out of the way, as he was about to shunt some waggons. She, however, did not do so, and was crushed by them and died immediately.[42]

As a rather tumultuous decade for the tip girl came to an end, there was one more reminder of their supposed immorality. Welsh artist Thomas Henry Thomas (1839–1915) produced his oil on canvas painting of 'Sackcloth and Ashes – tip girls leaving work' in 1879 and it was exhibited at Merthyr the following year. The title is taken from several Biblical books (Esther 4.1.3; Isaiah 58.5; Matthew 11.21 and Luke 10.13) where the wearing of sackcloth and having ashes sprinkled on the head is a sign of penitence or mourning. The quote from Matthew 11:21 describes people who 'have put on sackcloth and sprinkled ashes on themselves, to show that they had turned from their sins!' In the picture the tip woman has turned her face away from the viewer.

Chapter 12

1881 Census

The pit women represented only a fraction of the colliery workforce, about 7%, yet from the publicity, it appeared much more despite the fact that other jobs women did were as, or more, laborious but did not attract the same sort of attention and so pit women became symbolic of women workers generally. Several efforts were made throughout the 1880s to establish how many female workers there were but the figures varied enormously.

Richard Meade's (1858–1882) table in *The Coal and Iron Industries of the United Kingdom* compared figures for the years 1873, 1879, and 1880 showing those aged 10–13 decreased from 31–10, but those aged 13–16 rose from 6,957–7,037, and those above 16 also decreased from 5,383–4,276. Resulting in 11,323 women working in the coal and iron industry in 1880.

Six years later the *Annual Report of the Government Inspector of Mines* report cited 561,092 workers in all UK mines including 5,568 women above ground, about half that of Meade's figures for just the coal and iron industries.[1] Robert Hunt's 1883 *Mineral Statistics of the United Kingdom of Great Britain & Ireland* gives the figure of 4,479 females[2] in the coal industry alone.

In 1888, John Ellis (1841–1910), a British colliery owner and Liberal politician, asked the Secretary of State how many women and girls were employed in coal mining to which the answer was females under 13 during 1887, two; between 13 and 16 years, 259; and above 16 years of age, 3,922 – making a total of 4,183.[3]

According to an 1882 article in the *Weekly Mail*, the number of people employed on the pit surface in South Wales in 1874 was 9,829 of whom 820 were females; by 1881 there were 8,513 of whom 531 were female showing a significant decrease.[4] According to Hunt's figures for 1883, there were no girls aged between 10–13 in South Wales, aged 13–16 there were two in Carmarthen, 12 in parts of Glamorganshire, and two for Pembroke. Over 16 years of age and there were seven in Breconshire (part of), one in Carmarthen, 440 Glamorganshire (part of), and 32 Pembroke amounting to 496. However, research from the 1881 census for this book show, despite Hunt putting the figure of 16 for girls aged 10–16, there were 121 in the census, and those results are only cursory meaning the true figures are probably higher.

As more progressive machinery was being developed it did mean more and more women and men were being laid off but it should also be borne in mind that women's jobs could be intermittent and part-time jobs were not recorded in the same way as an 'occupation'. Even so, once again it can be shown how unreliable historic statistics can be.

1881 Census

For reasons not understood, the 1881 census accessed via *Ancestry* is the only census which returns keyword searches and most of the data for this year has been recovered via keyword/phrases. As searching using the methods for the 1841 and 1851 census were not practical, given the vast amount of material it would be extremely time-consuming to go through pages manually, it has to be accepted that the results are cursory at best and do not reflect as accurate a figure if individual pages had been examined.

The keyword/phrases were taken from job descriptions from previous censuses and newspaper reports and this method resulted in the recovery of 752 females, a statistically useful number to look at various aspects of the women's lives. However, not all entries gave complete data so figures used in the analysis will not always add up to 752. Women who worked at ironworks have not been included even if their jobs involved coal.

One of the search terms included *coal miner* as, despite the fact that the women and girls were not miners as such, this term has often been used to describe them. After inputting the keyword/phrase a summary of an individual's entry appears but where there are doubts each name has to be checked against the original enumerator's form. For example, despite the term *coal miner* appearing a number of times for women on the summary, when checked against the original it often reads *coal miner wife* and so these had to be discounted. Some, when checked, had the term crossed out but it still appears on the summary such as Caroline Griffiths who appears in the census list for Merthyr as a 'coal miner' but this is crossed out on the original form. Several are indicated by ditto marks in a long list and this could simply be the enumerator forgetting to leave the woman's name out. Only when it appears that the woman is genuinely being described as a coal miner is she included.

The largest county as would be expected is Glamorganshire (407 results) followed by Monmouthshire (265); Brecknockshire (37); Pembrokeshire (34); Flintshire (4); Carmarthenshire (5).

Forename

The most common name for all the women was Mary (94 examples) which is in keeping with the census returns of 1841 and 1851. In fact, throughout the UK in the nineteenth century the name Mary, due to its religious connections, was to remain the most popular female name and it included variations such as Mary Ann, Mary Jane, Mary Elizabeth, which accounts for a further 162 individuals.

The second most frequent name is Elizabeth (82) and variations on that name, followed by Margaret (61) and variants, and Ann appears 56 times, most commonly without an 'e'. Popular names were often added together for example Mary Ann or Maryann; Sarah Ann; Eliza Ann; Esther Ann; Elizabeth Ann; totalling 60 variations for the name Ann.

After which the most popular names are Sarah (52), Jane (41), Hannah (23), Catherine (23), Martha (19). Few noticeable Welsh names or Welsh spellings of English names are included, and those that do appear are Gwen, including Gwenny (5), Gwenllian (3), and Gwladis (1). The only other names of note are Kezia, a Hebrew name; and Sora, an oriental name, e.g. Japan, Korea.

Surname

A total of 216 surnames were identified with the most frequent being, Jones (73), Davies (57), Thomas (40), Evans (35), Lewis (27). Most of the surnames are those traditionally associated with Wales indicating that of the 752 women and girls most probably originated from within Wales; although a few other examples exist indicating a religious connection, such as Abraham and Isaac, and a few associated with other countries such as Loredan, a Venetian name, and O'Connell, an Irish name but of course these families may have lived in Wales for generations.

Age

In the 1881 census returns the youngest age cited is 11 (it was legal for children this young to work) for which there are two individuals: Catherine Richards, born at Ystradyfodwg, Glamorgan described as a *coal miner* living in a household of six at 23 Dunraven Street, Ystradyfodwg headed by her dressmaker mother (who is married but the husband is not included in the household). Three of Catherine's brothers, one of whom was 14, are coal miners and there was one scholar. Elizabeth A. Whitney, born at Merthyr and listed as a *miner tipping coal*, lived at 5 Lower Cwm, Upper Merthyr Tydfil in a household of seven headed by her coal miner father. Whitney's sister Mary M. (16) was also a *miner tipping coal*. The mother is listed as housekeeper, and there is one scholar and two infants.

The oldest women were in their 70s: Elizabeth Williams (70) was a widow living at 51 Whitty Court, Lower Merthyr Tydfil with her daughter, Jane Williams and an infant. Elizabeth is described as *Filling Trucks (Miner) Coal*, and while Jane may have married another Williams, it is also possible she was the unmarried mother of the infant. Martha Thomas (78) was not actively working but described as *Formerly Mine Labourer Coal*. She was born in Carmarthenshire but her address is simply listed as 'Hill' in Begelly, Pembrokeshire where she lived with her niece Sarah Thomas (25) who was a *coal carrier*.

The highest group of ages is in the 11–19 category of which there were 285 girls, with 60 aged 17, the largest recorded age of the 752 females. This is in keeping with previous statistics which show the most common 'tip girl' was a teenager.

Of the 20–29 age group there were 268 with an average age of 23; the largest group being those aged 20 of which there were 49 followed by the 21-year olds (42) and the numbers progressively dwindle until those aged 29 only account for 17 women – indicating most women probably worked until getting married in their mid-20s. Among the higher age groups, those aged 30–39 have 99 women and the 40–78 have 101 women. Of the latter group a handful lived with fathers, daughters, sons-in-law or brothers-in-law, one lived at the workhouse, and four were boarders/lodgers of which two houses were headed by widows. Eight women lived with their widowed mothers, 17 were heads of household with no status given, 26 lived with their husbands, but 31 widows were heads of the household. Of the 40–78 age group 42% were widows while 26% lived with husbands.

In fact, of the 752 women, 239 (32%) lived with heads of households who had lost spouses. Where male heads of house accounted for 337 (54%) only 16 (5%) were widowers. However, out of female heads of houses who accounted for 246 (40%), a massive 178 (72%) were widows. As this is a study of the tip girls and not their families, the ages of the widows/widowers were not collected but this would be an interesting study to compare if the more dangerous work of a miner resulted in more widows than the average population.

Occupations

The work of the women is most commonly described in generic terms such as *working/labourer* or as *Coal Miner Lab; Colliery Lab; Labourer at Coal Pit; Labourer at Top of Coal miner Pit; Labourer colliery; Coal labourer;* or simply, *at coal mine*, and there is a wide variety of descriptions around these terms. There are also a number of variations around *tipper* or *tipping* such as *coal tipper; (coal) miner tipper; tip girl coal miner; coalscreen tipper;* or *tipper*. This in turn led to the name they were most famously known for as *tip girls/women*. Alternatives were *Colliery girl; Colliery labourer* and very occasionally *pit girl*.

The word 'miner' is often incorporated such as *(Miner) Working at Coal Pit; Coal Worker (Miner); Coal Miner Labourer; Working at coal (miner); Lab at Works (Miner Coal)*.

Sometimes there is a more detailed description of their work such as *unloading* or *landing* coal and despite being known for sorting coal on the screens there are relatively few mentions of this work, only 16 examples. Other jobs included *coal washers/cleaners;* some were assistants, one to her father, two to banksmen, and one a *coal miner's labourer*. Some *trimmed coal* meaning to cut it down to size, *weighed coal* or were *coal carriers*. Relatively few were mentioned as oiling trams. There was one *messenger at office colliery;* one *Colliery Errand Woman;* and one *colliery manager*, other jobs included *Picking Rubbish at Coal Pit* and there were seven hauliers, women who worked with horses. Where a male term existed, such as *banksman*, there was no effort to make the term general neutral or female and so the women were given those names. There were also six proprietors of coal mines and two had shares in collieries.

The *colliery manager* was Elizabeth A. Gittins (24) born in Mostyn, Flintshire who lived at Rhewl in a house of nine with her father who was head of the house. He was also described as a colliery manager and Elizabeth had three brothers (9, 12 & 15) who were coal miners. It seems unusual that a woman, and a young one at that, was a manager, and her occupation is marked with ditto marks directly under her father so it may be a mistake.

Jane Jones (17) was a *messenger at office colliery*, born in and living at Blaenavon, No. 16 Victoria Row, with her widowed mother and five people including three brothers, an iron stone miner; a blacksmith; and a 13-year-old messenger in the steel works. The *Colliery Errand Woman* was Elizabeth Hillings (60) born in and living at Begelly, Pembrokeshire, at an address simply listed as 'Hill' with her two coal miner sons and a daughter who was a domestic servant.

Occupancy of House

The 752 females lived at 630 separate addresses.

The lowest occupancy was 12 women who lived by themselves, four in their 30s, two in their 40s, one aged 55, and five women in their 60s. Elizabeth Williams (64), a *Collier woman*, had been born in Cheshire and Sarah Griffiths (60), a *Coalminer wheeler*, was originally from Ireland but all the others were from Wales.

The households that held five individuals was the highest group (104), followed by six people (93); and then four people (77). The largest occupancy was 14 – Catherine Sims (18), a *Labourer top of colliery*, was born in and worked at Merthyr and lived at 8 Bell Row with her housekeeper mother; married sister; fireman brother; labourer at the brick works sister; five scholars; one infant; a sister in law; and another infant. Out of the 14 people only three were working.

The second highest was 13 people of which there were two households – Ann Samuel (18), a *Labourer Top of Colliery*, was born in and worked at Merthyr, living at Baeka Farm. Her father was a *colliery lamp man*; her brother a haulier underground; and another brother (13) was an assistant in the lamp room. The mother was housekeeper and there was a sister with no occupation; three scholars; three infants; and an aunt who also had no occupation. In this family, only four of the 13 people worked and two of those were teenagers.

Another of the 13 occupancy were Louisa M. Thomas (18), born at Aberdare who lived with her mother Rachel Thomas (57) at Ysguborwen House and both are described as a *coal owner*; the other occupants were Rachel's son a solicitor, two sons at university; a married niece; and seven servants. Louisa was the youngest daughter of Samuel Thomas, one of the pioneers of the Welsh coal trade, and when she died in 1904 aged only 39, she left £80,704 (about £10 million today) in her will.

On the other side of society, six of the women in the 1881 census lived in the workhouse. Five at Wrexham Union Workhouse and one at the Pontypool Union Workhouse. Elizabeth Baker (24), Elizabeth French (28), Ann Griffiths (37), and Jane Blunt (38), all born in Denbighshire, were *worker on coal bank* living at the Wrexham Workhouse. Hannah Bartlett (20) at the Pontypool Workhouse was born at Bleanavon, Monmouthshire and was *unloading coal at colliery*.

Women who lived with their husbands only accounted for 11% of the total which is not surprising as most women gave up work once they married. Some young women carried on working before expecting a baby, such as

Margaret Thomas (18) who was a *coal miner* living with her husband and a boarder. The eldest is 69 also described as a *coal miner* living with her *coal miner* husband also 69 and a grandson. Most are described as *coal miners* with a few labourers but there is also Eliza J. Lewis (36) a *Colliery Clerk* – however her husband is described in the same way so it may be a mistake particularly as there were three infants in the house. Similarly, Catherine Lewis (58) is described as a *coal cutter* someone who cuts at the coal face, which is unlikely as it was illegal for women to work underground, and her husband and two sons are described in this way so it may be a mistake. Jane Jones (38) at Pontypridd lives with her husband and four young children, but he is described as 'possible black lung' (pneumoconiosis, the inhalation of coal dust building up in the lungs making breathing difficult) which may explain why Jane was working. The same is true of Elizabeth Jenkins (56) at Merthyr, her husband is also described as 'possible black lung'.

A great deal of potential remains for a wider study of the 752 women, where they lived and possibly worked, their families, and other aspects, but it currently remains outside the scope of this book.

Chapter 13

Angels of Humanity

Throughout previous decades attempts to prevent women from working in the coal and iron works were persistent, but by the 1880s it had become an obsession. Article after article, letters, editorials, and speeches in the House of Commons flooded through and this time the social reformers were determined to end the women's employment.

At the National Conference of Miners, held in Birmingham in 1883, the resolution put forward was that 'such employment was degrading in its influence on the character of the women, and that it was detrimental in its economic and moral effects in the domestic life of the miners, and with the view of carrying the resolution into practical effect the delegates present agreed to use strenuous efforts to bring about the abolition of female labour at mines.'[1]

The same year, William Royal, who worked at the Gelly (Gelli Colliery, Ystrad) Colliery gave a speech before a 'great demonstration of Rhondda miners at Ton Ystrad' supporting the abolishment of female labour on the pit tops, to cheers of 'hear, hear' from the audience.[2]

Most of the arguments concentrated on the Wigan women and most were repetitions of those which had gone before, it was an evil practice, the women were degraded by such work and the accusations of immorality persisted, as well as a growing alarm about the number of working women 'forcing' their way into male industries.

In the early 1880s women's employment was increasing. The mills in north England had seen women flock to them so that 'domestic servants are scarce' and their wages comparatively high. One of the major problems, noted the *Cardiff Times* in its piece *Female Employment*, was that 'the home is not that place of social comfort and pleasure when the mother and daughters are all out at work. It is in the colliery and the iron districts that women sinks to the lowest depths of labour degradation.' They drew comparisons with English women who 'labour hard at the forge making chains, nails and other things of a similar description from early morning till late at night, their pay not being like that of a Lancashire factory lass, from 12s to double that amount per week, but only 7s or 8s.' But at least they did not come into contact with men unlike women at coal pits. Quoting the latest reports of the Inspectors of Mines the journalist claimed there were 307 girls between the ages of 13 and 16 employed at the mines, and 4,344 above 16, of which over one-fourth were employed in the South Wales and Monmouthshire colliery district. The *Cardiff Times* grumbled:

> the kind of labour at which these women and girls are employed is unsuitable is generally admitted. Some time ago we happened to go over the works of a large iron and coal company in this district, and there saw a number of girls engaged in pushing trucks – or trams, as they are called – of coal, away from the pit-shaft as fast as they were hoisted up from below. It was impossible to judge of the ages of the girls, for the coal dust so hid their faces that they might have been any age from sixteen to sixty. Their dress did not assist in solving the problem, but my guide informed me that their ages ranged from seventeen to twenty-three or twenty-four. They would, he said, drink, swear, and fight like men, and many of them smoke as well; whilst their moral character in other directions was equally low. It was, he stated, seldom that the pit girls joined in the local singing classes or chorus; their amusements and relaxations were of a different nature. But they have their enjoyments, nevertheless.

The journalist reassured readers that they did dress up smart on a Sunday – 'boots with military heels, fashionable dresses, mantles, hats, parasols, and all the rest of it.' While acknowledging the women and girls did not consider their work either hard or degrading, the writer patronisingly added they simply did not know any better but did admit it was hard on their health:

> it soon tells on them, and a pit girl after a few years at the work, looks ten years older than she is, and after 25 ages very fast. With regard to the degradation, the way these unfortunate females hide their faces when strangers come near them when at work is sufficient proof that they feel it. For the reasons we have adduced we are glad to find that colliers themselves are taking up the question. At the National Conference of Miners, held at Birmingham a resolution was passed to the effect that, 'having heard that a very large number of women are employed about the pits in South Staffordshire, Lancashire, Wales, Cumberland, and a few other districts, we deprecate such employment, believing it to be degrading in its influence upon the character of the women, and that it is detrimental in its economic and moral effects on the domestic life of the miners; and we pledge ourselves to use out most strenuous efforts to bring about the abolition of female labour about our mines.[3]

In 1885 Ellis Lever, a wealthy Cheshire coal contractor, and a frequent correspondent to *The Times* about improvements in mining, wrote complaining about a comment by a Thomas Norbury who had described pit women as 'picturesquely clad'. Lever refuted any female could look picturesque 'dressed in male attire of the coarsest kind, all greased and begrimed with coal-dust, and their faces and hands as black as those of chimney-sweepers.' He cited figures from the *British Medical Journal* which claimed in 1884 there were around 4,458 women and girls employed in Britain, 329 between 13–16, and three between 10–13, adding, 'it ought to be one of the first legislative acts of the new Parliament to forbid the continuance of such a baneful practice' adding that the only reason for their employment is that they do a certain amount of work for less money than it would be done by men.[4] Lever admitted their work was not easy as it consisted of 'taking the corves [wagon] loaded as they come from the bottom of the shaft to the screens and wagons and tipping them over. They have then to take the corves back to the bank.' And he was no fan of the miner, 'the men, and the women too ... are coarse in manner and in speech, and I should shock your readers were I to attempt to convey even a faint idea of the obscene, disgusting, and blasphemous language they habitually hear and too soon imitate.' The mothers of families, 'but too many, alas unmarried' would he claimed, be 'far better employed in caring for their offspring and in fulfilling more womanly duties: than following this degrading employment on the pit banks. In colliery districts where females are not allowed to work at the pits the men themselves are of a superior type.'[5]

These types of articles that criticised women were becoming more frequent, such as a piece in 1882 regarding a lecture in New York by social reformer Professor Felix Adler (1851–1933) on *Woman Slavery* in which he claimed women were employed because 'more work could be got out of them than out of men. They were docile and submissive.' Had he seen the Welsh women dealing with the blacklegs he would not have called them docile and submissive. He did point out that the women he had researched were paid 8s a week but had to pay the baby tenders, the 'firers' at the forge and other expenses, leaving them only 3s 6d a week. He compared them to agricultural districts where women and children worked in gangs with overseers driving them 'from field to field' dressed in 'boots and semi-male attire' but this was as nothing he claimed, compared 'with the sights in the collieries.'[6] Many other women doing hard labour wore trousers but they were rarely mentioned, it was mainly the pit women who were criticised.

Women did work in the same harsh conditions often doing identical jobs as men for lower rates of pay which could lead to protests and both Angela V. John and Val Lloyd write of a strike at the Hafod pit in Rhosllannerchrugog,

North Wales in the late 1880s. In a taped interview, for what was then the Sound Archive of the Welsh Folk Museum, Mrs. Jemima Evans claimed she had been working since the age of 9 at the screens sorting coal with her sister. If this is correct then either she was working illegally, as compulsory education had been introduced until the age of 10, or her parents had applied for a dispensation certificate that could be supplied for children who were considered bright enough to leave school and start working. During the women's strike for higher wages a group got together to challenge the manager Barrett and as they marched in procession, they sang a song *'Merched yr Hafod yn mynd yn y ffloc'* [Hafod girls go in a flock].[7] Jemima, who took part in several eisteddfodau, had a lovely voice and recorded the song in 1969.[8]

American journalist, Wirt Sikes (1836–1883) known for his writings on Welsh folklore and customs, wrote in his book *Rambles and Studies in Old South Wales* (1881):

> perhaps the roughest work which women do in Wales is that of the tip-girls. they are indifferently called tip-girls or pit-women, their work being to make themselves useful at the mines ... The Welsh pit-woman, like the Welsh miner, is commonly a worthy church-going person, not infrequently possessed of a rosy prosperity of aspect one would hardly see in such a class. There is even beauty among them; I have seen more than one tip-girl whose face was really fascinating. Of course a certain coarseness prevails as a rule; refinement and coal-dust are naturally not quite synonyms. The work of the tip-girl is at the bank or pit's mouth in the colliery, where she watches carefully every tram that comes to the top, and knocks off with a pick the slag and stone that may have been unobserved by the colliery, and throws out any stones that are tipped into the waggons. She is also useful at odd hours in waiting on the miners in various ways. During the depression which recently prevailed in the Welsh coal-trade, many collieries being idle, the tip-girls and their Mentors advised them to refine themselves a little, with a view to qualifying themselves for the higher post of domestic servant.[9]

All of these attitudes were to come to a head in 1886 when the government announced they were preparing a new Mines Bill and would once again, consider banning women working in the coal and iron industries – once again, people began to take sides.

In April a large and 'enthusiastic meeting of colliers, labourers, women, and girls, employed in and about collieries, was held at the Temperance-hall, Tredegar, to protest against the proposed abolition or female labour at the pit's mouth.' The *South Wales Echo* in its piece entitled, *The Employment of Women at Pits* noted this was 'a question seriously affecting the welfare of Tredegar, as the Tredegar iron Company alone ... employ upwards of 200 women and girls.' One of the speakers at the meeting remarked that 'there is no question that the work done by women and girls at the pit's mouth is far healthier, more moral, and in every way superior to the work in which thousands of women and children are employed in cotton and kindred factories.' Those men who spoke, there is no record of any woman speaking, highlighted the difficulties that would be faced by 'the large mass of widows and others who were now engaged about the collieries in employment they had followed from their childhood ... No other door would be open to then; except to the workhouse.' The motion to support the women was carried unanimously.[10]

In March, the Vicar of Pemberton at Wigan, the Rev. Harry Mitchell, called a meeting of the pit brow lasses in order to object to the proposed legislation prohibiting their employment on the surface at collieries. Over 100 women attended, many walking miles 'through wet field and miry lane'[11] to be there; a few were placed on the platform in their working clothes. The Mayor of Wigan's wife, Mrs Park, presided and read supportive letters from Lady Latham and others. The Mayoress stating that those who called the women immoral had not personally investigated the subject and nothing was further from the truth. Rev. Mitchell complained that London men were passing judgement on rural women and that the public had heard only one side of the story, stating, 'their dress and black faces did not unsex them; the black was only skin deep. As to their dress, he ventured to think that in 20 years' time they would be looked upon as the pioneers of civilisation in the matter of women's dress'. 'We must,' he said, 'try and raise a subscription for a special train to take 400 of 500 of you up to London for the purpose of putting you in evidence – pit clothes and all – and of shewing to the London world that you are not the degraded, unsexed, health-injured creature depicted by your traducers, but are, on the contrary as good an example of honourable and vigorous womanhood as England itself can produce.'[12]

That same month another meeting was held at the request of the pit women and organised by Rev. George Fox. This time 200 women turned up. More letters of support from Lords were read out and it was agreed that a petition would be signed and sent to the government.[13]

In May, a piece appeared in the *Manchester Guardian*, reprinted in the *Cardiff Times*, entitled *Welsh women at the Pit Brow*. According to their figures '981 "tip-girls," as they are called' were engaged in colliery work in Wales and they provided a brief description:

They are employed in "screening" and in "tramming," and in various subsidiary operations. Where ironworks are attached to the colliery a variety of light work is open to women. At Tredegar, for instance, women are employed about the ironworks, chiefly to sweep the floors around the blast furnaces in the engine-rooms, they also make bricks and pile them in waggons. Some who are unequal to rougher work carry account books between the collieries and the head office.

Most were under 16 but others were young un-married girls or widows, married women, 'do not work at the pits in this district, nor to any great degree in the whole of South Wales.' This is not true, the cursory examination of the 1881 census shows nine married women (6 had infants in the house) were working in Tredegar and 80 in South Wales.

The writer went on to give a ringing endorsement of the women:

The tip girls of South Wales are a smaller race than their sisters in Lancashire; their frames are slighter, and one misses the massive proportions which distinguish many of the northern girls. They seemed sturdy, however, after their fashion, and their mobile faces showed less of the gravity which a keen eye has noted as a characteristic of Lancashire pit girls. But the Welsh girls are not grave they are gay and buoyant, ready with a smile, and sing heartily at their work and on their way home. Visitors to the collieries can testify that the pit-brow rings again with the sound of the rich voices for which the Welsh are famous. The girls gather in a group during any temporary stoppage, and sing in parts plaintive Welsh airs or simple hymns. The costume worn by the women consists of a large wide pinafore or smock, completely covering the dress, made of some coarse washing material, and somewhat resembling the aesthetic fashion for children's frocks. They wear a handkerchief round the head, clean every morning, and over it a felt hat, generally decorated with a shabby ostrich feather which seems to be a recognised part of the costume. Bright beads are also used – evidence of a craving for colour. Needless to say, the handkerchief is worn Welsh fashion, the ends falling over the shoulders. Trousers are not included in the costume of the tip-girls in Wales. The girls in nowise dislike their work. A few admit fatigue, but when asked if they are too tired to clean up their houses when they get home the reply is promptly given, "Oh, no not too tired for that." The only way in which they desire to better their lot is by receiving more wages—a very natural desire. Wages are of course lower in Wales, where there is no other employment to turn to, than in Lancashire. The usual wages for women are 7s a week. In the good times when the coal trade was artificially prosperous they sometimes earned as much as 12s; but things are changed since then. However moderate the earnings of these girls may be, there is little or no other employment open to them. Religion and music combined are the chief resources of tip-girls when their work is done. Most of them are members of Dissenting chapels, every variety of which is to be found in a small Welsh town. Two or three times a week there are evening services and choir practices, which the tip-girls attend regularly. They are for ever practising for the various eisteddfodau held in different parts of the country, and their knowledge of musical terms and of the different notations and technical points in music is remarkable. While the religious organisation supplies a simple amusement for the evenings, it is at the same time an effectual guarantee of good behaviour. In Tredegar a tip-girl is rarely seen in a public-home, and the moral character they bear as a class is of the best. A manager is always on the spot during the dinner hour, and any irregularity would lead to prompt dismissal. Doctors having wide acquaintance with colliery districts give evidence to the good health of the women—both at the pits and in their homes after marriage. The active life that they lead is found to be the best preparation for any demands which may be made upon their strength in later life. They are not unfitted for domestic occupations; are able to bake their own bread and knit their own stockings. The homes of women who have worked at the pits are no disgrace to their mistresses. It is only to be expected that they should vary in degree of neatness, but their average is a tolerably high one.[14]

Three months later, when the Inspectors of Mines report was released, it too endorsed the women, and it was widely quoted in the press:

> the question of the propriety of employing women on the pit banks is attracting a good deal of attention, and the Lancashire women especially have been subjected to considerable abuse by persons who pose as their friends; their moral character has been gratuitously libelled, and their working dress pronounced bold and unbecoming. So far as my observation has gone, I have seen no good reason for legislation to prevent these women earning a livelihood at the occupation they have chosen; they always appear orderly and industrious, and it is a favourite employment, especially where the health will not bear confinement, and their dress is very suitable and appropriate.

The *Cambrian News* in its coverage noted that 'representatives of the miners have stated that the husbands and brothers of these women are averse to their employment at the pits' which was not in keeping with the Tredegar men, or elsewhere and the Inspectors questioned this account. If, they argued it was true then 'why do they sanction their following this employment? It hardly needs an Act of Parliament to enable a husband or father who disapproves to prevent his wife or child being so employed.'[15]

Despite the growing approval of the women, some still wanted changes.

In the new year, 1887, the Coal Mines Regulation Bill began to be debated. It included a series of amendments one of 'the most important was the gradual discontinuance of female labour in collieries by prohibiting the taking of women into such employment after the Bill.' Other considerations included raising the age that boys could be employed from ten to twelve years; and that relatives, or their representatives, of deceased miners to attend coroners' inquests for the purpose of questioning witnesses.

By February it was apparent that Rev. Mitchell had managed to make up a deputation of the Wigan pit women and they were going to Westminster to present their case. The Home Secretary had agreed to meet them, commenting that it 'appears harsh that male legislators should say that women should be shut out from the meaning of earning their own livelihood.' Nonetheless, he wanted to further consult with mine owners and the Royal Commissioners before meeting them.[16]

As usual it brought forth a flurry of letters in the press.

A letter from 'D.B.E. of Maesteg' appeared in the *Western Mail* stating, 'in South Wales and, I presume, in the other mining districts represented by the deputation women are only employed in light and perfectly safe labour, such as oiling trams, carrying stores, &c., and it would be a cruel injustice to take away from these poor girls the means of earning an honest living, and, perhaps, in many instances drive them to that last resource of despairing womanhood – the streets.'[17]

D. Morgan from Aberdare wrote a letter to the *South Wales Daily News* taking issue with Walter McLaren, the MP for Crewe who claimed that 6,000 women were employed on the pit banks. Morgan argued there were only 5,568. He questioned if similar measures against women in other industries for example the woollen trade would also be brought in and that 'in the good old Book … the women are naturally weaker than the male sex; therefore, we argue that the lightest work in society should be selected for them' before asking how McLaren would feel if he was 'compelled to push 600 trams (about 7½ cwt. each) about the top of a pit bank and oil them, and splutter the coal tar oil on his clothes? I expect that Mr McLaren would soon turn round and say that such labour is not only unwomanly, but also unmanly.' Morgan continued, 'it is argued that the prohibition of female labour will bring ruin to 6,000 by compelling them to go to the workhouse or to be destitute on the streets. I have had much experience in both cases, and I argue that the neighbourhoods in which there are no women employed at pit-banks are quite equal to the others. Now that we have had the advancement of education I argue that female labour should be transferred to the clothing and grocery establishments, and such like, and let some of the lusty fellows who are in the said establishments be drawn on to push the trams and perform the filthy and heavy work which is required on pit banks. It is no use arguing that those women whom we have on pit banks are fond of their filthy position, with few exception, I have made it my business to interrogate many of them on the matter, and their answer has been that they don't wish to continue such labour if they could get something better and of an honest character. I hope that the member for Crewe will see his way clear to support Mr Burt's amendment, especially if he is in sympathy with the female sex.'[18]

The Pit Women go to Westminster

Rather than the 400 or 500 pit women Rev. Mitchell hoped to get together to visit Westminster, it was a deputation of around 50 women from nine different towns and villages in Lancashire who would go, and the Home Secretary had agreed to meet them. They went independently of the mine owners and paid their own expenses, but they were accompanied by a 'large number of ladies and many members of Parliament' including Mrs. Park, Mayoress of Wigan. While most of the pit women wore 'the ordinary dress of civilised society' several were 'attired in the pit costumes' so the Home Secretary could 'personally judge the value of the statements which had been made as to the character of those costumes.'[19]

At Parliament the deputation was met by Walter McLaren (1853–1912) a Liberal MP for Crewe, and Colonel Blundell (1831–1906) Conservative MP for Ince, near Wigan, who gave the women guided tours to parts of the building and allowed them to peep into both Houses, the Commons and the Lords.

After they had settled, a number of questions were put to the women but their replies are not recorded and few of the accompanying miners spoke, most of the talking was done by MPs and other prominent men. 'Ladies', such as Lady Crawford, Mrs. Josephine Butler, and Miss Muller, members of the Society for the Promotion of the Employment of Women, also spoke in defence of the women as their cause was becoming tied up with the suffrage movement who supported the rights of women to work.

Conservative MP for Whitehaven, Cumberland (now Cumbria) George Cavendish-Bentinck (1821–1891) presented two memorials from colliery managers against the 'obnoxious amendments' abolishing female labour at the pit-brow. Miners' delegate from South Wales, Archibald Hood (a Scotsman) (1823–1902), a coal owner and an important figure in the industrial growth of the Rhondda Valley, was the managing director of Glamorgan Coal Company and former president of the South Wales Coalowners' Association, protested on behalf of the Welsh women; as did Frank Ash Yeo (1832–1888) MP for the Gower, a colliery owner and director of the Swansea Bank. Despite these men with Welsh coal interests speaking, it does appear that no Welsh pit women joined the deputation.

The following day the pit women were introduced to Henry Matthews, (1826–1913) the Home Secretary (he was later ennobled as the 1st Viscount Llandaff, and in modern times is described as the 'Unknown Home Secretary' despite having the longest tenure until Theresa May (1956–) who held the job from 2010 until 2016) who then led a discussion in the House.

Matthews told the Commons he had been informed by the Inspector of Mines that in 1885 the number of women working on the pit's bank was little short of 6,000.[20] Yet that figure, throughout the decade, had ranged widely from 4,183 to 11,323 – it seemed nobody from the government could come up with a consistent figure.

Matthews went on to tell the house that the women's work:

> consists of picking over the coal as it comes from the pit and removing the worthless pieces. The employers it is said, prefer that this should be done by females, on the ground that these do the work with more care than men. The women themselves say the work is light and extremely healthy, instances being given in which mill-hands whose health was failing had recovered on taking to the pit-brow. The pay is from 1s. 10d. to 2s. 6d. per day, and those who engaged in the work wear during their hours of employment only a composite dress, which suggests the attire of both sexes, and is a sort of tough idea, a primary stage, of the garments which some ladies on both sides of the Atlantic say should be adopted by their sex generally. It is said that the girls are most respectable and modest.[21]

Matthews was opposed to what had been called meddling government interference with full-grown people, who knew their own business best and that for them in London to attempt to decide what Lancashire girls should or should not do was a very unwise proceeding.[22]

Despite this, support in parliament was mixed, many of the MPs having interests in coal mining so Matthews suggested forming a Committee to discuss the matter due to complaints from several members that the second reading of the Bill was carried through the Commons so quickly that there had been no opportunity for discussion.

In addition to the committee, and prior to the forthcoming miners' conference, men from all parts of the UK met at the Swan Hotel, in the Temple area of London and MPs mixed with trade unionists and mining representatives to discuss matters. South Wales was represented by David Edwards (Dowlais); David Morgan (Aberdare); John Morgan (Ystrad); William Evans (Treorky); W. 'Mabon' Abraham MP.

Trade Unionist William Pickard (1821–1887) from Lancashire complained that the women's case had been greatly misconstrued and misrepresented by the recent deputation and that the women's work was not light but they could be daily found doing men's work, but at women's wages. He argued if parliament was to allow the women to continue working, then, when doing the same work as men, they should be paid the same. However, he too could not resist the familiar barb, that it was 'almost impossible for young women who worked at the pits' to be suitable mothers, they could not acquire a knowledge of domestic economy. That the employment of women tended to keep down the position of the 'unfortunate colliers'.[23]

Mabon said he did not wish to make a speech but coming from a district where a few girls and women were employed about the mines he was proud to inform them that he was sent to the House by the miners of that district and that he was paid by them for being there. He represented, he said the miners, who were against the employment of girls and women about the mine – the meeting at Tredegar did not support his argument. Nevertheless, he urged MPs to visit mines for themselves, 'Let them see young women and young men going together to the side of a ditch or brook to obey the necessities of nature because there was no place else provided, and how would hon. members like their female relatives to live such a life? In some parts of the country this labour about the pits was degrading and immoral to women.' Mabon claimed the MPs did not have a proper picture of things, to make the picture of the deputation complete a few things were necessary such as the tram, the oil can, the grease pot, and the cloud of dust. 'The employment of female labour at mines would have to cease,' Mabon stated before providing figures that he said showed the waning of female employment – in North Stafford, in 1873 there were 1,142 women and now only 320. In south Stafford 1,433 now 257. In South Wales twelve years ago, there were 820 now only 427. 12 years ago, the total of females employed about the pits was 6,899 now it was 4,431.[24]

'The angels of humanity,' continued Mabon, 'should not be allowed about mines, amongst the grease and the coal dust and other disagreeable surroundings to be found there.'

A comment that drew forth fury from Sir John Gibson (1841–1915), the editor of the *Cambrian News*, a long-time supporter of women's suffrage and author of *The Emancipation of Women* (1891). He claimed Mabon 'talked a good deal of nonsense' and in his editorial thundered, 'Are not the hundreds of thousands of women employed in making matches at threepence or fourpence a gross, also angels of humanity! Are not the prostitutes who throng the streets of large towns, angels of humanity; are not the women who sort dust heaps and perform all sorts of foul drudgery angels of humanity?' He went on to make the valid point 'that the government should improve all conditions of labour' and 'there must be an end of prohibiting women from work under the pretext of caring for their health, their beauty, and their morals. Work mars the beauty of men, deforms their bodies, degrades their morals, and destroys their spiritual perceptions but who would dare to propose that men should be prevented from engaging in any employment, however dangerous and debasing.' He went on to question what happens to those women who never marry or who are left alone to raise children, 'The "angel of humanity" humbug is very nauseating out of the mouths of men who must know that the inability of women to earn a living drives them to prostitution or pauperism ... there is something very shabby in trying to exclude women from honest labour under the pretence that they are "angels of humanity," and leaving them to starve or become fallen angels of humanity'.[25]

The editor of the *South Wales Daily News* had also considered the matter in depth. Reviewing women's history of being dependent on men he congratulated 'womankind in this country that they have now a personality of their own in the eyes of the law' but was not 'quite prepared to go the length of maintaining that all occupations should be equally open to men and women. We still believe in a natural distinction between the sexes, and a natural fitness of men for some kinds of employment and of women for other kinds.' The editor argued that no legitimate employment could be regarded as degrading but also fell back on the marring of beauty argument, 'while the employment itself may be perfectly honourable and above suspicion, it may mar and bloat the natural beauty of women, rob them of all their grace and dignity, and unfit them to be at the head of even a humble household.' The backhanded compliments continued, 'There is a great deal of sheer rubbish said and written about women's equality with men. In many important features women are far superior to men, but in many others they cannot reach the height which men have reached. There is no female Homer or Vergil, no female Dante or Ariosto, no female Plato or Aristotle, no female Francis Bacon, Isaac Newton, or Charles Darwin. There have been, and there are now, women of rare and splendid intellectual gifts, but no such giants as those we have mentioned.' It never occurred to the editor that women had not made these achievements because as he admitted himself in his introduction, women had been shackled to men and had not been permitted an equal education. He reluctantly concluded, 'It is beneath the dignity of a woman, and its natural consequence is to unsex those who are engaged in it. We are, therefore, in favour of women being banned.'[26]

The Decision

On 23 June 1887 the House of Commons voted on an amendment to the Mines Regulation Bill as to whether girls under 16 should be banned from working at the pit brows. Fourteen Welsh MPs voted for the ban, including Mabon, eight voted against, and thirteen were absent. Despite this, the overall vote was 188 to 112 and so the amendment was negated.[27]

When the Bill came to be written, Home Secretary Matthews stated that women could only be prevented from working if that work was prejudicial to character and morals or health, however, the pit women had satisfied him that their work was not open to either objection. He thought their costume looked perfectly 'descent, respectable, and proper' and their testimony was of a 'high character and eminently praiseworthy industry' of the pit-brown women. He would resist attempts to prevent them working, and the amendment to prevent women working at the pit brow was not included in the Bill.[28]

Possibly because of the continued confusion about the number of women working, when the Coal Mines Regulation Act, 1887 was published it contained a clause that all employees had to be registered separately with their name, age, residence, and date of first employment and had to produce the registers if requested to do so by an inspector. This would have provided a wealth of information about the women but sadly most of these records have been destroyed.

Chapter 14

Rough Grace

The pit women had finally won the right to be left alone. They had saved their jobs, been found innocent once again of immorality, their clothes had been accepted, they had been embraced by the women's suffrage movement, and the radical dress movement campaigning for women to be allowed to wear trousers – now they hoped to be left in peace to get on with their lives.

Things, however, were not going to be that easy.

Images of the Wigan women continued to proliferate, they had remained a curiosity for the public and became poster girls for the suffragettes and the radical dress movement but there were less images of Welsh women. Some exist, such as that at Abergorky Colliery, Treorchy, c.1880s, of women standing beneath a pit head and dressed in a style similar to the Clayton women; and Munby sketched a Pembrokeshire tip woman knitting away, trying to keep her wool clean, while waiting for the arrival of some coal trams.

There is another image for which some detail was supplied by Ebenezer Lewis in the magazine *Camera* for July 1887, the editor, describing it as 'full of interest—for it not only shows the workers, but the scene of their labours far away in the Rhondda Valley'. It would appear that Lewis, a coal owner and also vice-president of the Cardiff Amateur Photographic Society, took the photo and supplied these notes to the magazine:

> The picture is a representation of pit-brow women at the Ynysfeio Colliery, Treherbert, near Cardiff. It is to be observed that the women's dresses are short all round, and that the costumes of each are almost identical, for there is an unalterable law of fashion at the collieries, as there is in the West End of London, all of the ladies being dressed accordingly. But, different from London, a fashion here remains in force for many years. The head-gear is convenient, being a cross between a cockle-shaped bonnet and a hat, the head being first covered with a shawl to keep away dust, on the top of which the hat is placed. The women invariably wear trousers, but being a little more modest than their Lancashire sisters, do not show them. It is notable that there are no woman employed underground in Wales, their occupation being entirely

confined to the operations on the pit brow. As a class they are eminently industrious and moral, their spare time being, as a rule, devoted to the study of music. It is not an uncommon occurrence, when passing a colliery, to hear selections from the oratorios, some of the vocalists being blessed with superb and well-trained voices. A few years ago, 600 vocalists, chiefly drawn from this class, earned the distinction of taking first prize from all comers at the Crystal Palace competition; and we have no doubt that at the forthcoming Grand National Eisteddfod at the Albert-hall, London, they will prove to be equally efficient, all well as a great attraction. The photograph was taken on a 7½ by 5 Ilford ordinate plate, using a Ross rapid symmetrical lens, No. 4 stop, four seconds' exposure, on a bright March day.[1]

Unfortunately, the image has not been found nor has a copy of the magazine, but at least Ebenezer Lewis confirmed that Welsh women did wear trousers but would not show them.

The rumbling argument about trousers even caused Oscar Wilde to weigh in on the subject writing on *Sensible Dress* in *The Women's World*:

> How sensible is the dress of the London milkwoman, of the Irish or Scotch fish-wife, of the north-country factory girl! An attempt was made recently to prevent the pit women from working on the grounds that their costume was unsuited to their sex, but it is really only the idle classes who dress badly. Wherever physical labour of any kind is required, the costume used is, as a rule, absolutely right, for labour necessitates freedom, and without freedom there is no such thing as beauty in dress at all. In fact, beauty of dress depends on the beauty of the human figure, and whatever limits, constrains, and mutilates is essentially ugly, though the eyes of many are so blinded by custom that they do not notice the ugliness till it has become unfashionable.[2]

Elsewhere, interest in the pit brow women was waning as were the numbers, for both women and men were being replaced by machinery. In 1886 the Inspectors of Mines report cited 5,568 UK women working above ground[3] and in 1891 the *Weekly Mail* claimed there were 6,000 in the UK working as pit brow women.[4] According to Angela V. John, between 1874 and 1890, numbers in Wales had halved, from 1,747 to 793[5] with some areas claiming no women worked at mines. The *Western Mail* claimed there were no women in the Rhondda but hundreds in Aberdare. To which the *Merthyr Times* wrote 'Bravo, chivalrous Rhonddaites! And may Aberdarians copy your example in properly providing decent and congenial occupations for their women.'⁶ Figures from the *Digest of Welsh Historical Statistics* taken from census returns shows the number of women employed in mines and quarries began a steady decline during the 1890s when there were 802 to 343 in 1901 and 268 in 1911.⁷

In 1897 a correspondent wrote to the *Western Mail* stating that 'One may go now throughout all the steelworks and scarcely meet with a sample of womankind, except those conveying the dinners of the workmen. Labour of the roughest kind is relegated to machinery, which neither tires nor falters, but pursues a steady and harmonious way, both in the steelworks and in the mines, and the half scream, half laugh of the girls and the coarse shout of the boys no longer offend the ear.'⁸

The following day a journalist, horrified at the claim there were no women in coal mining in Wales, also writing in the *Western Mail* produced an extensive article, with images, entitled *Women Colliers in Wales*. This 'astounding statement' the writer assured his readers, was far from correct and he would provide details that would be 'startling' but for the fact that they could be verified by visiting Merthyr, Dowlais, Aberdare, and Monmouthshire colliery districts.

In the Aberdare Valley there were girls and women 'doing ordinary labourers' work, mostly:

> at the colliery screens, shovelling small coal – very hard and wearing work for a woman, I should say – exposed to all weathers, and when I and your artist visited several collieries … we found them, both in Aberdare and in Merthyr, working out in the pouring rain, except when they happened to be in the screen-sheds or standing knee-deep in a small coal wagon, levelling the surface of the load beneath the screen itself.

An illustration was included showing a woman standing in a coal wagon shovelling coal.

Others, the writer noted were pushing trams, oiling tram wheels, keeping the roads clean, and attending the fires, all jobs unchanged for decades. They were paid 6–8 shillings a week, pay that had hardly changed since the 1870s although their hours were now shorter and could not exceed fifty-four hours a week. However, as Liberal MP Henry Fenwick (1863–1939) pointed out in 1888, the 54 hours did not include meal times so the actual figure was 63 hours per week⁹ (the modern standard working week is 40 hours).

The *Women Colliers in Wales* writer continued, 'the sight of the black-faced girls, with blue handkerchiefs tied around their heads, beneath a hat which seems to be in fashion among "women colliers" only – and that only when at work – is so familiar, apparently, in some of the larger towns as to make people utterly forgetful of the fact that women are now popularly supposed to have left that sort of work for ever.' The writer described how the first person he met in Merthyr was a tip-girl coming from work to go home to dinner yet a few minutes later he met a gentleman who assured him that female labour had long ago been abolished. There were:

> half a dozen or so working at the Cwm Pit of the Messrs. Crawshay, at Nantwen (Bedlinog), at the Dowlais Collieries, and at the screens of the Cyfarthfa Works, where the coal is brought from the mountain levels of the vicinity. I am told they are at work in Abercanaid, and that about four years ago one of these surface-work girls was accidentally killed in the colliery yard. They are at the Gadlys and Abernant Pits, in the Aberdare Valley, and, as I have before intimated, extensively employed in Tredegar, Sirhowy, and other Monmouthshire districts. One colliery official told me that he, a few years ago, knew a girl employed as a haulier, and she managed her horse better than anyone else could possibly manage it.

Disproving the criticism that tip girls were ruined for life, the writer mentioned he knew the names of 'several well-to-do tradesmen whose wives – most respectable and highly-respected women (locally they were referred to as "ladies") – had at one time been employed on the tips.' Another man he spoke to informed him there were few under 16s, although the act allowed employment over 13, and most were 'daughters of labourers or of widows' and that they preferred the work to 'the eternal drudgery of the household "slavey"' namely domestic service. In a brief exchange he had with one young woman she told him, 'we are free after five o'clock, man!'

'But shovelling small coal and bending to your work in that way is hard labour.'

'Yes, until you get used to it,' was the reply, 'but we don't always do this.'

The preferable working conditions at the pit brow were covered in another article, also for the *Western Mail*, in 1897 'their lot is ever so much better than many farmhouse servant girls in some rural districts in Wales. In certain places, in Cardigan and Carmarthen especially, the condition of farm girls is often only one short remove from that of slavery.'[10]

The *Women Colliers in Wales* writer reviewed the new regulations:

- No girls and women to work more than 54 hours in one week and ten hours in a day
- not to be employed between 9pm and 5am
- not on a Sunday nor after 2pm on Saturday

- eight hours interval between the period of employment on Friday and that on Saturday and twelve hours' interval between each other period of employment
- the working week was to begin at midnight on Saturday, and to end on the succeeding Saturday
- If employed continuously for more than five hours, an interval of half an hour to be allowed for a meal. Or if employed for more than eight hours, an interval or intervals for meals amounting to no less than an hour and a half
- Not to be employed in moving railway wagons

Another addition was Clause 22 under 'Sanitary Regulations' which stated that if both sexes were employed the local authority had the right via written notification that owners had to construct a sufficient number of water-closets, earth-closets, or privies and ash-pits for the separate use of each sex. When the journalist asked about any sanitary provisions at one mine, he was told there were none and besides, there was 'a wood close by'.[11]

Despite the waning numbers of women working at the mines, alternative employment was still scarce. According to evidence collected by the *Royal Commission on Labour*, the openings in Wales were few compared to the number seeking work. Complaints made to the Commissioners highlighted low wages and scarcity of jobs, except among shop assistants who would often complain of long hours and uncomfortable homes as most had to reside at the place of business. Competition for jobs was so high it meant employers could dictate wages and colliery women were getting left out. 'Formerly a considerable number of women were employed at the collieries, iron, and tin works, but during the past twenty years the number has steadily diminished. Two reasons are given for this, viz, the restrictions put on women's work under the Factory Acts, and the introduction of machinery, which has done away with the necessity of employing so much unskilled labour.'[12]

Some did find unusual employment such as the woman hired by Leonora Philips (1862–1915), wife of Pembrokeshire MP, Wynford Philips, a lady known throughout Wales as a 'vigorous and zealous politician and social reformer' and a member of the Women's Progressive Club:

> The Progressive Women are very progressive indeed, for instead of the burly porter Mrs Wynford Philips has engaged a pit-brow lassie, with sinewy arms and muscles, to lift about the lady members' boxes and portmanteaux. And this Amazon of the hall – who presumably will be able to accept a tip as gracefully as the male genus – will be attired in smart tailor-made dress.[13]

According to one account, there was even a woman working illegally underground. In David Owen's book *South Wales Collieries* Vol 3, there is a picture supposedly of a female hewer from Waun Bant level of the Garw valley mine from 1897.[14] However, as Ceri Thompson points out:

> she has a 'peg and ball naked flame lamp, a coal cutting mandrel under her left arm and, what looks like a wooden block under her right arm (firewood?) but her clothes look hardly suitable for cutting coal on the coal face which meant her lying on her side and cutting a channel at the base of a, probably wet, seam, however she could have dressed up in better clothes for the occasion. On the other hand, she could have been employed carrying sharpened mandrels to the colliers on the coal face, as it was usually a boy's task to do this. I wonder how old she was as its difficult to tell in the image.[15]

For those women who were still working things were still inequal particularly when it came to relief money. During a strike in 1898, Tredegar tip women were financially supported by local relief committees but the Ebbw Vale women were not.[16]

Where women were working, accidents and deaths were still being reported and it is from these reports that certain dangers and health conditions can be recorded.

Harriet Rogers from River Row, Treorkey was picking coal on one of the Tylacoch Colliery's tips in 1882 when she went to warm herself at the large grate or 'devil' in which fire was kept for the tippers. Turning to warm her back, her clothes immediately caught fire and before any assistance could be given by another tipper who was close by, Harriet was completely enveloped in flames. Her dress, embedded in coal dust, would have burnt rapidly, nevertheless, she had the presence of mind to roll down the slope of the tip while the tipper ran after her. A portion of her dress was entirely consumed and she was terribly burnt around the lower extremities and was carried home but there was little hope of her recovery.[17] Mrs Roberts, from Parry Street, Ton, was run over by a number of loaded trams in 1898 while she was picking coal on the Maindy Colliery tip and her leg had to be amputated below the knee.[18]

In 1894 Rebecca Gibson (18) of 152 Simm's Square, Aspull in Lancashire, was a former tip girl but had 'strained herself by carrying a heavy weight and suffered continuous pain', probably a hernia. She was living with her widowed mother for two years so her health had deteriorated when still only 16 years old. According to Rebecca the internal injury also affected her eyes and she had to wear glasses, so having seen newspaper reports about miraculous cures at St Winefride's Well in Flintshire she and her mother decided to visit. Having bathed, and kissed the relic of St. Winifride she felt a 'kind of buzzing in my side and a sense of relief, the constant pain I had felt there disappeared' and she later stopped using her glasses. The story does, however, have the feel of an advertisement and may well not be true.[19]

Other women were witnesses to accidents. In 1892 Martha Williams, a tip girl, witnessed an accident at Rhymney that killed one man and injured three others[20] and in 1898 a woman called Bellis, who was picking coal at Sandycroft Colliery, Flintshire, witnessed the death of John Carver, a head banksman. The inquest, held at the Primitive Methodist Chapel, Vestry found John had fallen from the cage bringing up the trams and died later. The inquest, as many of these did, returned a verdict of accidental death with no blame attached to anyone, particularly the mine owners.[21]

A number of the pit women themselves also died in accidents, particularly with trams. Margaret Andrews residing at Chapel Street, Abercanaid, was employed at the screen at the Zaron Lever, Plymouth and was in the act of shifting a tram when another ran into it killing her in 1886.[22] Sarah Lewis (60) from Commercial Street, New Tredegar, was picking coal on the tramroad from the White Rose Level when she was killed by 'a journey of trams'. James Shortman, the driver, said he had called out to her but Sarah being deaf had not heard him.[23] Mary Jane Evans who worked at Werfa Colliery was run over by waggons on a surface incline and died in 1896 aged 20.

Coal tips were often not secure and could collapse, and occasionally tip women were mentioned in relation to this particular danger. Mary Ann Conniff (28) with her niece Margaret O'Toole (10) were engaged to pick coal from the tips at Sirhowy, Ebbw Vale, when after burrowing into one it collapsed killing them both. When a man tried to rescue them there was another fall and he was killed.[24]

At least, accusations of immorality seemed to have abated although a few stories appeared in the newspapers. Of course, there could have been many more that did not mention the women who worked at the mines.

At the South Wales Assizes in 1892, a concealment of birth case was brought against Fanny Garbett (22), a tip girl. Fanny was single, living at 4 David's Street, Vochriw, Caerphilly and, as was usual at this time, shared an outside closet, or toilet, with others. One morning Mary Kingsley went into the closet and found a child down the toilet. Elizabeth Ann Hawk who worked with Fanny at the Bargoed coke ovens had noticed a change in her appearance and accused her of being pregnant which she denied. Amelia Garbett, Fanny's stepmother, said the same. When arrested Fanny confessed that the child had been stillborn and so she had disposed of it down the toilet. The stillbirth was confirmed and on an appeal of mercy, she was given a month's prison sentence with hard labour.[25]

Elizabeth Susannah Davies (24) was accused of murdering her illegitimate child in 1890. She lived at 2 Railway Terrace, Treharris with her mother Mary Davies, her two brothers, a sister, a lodger Richard Phillips who was a collier, and her five-year-old illegitimate child. She was a former tip woman at Treharris. One morning Richard saw Evan (12) one of Mary's sons, digging in a corner of the garden and the boy called him down to look at something in the hole that looked like flesh. Another son and daughter were also called down but they laughed it off saying it was nothing but an old fowl. However, a few days later Mary called Richard upstairs where he saw the body of a child wrapped in a sack and Mary told him she was nearly breaking her heart over the affair but he knew nothing further until the police visited the house to dig up the garden. It is not known who informed them, but a sergeant had asked Evan to show him the spot and he started to dig, removing a heap of ashes, before finding a body wrapped in canvas about fourteen inches down. An arrest warrant was issued for Elizabeth, who had gone to Carnarvon to stay with a sister at the Blue Bell pub. In the meantime, a post-mortem, held at the Navigation Hotel, Treharris, on the baby girl showed she had a 'separate existence' meaning she had been born alive but there was a fracture on the top of the head and the umbilical cord had been cut but not tied so death may have occurred from a haemorrhage. The baby had been buried for about six weeks. In court, Mary said she was married to Humphrey Davies who now lived in Merionethshire, but when he had visited, he told her he thought Elizabeth was pregnant, and a neighbour said the same, but Mary dismissed both claims. One Sunday she had gone to church leaving her daughter in bed and when she returned at 9 am Elizabeth was still in bed but Mary thought nothing of it. On the Wednesday, Elizabeth left to visit her sister and, on the Saturday, Evan called out to her that he had found a dead cat in the garden and she told him not to bother with it. However, she later found it was a child, took it into the house, wrapped it in canvas and reburied it. As there was little evidence against Mary she was discharged and, in the end, the court could not prove Elizabeth had given birth to the child, or who had originally buried it so the case was dismissed.[26]

Only one other case recovered in the newspapers for this period that specifically mentions tip women is from 1887 when, at Pontypridd police court Catherine Parry, a pit girl, of Tylorstown charged Lydia Parry and Sarah Ann Parry, two other pits girls, with assaulting her. Lydia apparently struck Catherine and threw her over a five-foot wall and Sarah threatened to beat her brains out with an iron bar. Lydia was sent to prison for fourteen days and Sarah was fined 10s and costs.[27]

Far more numerous cases featured in the newspapers are of women stealing coal from collieries, and women appear more frequently than men probably those from economically deprived families. One of the difficulties with these cases is that they are referred to as 'picking coal' but this is a term also used as a job description so it can be difficult to distinguish which women are legitimately employed, and who were tempted to take some coal home, and those trespassing with intent to steal.

These cases appear frequently from the 1700s and a number can be found in the Glamorgan Court of Quarter Sessions, at Glamorgan Archives. Catherine Jenkins of Neath was charged with stealing coal in 1767.[28] In 1858 Catherine Payne, a single woman from Merthyr, was given a week in Cardiff prison for stealing 60lbs of coal worth 4d[29] and Ellen Kennedy also from Merthyr in the same year, was given 14 days hard labour for 25lbs of coal worth a penny.[30] Margaret E. Leyshon, Ann Jones, Elizabeth Salter, and Mary Susan Evans, of Penycraig were charged with stealing 120lbs of coal valued at 8d from Pandy Colliery and selling it elsewhere. Salter was fined 1s and the others 2s 6d each.[31]

In 1862 Mary Griffiths a tip girl was charged with stealing 28lbs of Cyfarthfa coal. She had already been found guilty of a similar offence and so was sent for trial.[32] In 1865 Louisa Griffiths, a tip girl, was charged with stealing 30lbs of coal in Aberdare but the case was dropped and she was discharged.[33] Mary Jane Carter, a young girl who 'appeared in court in the garb of a tip girl', in 1869 was charged with stealing 22lbs of coal. P.C. Watkins had seen Mary coming out of Plymouth yard at 6 pm carrying the coal and although she begged him to forgive her, he said he could not as she had been cautioned so many times before. Watkins said it 'was a great habit of the girls to take lumps of coal away as they left work in the morning.' Mary claimed her clothes were dripping wet and she had taken the coal so she could dry them but her claim was ignored and she was sentenced to ten days imprisonment.[34]

In 1895 two young 'poorly clad' tip girls, Bridget Thomas, of Evans Terrace and Sarah Thomas, Neath Road, Plasmarl, Swansea were summoned for stealing coal, value 3s, the property of Mannesmann Tube Company Ltd. The girls, and six others, were seen on the coal bin attached to the Tube Works, and were filling their aprons with coal. Both had similar offences on two occasions and were fined 2s 6d.[35]

The *Merthyr Express* titled one piece 'Colliers in Petticoats' about women stealing coal in Merthyr in September 1871[36] but it is unlikely the journalist meant they were working underground and used the phrase for sensational purposes only.

Mrs Catherine Mellin from the Eagle's Bush Colliery Company, Melincrythan, Neath, was spotted by P.C. Phillips who saw her picking 24lbs of coal at the side of the tramway. When she saw him, she threw it into the pond near the foundry and begged him to forgive her but he arrested her. However, the court dismissed the case on the grounds there was no felonious intent, a decision applauded by those listening to the case.[37]

Children were also sent out to pick coal sometimes with disastrous results. A seven-year-old daughter of Thomas Guntor, a collier from 45 Ogwy Road, Nantymoel, Bridgend, was with her brother picking coal from the Wyndham Colliery rubbish tip in 1897. As it was illegal for her to be working at this time, she must have been trespassing with the intent to steal. She sat down to rest next to a pulley with a wire rope which had been stopped but when it restarted it frightened the child who fell and was drawn into the pulley by the arm which was severed. Some men tried to reach her but she had started for home leaving the severed limb on the ground. Doctors were called and did all they could for her.[38] In 1896 a young child, Rose Hardwick from Pentre Clais, Nantyglo, was picking coal at Coalbrookvale Deep Pit when she slipped into a pond and drowned.[39]

Cases continued to rise in the twentieth century. One manager, complaining to a magistrate said he had repeatedly warned the women but a customer was putting in claims of £3 a month due to short weight and he felt he had no option but to press charges.[40] Indeed, magistrates were becoming frustrated because as one woman said, there were 20–30 people every day on just one tip,[41] and by 1909 the police has resorted to patrolling the tips in civilian clothes.[42]

Fiction

From 1877 onwards a number of novels included references to tip women but most often they were supporting characters or the love interest of the man, few had the woman as the heroine. Of those that did one of the earliest is R. T. Casson's novel *Mary Armitage: the Miner's Daughter* which appeared in 1877. Casson was a minor Welsh writer about whom little is known other than at one point he worked for the *Western Mail* and later became editor of the *Weekly Courier* in Liverpool. He had several novels and poems featured in the Welsh, and other, press including three about miners, *A Story of Collier Life* serialised in 1885 and *Lucy Lofton, The Miner's Daughter* in 1888.

In *Mary Armitage*, the heroine is a tip girl and her mother asks,

'But Mary, why did you go to work on the pit-bank? Surely, if you wished to be independent, you could have chosen some occupation more suitable to you than that of filling and pushing about coal trams?'

'What could I do? I have not learnt dress-making, and am not learned enough to be a governess. It was necessary that I should begin work at once.'

In the tradition of the time, Mary of course ends up getting married.

One of the most famous fictional tip women is by Frances Hodgson Burnett (1849–1924), an Anglo-American novelist and author of *That Lass o' Lowrie's: A Lancashire Story* (1877), her first novel that appeared in the same year as Casson's *Mary Armitage*.

Burnett subscribed to the prevalent view in the 70s of the flawed beauty of pit women:

> who wore a dress more than half masculine, and talked loudly and laughed discordantly, and some of whom, God knows, had faces as hard and brutal as the hardest of their collier brothers and husbands and sweethearts. They had lived among the coal-pits, and had worked early and late at the 'mouth', ever since they had been old enough to take part in the heavy labour. It was not to be wondered at that they had lost all bloom of womanly modesty and gentleness.

The heroine, Joan Lowie, stands apart from these women and her genteelness is the butt of jokes from the other women but she succeeds in marrying a professional engineer, an outcome some felt not possible for a working-class woman at this time, however exactly that had happened to Eliza Harris from the 1830s when she had married Henry Crawshay, the son of William Crawshay II, the influential iron-master.

Despite Burnett, and all the others throughout the decades claiming pit women lost their beauty, this is not borne out by the existing photographs. The faces of the Wigan women and those from the Clayton images show healthy and often strikingly beautiful women.

The last novel of note to feature a tip woman as heroine is *A Pit Brow Lassie* by John Monk Foster (1857–1930) published in 1890. Foster was born in Wigan and the novel follows collier Luke Standish's love for pit woman Kate Leigh who also stands out from the other pit women in beauty and genteelness. In the novel, set in the 1860s/70s, Foster claims miners wished to end the women's employment:

> The cry against female labour about mines had at this time not grown strong enough to deserve notice. It was then only talked of in secret at Miners' Union Meetings, and the whole movement against the pit brow women had its origin in the worst of motives. No feelings of charity

actuated the men who took up the cry; they had no chivalrous regard for the weaker sex; it was not because they deemed the labour too arduous or that it had a tendency to demoralise the worker; it was because they regarded pit brow women as rivals in the labour market and, wished to have the whole field to themselves.

Casson's *Mary Armitage* is the only novel with a Welsh tip woman as heroine but there is a mention in one of the classic novels of Wales (despite the author rarely spending time in Wales). *So Green was my Valley* (1939) by Richard Llewellyn (1906–1983) was set in the late nineteenth century, and the narrator's brother, Ianto, disapproves of male attention towards their sister, Angharad. He perpetrates the image of the pit-woman as being immoral when he states, 'I will not allow my sister to be treated like a pit-woman … but so quietly that only a few could hear.'[43]

The only children's book discovered that includes a Welsh tip girl was published in 1996 by Gwasg y Dref Wen entitled *Susan Rees: A Pit Girl* as part of their Welsh History Stories, written by John Evans with illustrations by Chris Rothero. One of the Clayton images was used as inspiration for the fictional Susan Rees and outlines some of the hardships suffered by young girls before the 1842 change in law banning females from working underground.

The only other literature to feature a Welsh tip woman so far located was a poem published in 1891 in the newspaper, *Seren Cymru* signed by 'Spinther'. This was James Spinther (1837–1914), a collier in Aberdare from 1854 to around 1859, who also wrote many poems but was more known for writing histories of the Baptist religion.[44] The Welsh language poem, entitled *Merch Y Tip* (The Tip Girl), conforms to the stereotypical image of the harsh life of a tip woman and not able to find love:

Yn Rhymni, gyda brig yr hwyr,	In Rhymney, on a winter eve,
Trwy'r gwyll a'r eirwlaw oer,	Through blinding sleet and snow,
Dylyfai'r gweithwyr tua thre	The workmen wended to their homes
Wrth oleu'r welw loer.	By moonlight dim and pale.
Daeth merch fach heibio, oddiar y tip,	A tip-girl from her work passed by,
Yn wleb a gwael ei llun,	Lonely and wet was she,
Dan sibrwd canu yn y gwlaw	Plaintively singing to herself
Ei gofid iddi ei hun.	Her doleful misery!
Hon oedd y gaingc, mewn acen leddf	Her piteous strain disturbed my heart
Gyffyrddodd fi i'r byw—	This weird and dismal sound—

"O! fi yw'r ferch fach fwyaf llom Ar wyneb daear Duw!"	"I am the poorest loneliest lass On God's earth ever found."
Edrychai imi'n boenus ddrych	Her humble mien proved this to be
O dlodi'r byd a'i drais, Anadlai galar yn y gan,	Her lot, and not her choice; Deep sorrow quivered in her song.
A dagrau yn y llais; Ehedai'r brudd ochenaid hon	And tears were in her voice; Unconsciously she, breathed a sigh
O waelod calon, friw - "O! fi yw'r ferch fach fwyaf llom Ar wyneb daear Duw!"	Her heart was in the sound – "the poorest, loneliest lass On God s earth ever found!"
Rianod hawddgar Cymru fad	Ye maids of Cymru, who are blessed
Sydd mewn cartrefi clyd, Yn llon fwynhau tynerwch serch smiles A phob rhyw foethau'n nghyd, O! fforddiwch ollwng deigryn bach O gydymdeimlad byw A'r eneth fechan fwyaf llom Ar wyneb daear Duw!	With parents' care and love, Who live and move in fortune's And sunshine from above; O! shed a tear of pity when You hear the mournful sound Of this the poorest loneliest lass On God's earth ever found![45]

New Trouble

Fiction aside, new trouble was brewing when, at the 1895 Miners' International Congress, men were still seeking to prevent female labour at the pit brow. In response, the Women's Employment Defence League passed a resolution the following year pledging to support the women.[46] However, by 1899 it was apparent the subject was going to come up again ten years after the pit women's 'rough grace and quaint dialect' had 'captivated' Home Secretary Matthews. 'It is doubtful,' wrote the *Pall Mall Gazette* in their piece *Women as Coal Miners*, that 'they will be left in peace in any future amendment of the Mines' Regulation Act' a pity the writer lamented as 'mining life will be gloomier in their absence, for the given animation and colour to many a pit-bank and coalyard,' but could not resist that old familiar bard, 'but in mining villages home life may benefit'.[47]

Chapter 15

Diminishing Numbers

It would seem that the *Pall Mall Gazette,* and others, were correct in their prediction that the pit women would not be left alone, despite the fact that their numbers were dwindling.

According to the Digest of Welsh Historical Statistics numbers had been falling in the censuses from 798 in 1871, to 112 in 1901, and 92 in 1911.[1] However, using the occupation summaries for the 1901 census, women working above ground in Monmouthshire alone amounted to 120, 91 unmarried women and 29 married or widowed, compared to the Digest which claimed there were 112 in the whole of Wales.[2] Figures published elsewhere continue to illustrate how unreliable the statistics were.

In 1905 when Germany was looking at banning their women from mines, William Brace (1865–1947), vice-president of the South Wales Miners' Federation, wrote an article for the *Weekly Mail* claiming there were still 6,000 women in the UK and the number was increasing. Brace thought there should be other labour available for women without 'our womenkind … being forced to do labour by no means congenial to their sex', while giving no thought to what so many people had been saying for decades, that there was no 'other labour'. Brace thought if the women were asked, they would vote against their work being interfered with, but that sometimes people had to be saved from themselves.[3]

In 1910 the report of the Chief Inspector of Mines quoted 5,963 women or girls employed in the UK[4] but in the 1911 census Occupation tables taken under the general term of *coal miner* there were 3,098 females. 148 aged 5–15; 1,017 aged 15–20; 671 aged 20–25; 963 aged 25–45; 266 aged 45–65; 32 aged over 65; with one female who was deaf and dumb. In Wales the total was 1,074 – Glamorganshire 429; Monmouthshire 280; Ystradyfodwg 98; Merionethshire 70; North Wales 59; Denbighshire 50; Brecknockshire 47; Pembrokeshire 31; Flintshire 8; Montgomeryshire and Swansea one in each; there were none in Carmarthenshire, Cardiganshire, Radnorshire, Caernarvonshire, Anglesey, and Cardiff.[5]

Unfortunately, keyword/s searches in the census for 1901 return no results and only 32 from 1911. One of the difficulties with the 1911 census is that the space available to enter a job description is not very long and often the wording in a preceding entry will run onto a second line giving the impression it is the woman's job. The 1911 census is also well-known in women's history in that it was boycotted because women did not have a vote and many camped out in fields and elsewhere to avoid being in a house on the date of the census. Certainly, the Wigan women supported the suffrage movement, for in 1906 a number had travelled to London to demonstrate for women's rights.

From the few examples recovered from the 1911 census, glimpses of people's lives can be seen. Harriet (26) and Mary (19) Roberts were both born in Flintshire but became coal screeners in Warrington near Wigan. Mary was living with her father and Harriet was lodging with them so was possibly a cousin. As the work dried up in one area, it is feasible women were moving to find work elsewhere particularly as had so often been stressed, other suitable employment was scarce. Others came from Ireland, Scotland, Somerset, and Lancashire to work in Wales.

One of the main arguments against women working was the damage to their health and in the Infirmary at Ty Bryn or 'The Spike', Tredegar's Workhouse, there were three coal workers, all married – Sarah Cunningham (28) from Tredegar, Catherine Foley (55) originally from County Cork, and Rhoda Thomas (65) from Somerset. It has to be wondered what illnesses brought them to the infirmary.

1911 Coal Mines Act

Irrespective of how many women were working at coal mines, in 1911 a new initiative to ban them started. Once again, the Wigan women took the lead in activism.

Sir A. B. Markham (1866–1916), a coal mine owner and MP for Mansfield, Nottinghamshire, wanted Clause 93 added to the Coal Mines Bill that:

> No girl or woman other than those employed on or before January, 1911, shall be permitted to be employed above ground on any mine, provided always that this section shall not apply to women who is engaged in the cleaning of colliery offices, or any other like purpose.

There were conflicting opinions in the committee room where they were planning the Bill. Charles Masterman (1873–1927) who worked closely with David Lloyd George and others on social welfare projects, including the National Insurance Act 1911, pointed out the number of colliery women was small and they were healthier than their counterparts in other industries such as fish curing, glass bottle making, or even agricultural work, and that by comparison, 'pit women's work was a paradise'. John Harmood-Banner (1847–1927), MP for Liverpool Everton and who had interests in Lancashire coal, handed around photographs showing pit women attired in white dresses which *The Graphic* reproduced on 12th August 1911.

Unexpectedly, there was strong opposition by pit women which was ignored, and the amendment was carried 15 votes to 13 and so added to the Bill. The Wigan women protested, and once again they resolved to march on Westminster, led by the Mayor and Mayoress.

> The deputation came in their working dress—though it was so new and so clean that one imagines its association with pit-head is a thing of the future. Some wore black granny bonnets, thick pilot blue jackets and skirts, covered with aprons of coarse sacking. Some had iron-shod clogs of the traditional Lancashire pattern; and they had been blacked till they Shon like looking-glasses. Others were in print frocks, with patterned handkerchiefs covering their heads and flowing over their shoulders, and beneath them bands of colored linen, covering the hair and the forehead, to keep the coal dust away.

Masterman dryly noted the deputation was 'more attractive in appearance than many which were seen there' and said they should have come a day earlier because the Committee, against the advice of the Government, had carried the clause. Nevertheless, Home Secretary Winston Churchill (1874–1965) had given Masterman permission to tell the women that when the Bill came before Parliament, they would do their best to oppose it. As this would take several months, Masterman suggested the women canvas MPs and others to vote against it.

'We will now take tea on the terrace,' announced Harmood-Banner and soon:

> there was a clattering of clogs on the flagstones of the house. The fashionably-dressed ladies, wives and sisters of members, looked somewhat astonished at the unexpected addition to their afternoon party. But there was no shyness on the part of the girls from Lancashire. On the contrary, they all acted as if hobnobbing with members of Parliament was quite the usual thing with them, and made themselves quite at home on the Terrace.[6]

They were then given a tour of the House and took it in turns to sit on the gold throne and the following day went sightseeing around London. On returning to Wigan they were greeted from the train by a great crowd.

Three months later in December, the Commons debated whether the clause banning all future work by women at coal mines should be kept in the Bill.

Viscount Wolmer (1859–1942), MP for Newton, Lancashire, objected to the amendment complaining that the wording was extremely vague and what was the purpose. The grounds for the amendment was that pit work was injurious to women's health but other work was injurious to women's health so how were they to define what was to be banned or not.

A doctor, T. A. Angior, of Wigan, whose surgery of 25 years, included a lot of colliery workers, said he did not ever recall treating a pit-brow woman for strain, or any internal complication or complaint peculiar to women as an outcome of their work. 'Physically,' he said, 'they are above the average. Their children are strong and healthy ... Some few of them push tubs [wagons], but as these are on small iron plates, and the muscular effort required is by the shoulders and arms, there is little or no risk of internal strain.'

Rigby Swift (1874–1937), MP for St Helens, Lancashire thought it was a purely imaginary danger 'invented and discussed by those who object to women working at all at the pit-brow' along with the imaginary immorality and with regard to bad language he blamed the men, 'I would remind the House that that is the fault of the men who use the bad language, and not the fault of the women who hear it.' While he objected to women working, 'I think that the proper sphere of woman's activity is her home. I think that her highest destiny in life is to keep house and be a joyful mother of children', he also recognised, 'that in the present state of society you cannot live up to that ideal. I realise that over six million women every day of the week have got to go out to earn their daily bread, and whilst that state of affairs exists, I do suggest that this House has no right whatever to take away from them the opportunity of what is an honest, honourable, and healthy employment.'

Markham defended his amendment saying, 'I do not wish now to enter into a discussion of the much wider question of the employment of women, but to deal with one particular point, namely, that of tub-shoving. It is all very well to say that the shoving of tubs is not an injurious occupation, but if the Noble Lord were in South Wales, where the tubs are 25 cwt., and where it takes two women to move them, by putting the lower part of their backs against them, would he say that is a proper occupation for women?'

William Edwin Harvey (1852–1914), an ex-coal miner in Derbyshire, agreed saying, 'Let hon. Members think for one moment of women handling tubs in South Wales, where they run from one to two tons in weight; and then think if they would like any of their female relations to do this kind of work ... What are these women paid on the pit-bank? They get 1s. 9d. or 2s. a day for work which is paid for in other counties at the rate of from 3s. 6d. to 5s. a day. The Lancashire coal-owners want to keep the girls so that they may have this cheap labour.'

Sir George Toulmin (1857–1923) MP for Bury, Lancashire and a newspaper proprietor and founder of the *Lancashire Daily Post*, disagreed saying, 'in Wales the case may be different. I have never heard of any case of strain or injury arising from this work amongst women.'

Possibly because going to the doctor cost money and hardly anyone actually bothered to ask the women themselves what their health conditions were. It is inevitable that pushing heavy trams about and lifting large lumps of coal would cause hernias and to claim women did not suffer from them is pure ignorance.

As with all discussions of the women, reverting the conversation back to men was never far away and William Ormsby-Gore (1885–1964), 4th Baron Harlech, MP for Denbighshire, asked if women were being protected from hurting themselves, why was this not extended to men? 'It appears to me,' he said, 'that this Amendment of the Under-Secretary is a plain dodge to encourage the course of discriminating between women's labour and men's labour. It is a protecting Amendment in the interests of a class. Why, if health is concerned, should men not be included as well as women? Nobody wants to do anything or to move anything so heavy as to cause injury to men. I think the Home Secretary has made that point perfectly clear. We must regard this Amendment as a dodge to discriminate between man's labour and women's labour. We are not satisfied.'

Harmood-Banner disagreed, 'there are big pieces of coal which we ought to be very glad to see lifted by men, and not by women or by girls. I should not like to lift some of these large pieces of coal myself, however stalwart I might happen to be.'

The notion of tip work being a healthy occupation was brought up again by Rowland Hunt (1858–1943) MP for Ludlow, Shropshire, 'There is plenty of evidence,' he said, 'from doctors and other women,' and when laughter broke out he added, 'Well, there are women doctors as well as men doctors, and there is plenty of evidence to show that this is a more healthy occupation than certain work in shops and factories.'

Stephen Walsh (1859–1929), MP for Ince, Cheshire, previous a coal miner himself and an official of the Lancashire and Cheshire Miners' Federation, tried to argue the economic conditions of his county were different to that of South Wales and South-West Lancashire 'where this labour is mainly carried on'.

He referred to statements made by William Brace (1865–1947), a Welsh trade unionist and MP for South Glamorgan, who had claimed that there were no economic necessities in Lancashire or in the other counties that did not exist in the various other mining districts. Walsh set out his figures to prove Brace was wrong. The mining district of Glamorgan, he claimed, contained, roughly speaking, a population of 900 to the square mile whereas the mining districts of South-East and South-West Lancashire, where the majority of women worked, contained a population of over 7,000 to the square mile. Portions of South-East and South-West Lancashire, he argued, were 'more congested than probably in any part of the world, with the exception of the thickly congested parts of New York' which meant, according to him, that Lancashire could not be spoken of in the same way as other districts.

Ignoring Walsh's point Markham moved back to the discussion of women moving tubs, 'You may call them wagons or boxes,' said Markham 'but they weigh two tons ...

> I have seen them coming home night after night. They have been working in the open air, the tubs they have been moving about are covered with grease, and you see these women with all their dresses or all the trousers they have worn smothered in oil and filth, and their faces are begrimed with fine dust. That is the kind of civilisation of the twentieth century we are endeavouring to attain to ... It is all very well for Lancashire. After all, there are 6,000 girls employed in this industry, of whom Lancashire employs 2,300. In other districts where coal is tipped out of a tipper on to a flat screen, clouds of dust come out with the coal, and in South Wales particularly the women stand right underneath, where all the fine dust is thrown on them. Can it truly be said, where women are working under these conditions, that that is going to make for better life and higher civilisation? In the districts where they are employed wages are low. In the Scotch coalfields there are 2,700, in Lancashire 2,500, and in South Wales 225. So far as South Wales goes there has been a constantly diminishing number. Employers of labour have not put on additional women, though they have allowed the existing women who are working at the mines to work as long as they choose. Last year, I am sorry to say, there was an increase of nearly 300 women employed in the mines, most of them in the Lancashire district.

This is something similarly recalled by George Brinley Evans working in the 1940s at Banwen Colliery, 'Then there was the dust! With each dram that was tipped, a jet-black cloud of dust rolled down the 'Big Shaker' into the screens. There was no water suppression or extractor fans so the dust fell right on to the heads of the boys picking slag and stone from the conveyors. More than a thousand tons a shift had to be screened so the clouds of dust were continuous. When the wind blew from the east, even the village itself didn't escape the all engulfing noise and dust.'[7]

Viscount Wolmer tried to defend the women, 'I wish to know what part of the work he [Markham] finds degrading. The only thing he seemed to find degrading was that they get their faces and hands dirty. I can tell him that Lancashire girls wash when they get home. If he were to go to Lancashire and tell these women that they are a degraded set of women I should be sorry for him in view of what would happen to him during the next quarter of an hour ... It is a perfect scandal that Members elected by men only should try to do a set of women out of their livelihood when these women have no adequate means of making representations on their own behalf.'

Charles Edwards (1867–1954), MP for Monmouthshire, claimed where there was a higher population there was a higher number of women employed, 'that is not so' shouted another MP, but Edwards was prepared to prove his statement. 'Speaking for a great constituency in South Wales, I say that we do not desire women's labour on the pit-brow. We are practically free from women's industry in the whole of the South Wales coalfield, and we desire to be entirely free from this particular kind of occupation, which the mining community regard as very objectionable and as particularly repugnant to their sense of the nobility of women.'

In the end, the discussion came to an end, the vote was taken, and the amendment was carried, no more women were to be employed.[8]

A law that lasted for only three years.

The First World War

During the First World War the number of women who worked at mines rose as the men went off to war. By July it was calculated the figure was 6,500 rising to 11,300 by November 1918. Wages were also higher and in South Wales women could earn thirty shillings a week (roughly £184 today) although this dropped when the war ended.[9] In 1915 the Home Office Departmental Committee considered removing the clause preventing new employment of women on the pit brow but concluded 'after careful deliberation of all the facts and evidence before them' they did not recommend it.[10] Where women were employed it was on a temporary basis.

Katie Olwen Pritchard interviewed a few women who had worked at the mines during the War for her book *Gilfach Goch in Cameo* (1973). She writes that the women continued to move the trams, or tubs, often weighing 10 to 12 tons each, emptying them of coal, rubbish and stones, or in some cases timber props or bricks.

Occasionally, the women were directed to the top of the pit to empty small coal into stoke holes for the boilers and to push the drams into the cages. During the week, large amounts of rubble from the trucks would fall over the sides on to the track and form tumps. On Sunday, the women were expected to clear the track and level the rubble that had accumulated. Some of the girls employed were only 15 years of age. Their day commenced at 7 a.m. If coal could be sifted out of the rubble, the girls would start work at 4 a.m. in order to fill bags of coal which they sold for a shilling (5p) a bag. Life was hard and conditions of work were very grim. The tips were high and bleak. There was no shelter from the cold biting winds or the driving rain. In addition to heart breaking conditions of work, the women suffered from the weight of heavy clothing, necessary to keep out the cold. Any garment, including old sacks were worn. These were thrown over the shoulders and tied around the middle to act as aprons. At the end of a winter's day, these were covered with ice and snow. Feet and hands became numb and only their indomitable resolve, strength of purpose, and the wonderful team spirit that existed among them, urged them to fulfil such a stupendous task. Rain was a hazard. Then the props were wet and slippery and when unloaded there was a danger of them slipping back into the truck, injuring the women who were handling them.

For their meals they would retire to a small hut which contained a fire where, if rations permitted, they would fry bacon or an egg on a cleaned shovel. One perk to the job was that if they found any fossils and cleaned them up, they could sell them to a collector. For the book, Pritchard interviewed Mrs Lottie Williams who related her experiences, recalling that 'life was hard but full of activity and humour. Many of the women were Salvationists, and after their day's work attended a band practice or a service. Others would attend their places of worship to engage in a Cantata rehearsal or Choir practices. They were a wonderful band of workers, loyal to each other and kind to the old and lonely. Their contribution to the war effort was superb and deserved the highest praise.'

Another woman, Mrs Minnie Pope, a miner's labourer, described being faced with redundancy and so she and another pit woman went to work in a Birmingham Munitions Factory where she was asked to produce a certificate stating her previous employment. It read: 'This is to certify that

Minnie Evans a Colliery Labourer has been Registered under The National Registration Act. 1915'. However, after only a few weeks in the munitions factory, they returned to 'grim, cold tips, and the warm hearted group that worked on them'. Coal, she said, was in her blood and she was the third generation in her family to work on the colliery surface. Her mother Maggie Evans (Dowlais) worked on the surface and had the 'privilege of supplying the workmen with a shovel, to cut the first sod of the Britannic Colliery'.

When the war ended the women ceased to be paid for working on the tips but many continued to unload the trucks in order to earn their living by selling any coal they could find among the rubble. A precarious occupation with little return and when they had collected enough, they sold it for a shilling a sack. However, with no transport available they had to carry the sacks on their backs to every part of the valley. Something reminiscent of Vincent van Gogh's (1853–1890) 1882 painting of women miners carrying coal sacks on their back.

Another pit woman who continued until men replaced them on the pit surface was Miss Ivy James a familiar figure in the valley, with:

> her hair cropped short like a man, a dark Tarn on her head, a long navy blue coat tied around the middle and strong hobbed-nailed boots, covered in coal dust. She would be seen daily working on the tip or walking around the valley with a sack of coal on her back and a bag of sticks under her arm. Weather did not deter her daily routine. This was her living, and her day started at 7 in the morning and continued until darkness fell. Life was hard and money scarce, but there were compensations in the companionship and the kindness extended to her by the workmen.

The money Ivy earned was hardly sufficient to maintain her and her widowed mother so she would take other jobs. After carrying sacks around all day, she would wash, have a quick meal, and start work at the Ogmore Hotel to help with the cleaning. At weekends she acted as a bouncer at the Six Bells Hotel where she was known for her remarkable strength, physically lifting and ejecting drunken customers who refused to leave, so that she became known as 'Champion Ivy'. One day, when crossing the tip with a bag of coal the manager called out 'Where are you going with that coal my man?' 'I'm not a man,' Ivy shouted back, 'I'm a woman!' 'Arglwydd Mawr!' (Great Lord), he replied and impressed with her strength promptly offered her a job emptying three wagons a day. From that day she worked regularly for years and was noted for her kindness as well as her strength. 'The old and infirm were never without coal while Ivy was able to carry it.'

The last woman Pritchard mentions in relation to the coal works was the postwoman, Miss Jennie Davies affectionately known as 'Jinny the Post', born in Llantwit Major in 1890. 'Jinny was always apprehensive when delivering to the colliery offices. The miners delighted in flicking their caps in her face so that she was as black as a collier and had to return to the Six Bells to wash before continuing on her rounds.'[11]

Recalling Lives

The women in Pritchard's book were not the only ones to recall their lives and during the first two decades of the twentieth century, several other tip women were asked by journalists to describe their lives.

Jemima Evans from Blaina was interviewed in 1900 who, at 'over 70 years of age' recalled in her younger days working for many years in the coal mines in the neighbourhood of Nantyglo. She was 'taken to the mines with her father at a tender age and remained at work until she was considered capable of taking charge of her own heading or "talcon." She has many amusing reminiscences of her working days, and relates with glee how on one occasion when the haulier tried to cheat her of a tram she knocked him off his feet in defence of her rights. She was considered a capable miner - or should it be mineress?' – and earned good wages at the craft.'[12] If true, it means Jemima was working illegally underground at the 'talcon', not only that but she had charge of her own part of the coal face.

A year after Jemima's story appeared, Sarah Wilde of Duffryn-terrace, New Tredegar, died at the residence of her daughter-in-law, Mrs Llewelyn Wilde, supposedly at the age of 103 years. She was a native of Monmouthshire and lived the greater part of her life at Rhymney, where for some years she worked 'underground chiefly in attending to the flares'. At least in Sarah's case working underground is feasible as she would have been born in 1798. She was, the journalist wrote, 'an inveterate smoker to the last – a habit which she had contracted while employed at the flares'.[13]

Three years later another story appeared in a piece entitled, *Woman who worked in a Mine. Interesting Ferndale Character*. Mrs Mary Bevan of Duffryn Street, Ferndale, was 'an interesting old Welsh character' who:

> in her young days was employed underground as a hitcher in No. 4 Pit, Dowlais. She was born at Ponthenry, a village situated a few miles from Llanelly, and being the eldest of a very large family had to commence work at a very early age to assist in bringing grist to the mill. Mrs. Bevan was a strong woman, but has become very feeble in her old age. She

recalls the time when her father and brother were employed at Dowlais, and the journeys she had to make every fortnight from Llanelly to fetch their wages - a distance of 45 miles. In order to preserve her boots she resorted to the expedient of carrying them under her arm for the greater part of the way, her explanation being that "boots were very dear." Another instance of economy may be cited. A toll was demanded for crossing the Loughor Bridge, and in order to avoid the payment she was accustomed to carry her mother and sisters on her back and wade through the Loughor river. Shortly after the removal of the family to Dowlais, Mrs. Bevan sought employment as hitcher at the No. 4 Old Balance Pit, Dowlais, and worked in the mine for two years. She was forced to leave her vocation owing to Lady Guest, the wife of the late Sir John Guest, raising objection to women being engaged underground. From here she went to the Dowlais Iron Works, and for 13 years was engaged in filling cinders from the furnace pits. At this period it was not an uncommon thing for women to be thus engaged, and on pay day they generally had an outing to Merthyr and indulged as freely as the men in calling for drinks at the various public-houses. The married life of Mrs. Bevan was of short duration. For many years prior to removing to Ferndale she lived at Vochriw and obtained a living by selling sweets. In her old age she frequently walked from Vochriw to Merthyr to purchase small goods, and is justly proud of a feat she accomplished during that time of carrying a chest of drawers on her head from Merthyr to her home some miles distant without any assistance. She has been at Ferndale for eight years, and is being cared for by her niece, Mrs. Griffiths.[14]

Another piece appeared in 1906 entitled, *Worked in a Pembroke Pit for Years*. This story concerned Elizabeth Butler, an 'elderly' woman who lived with her two 'elderly' sisters, Martha, and Mary at Landshipping in a 'quiet little cottage home'. Elizabeth, the piece claimed, 'is one of the very few women now living who once worked in a colliery'. She was employed at the Garden Pit Mine, Landshipping for several years at 'the noble sum of 4½d a day, the man's wages at the time being 1s a day'. Two of their brothers had died in the flooding of the mine in 1844, just two years after Elizabeth had been banned from working underground, a fortuitous escape thought the journalist.[15]

Other women freely admitted they had worked illegally, such as one elderly lady talking in the 1920s who recalled that when she was employed at the Kilgetty mine (south Pembrokeshire) in the late nineteenth century. She would work underground if it was required, but when a mines' inspector visited, she stayed at home but was still paid. 'There was obvious connivance here between employee and employer, which was itself a reflection of the need for women to find work within an economy offering few employment opportunities, and perhaps to supplement the meagre wages of their menfolk.'[16]

Newspapers

A number of other tip women appeared in the newspapers. One from 1908 played on the immorality angle, *Pit-top morals: Amazonian surface girl and colliers*. Annie Lloyd (18) of Tredegar sued Thomas Henry Watkins a colliery engineman, because, she claimed, he had injured her by pulling her about at the top of the colliery in front of the other tip girls.

Annie and her mother had met with Thomas on the pit brow to ask his intentions with regard to her pregnancy and Thomas claimed she threatened to batter his brains out if he did not admit paternity, and then hit him on the head with a stone. Annie's version was that she seized him by the collar, smacked him in the face, and took his tea-jack from him. Naomi Lloyd, a tall 'excitable girl' who also worked at the pit mouth, said Thomas pulled Annie about so much that her clothing 'was all torn to garters'.

When the case came before Tredegar Police Court, Thomas claimed he had never disowned the child but when his defence solicitor, F.P. Charles, asked about another man, Thomas admitted that a collier, Tom Aurelius was close with Annie and that she had received a letter from him. Annie did not deny it, but said she hardly knew Tom. Charles then read out the letter which said, 'I arrived home safe. It was cold coming over the mountain; but I was thinking of you all the time, because you are such a little dear,' causing those in court to laugh. Charles read further extracts to more 'loud laughter' and when Annie laughed as well, he pointed out it was not a laughing matter. Annie replied, 'it is no use crying about it.' 'You will,' she was told, if her evidence was not believed. Charles continued reading from the letter, 'I am taking the pleasure of asking you for your photo. And yet you say you do not know this man?' when Annie continued her denials, Charles pointed out that Tom had wanted to put her photo next to his, and he asked what the crosses were. Annie said, 'kisses, I suppose.'

In the end, the case was dismissed for lack of evidence but outside Annie attacked Thomas, striking him with her fists on his head as well as attacking another man. She was arrested and taken to the police cells while a large crowd of women followed Thomas and his father through Bridge Street hooting and yelling. Three months later, Annie tried a second time to sue Thomas, this time in Merthyr but the magistrate refused saying having lost in one district did not mean she could try elsewhere.[17]

Elsewhere in the newspapers, there were a few reports of accidents.

At Penycae, Ruabon, Martha Lloyd who was engaged on the screens at the Vauxhall Colliery was knocked down by some wagons on a siding resulting in a compound fracture of the left leg and extensive bruises on her body. The accident took place at 10.30 am and her colleagues had tried to take her to Ruabon Hospital but they did not admit females so she was taken home some three miles away. She was not seen by a doctor until 2.30 pm by which time she had succumbed to her injuries. The coroner returned a verdict of accidental death, with the riders that 'there should be a telephone connection between the collieries and the doctor, that female labour at collieries should be dispensed with, and that a resolution to that effect be sent to the Home Secretary.' The colliery manager said he had ceased engaging new girls, and in a short time, he intended to do away with them altogether.[18] A later piece in the *Wrexham Leader* confirmed that the employment had stopped.[19]

Alice Smith (16) working at Avon Colliery, Abergwynfi was caught in a journey of trams and her foot had to be amputated just below the knee.[20]

Chapter 16

Endings and Beginnings

Following the ruling of 1911 that no new women were to be employed, it would seem the age of the Tip Girl was over – but as with anything to do with these stalwart women that was not the end. The women seem to cling to their jobs, although only snippets of information trickle through in the following decades.

Angela V. John notes a woman, Maggie Davies of Ty Trist colliery, Tredegar, who in October 1920 faced the prospect of a strike without any support from the unions. She had worked for 44 years at the pit and recognised that 'we will be on the stop without a penny coming in, and with the price of food being what it is today we want all the money we can earn to keep going. It is looking black enough for the girls. Some of them were in the Federation once, but dropped out and it has not been tried since, so there will be no strike pay. We have no voice in anything and have to fall in with the rest of them.'[1]

It was not until thirty-four years later that another attempt to stop their voice was made in 1954 in the proposed Mines and Quarries Bill.

Lord Macdonald of Gwaenysgor (1888–1966), MP for Ince, moved that an amendment should be added that replicated that of 1911, that 'no female shall be employed at a mine or any work involving the getting, processing or preparation of coal unless she was in the employment of the mine on that date.' Macdonald, who disapproved of women working at the pits, made it clear that it did not mean 'the total prohibition of female labour on the colliery surface—they can still remain in certain jobs there. Nor does it mean that anyone now working in jobs which will be prohibited if this Amendment were carried will cease until she wishes to cease. That needs to be made perfectly plain ... Nobody will be sacked because of this Amendment. Women may continue to work on the surface as long as they wish, apart from the jobs specified in the Amendment.' According to his figures, only some 400 women were employed in Lancashire, the number having come down over 1,000 in the last few years and he returned to the argument that some people had to be saved from themselves. That the danger of the work causing hernias had to stop – without giving thought to other female work that caused the same damage – and he was concerned about pneumoconiosis, quoting an 'actual case' of a Miss Stretch who had apparently died of this –

again, he did not spend time considering the thousands of men who had died from it. Also, Macdonald wanted the women's jobs to be given to disabled men.

The Earl of Selkirk (1862–1940) assured Macdonald the government would look into the matter but noted that 'what is involved here is really a head-on meeting of two great crusading movements. On the one hand, there are those who have fought for a long time to establish that nobody should be compelled for economic reasons to do undesirable work. On the other hand, there is the undertaking which we made in the Declaration of Human Rights, that everyone has the right to work, to free choice of employment, to just and favourable conditions of work and protection against unemployment.'

'Even in the coal mines?' asked another MP.

'That is what is declared in the Declaration of Human Rights,' Selkirk replied, 'something that applied to both men and women.' However, they had a responsibility he claimed, that women did not harm themselves which is why they had been banned in 1842, but 'I have never been quite clear,' he added, 'why men should be allowed to strain themselves, but that is by the way.' He had listened, he said, 'very carefully to the noble Lord, Lord Macdonald of Gwaenysgor, and, with great respect, I consider he gave no reason at all which I should say was specific as to why women should not be employed on this work. He mentioned pneumoconiosis. When anyone suffers from that dreadful disease, of course it is most unfortunate. What he did not mention was this. At the present time, under the Pneumoconiosis Benefit Scheme, which was passed by this Government, there are thirty-three women in receipt of total disablement benefits. Not one of them comes from the coal industry. Eighteen come from the pottery industry, fourteen from the asbestos industry and one from sand blasting.'

To which Macdonald doggedly replied, 'there has been one from the coal mining industry.'

'I agree. But,' argued Selkirk, 'are you going to exclude the women from the pottery, the asbestos and the sand blasting industries? The noble Lord greatly underestimates women. I have never heard that women wanted to be excluded from work because the danger involved is the same as it is for men. Have you ever heard women asking to be excluded from fever hospitals? Where they ask to be protected is where the danger they face is greater than for men. That is a very material difference indeed.' Selkirk spoke of his visit to a mine where the women's work consisted:

> simply in picking out stones from the coal on a moving belt, after the smaller coal has been removed. The work, as I saw it, was under cover.

It was certainly noisy and it was certainly dusty; the women worked in overalls provided by the National Coal Board. There are two points at which I looked particularly: first, the amenities, whether they had proper washing facilities, canteens, rest rooms and facilities of that character; secondly, the nature of the supervision. I looked particularly to see whether there was some sort of female supervision over the women. So far as the general amenities were concerned, I was fully satisfied with what the National Coal Board provided. I understand that in the great majority of the mines concerned special regulations exist which lay down the type and nature of those amenities. I think we can rest assured that this matter is fairly well covered, so far as amenities are concerned.

In all he visited seven pits in Scotland and in Lancashire, which employed women. 'The girls were absolutely unanimous that they liked their job. I think this was most important: that quite a number of them had been employed on other work and they were very strong in expressing the view that they preferred working on the picking tables.'

George Hall, 1st Viscount Hall (1881–1965), then rose to speak. He had been born in Penrhiwceiber, Glamorganshire, after his parents, like thousands of people who migrated to the South Wales Valleys from the West Country in the late nineteenth century, followed the expansion of the coal trade. Aged only eight his father died and Hall went to work at Penrhiwceiber colliery to support the family. As he addressed the matter in the House, he claimed the only women left working were 690 in Lancashire, 150 in Cumberland, and 150 in Scotland. 'It is quite true that they are a diminishing number,' he said, 'That is why we are so anxious not to interfere with those women.' Besides:

> there is not quite so much dust as there was formerly. Dust repression at the coal face has cut down the amount of dust at the screens by something like 20 to 30 per cent. But there is dust. It is dirty, it is dangerous, it is draughty and it is noisy work. Surface accidents at the collieries of this country last year were: 48 fatal accidents, 195 serious accidents and 22,300 accidents disabling workpeople for more than three days. These women have to pass over the pithead, over the pit surface, to get down to the screens. In regard to the screens themselves, and people handling machinery, loose coal and stone, there were last year four fatal accidents, 9 serious accidents, and 5,000 accidents which disabled people, men and women, for more than three days.

Hall pointed out that Clause 93 of the Coal Mines Act 1911 stated that women or young people should not be employed at a mine to lift, carry or move a load so heavy as to be likely to cause injury, but who, he asked, is to stand by and judge the weight? He accepted that some women regard themselves as quite as strong and physically fit as men and if a stone on the belt passed through, if the woman was closer she would probably lift it, even if it was, he argued, 'to show the man that she can do it'. Hall continued, citing Clause 124 that women and young persons should not work in excess of nine hours in any one day. 'From what I saw on the screens,' he said, 'I should not like to remain at work for nine hours in that dust and filth and noise, to have half an hour at the end of four and a half hours, and then to work for another four and a half hours.'

He noted as an aside that a protest had been sent to him from the Status of Women Committee who objected to the governmental classification of women with young persons, a legal definition that had been brought in as part of the 1842 act banning women from working underground. Hall admitted, 'even the Government themselves do not classify women with adult males. In every classification, in every reference to classification, the women who are employed are classified, irrespective of their age, with young men under eighteen year of age, some of them under sixteen years of age.'

Hall claimed that out of twenty coal mining districts in Great Britain only three employed women and there were fewer than 1,000. 'There is,' Hall continued, 'sufficient work at the pithead—more congenial work, such as work in canteens, work in offices, upon which girls of fifteen and sixteen can be employed, because there is a dearth of clerks.' In other words, only catering and administration work were suitable for women.

In the end, the Amendment was agreed to and, once again, it became a law that no new women would be employed at coal mines.[2]

What happened to the numbers of women after this is difficult to measure. Post-1911 censuses are difficult to access with the exception of a few extracts. From 1939 Martha Jane Williams (39) a single woman living in Crickhowell, Breconshire, was a patient at the Public Assistance Institution and listed as a retired colliery surface worker. Others are listed as working underground but this is most likely the same problem from 1911 where a man's listing has spilt over onto another line giving a false impression this is the woman's job.

As the years rolled by the exclusion of women in mines was retained, even in 1979 when the United Nations General Assembly adopted the *Elimination of All Forms of Discrimination* against Women, which urged laws restricting women's work hours and some categories of jobs should be repealed, the UK did not do so. The USA had allowed women back into the mines two years previously following a sex-discrimination lawsuit in 1974 that opened the pit gates to women. In 1980, women from Virginia spoke to the *Observer*

Magazine about their work as female miners and their experiences in the brutal working conditions, the sexual harassment, and the discrimination.[3] 'Appalachian social mores,' said one woman, echoing voices that had drifted down since 1842, 'insist that a virtuous woman would shrink from working underground in the filthy, dark world that has belonged to men.' Pictures of the American women miners are held in the Raissa Page Collection, in the Richard Burton Archives, Swansea University.

The only time a woman was allowed to work underground in the UK was as a doctor accessing injured colliers and in August 1978 the NCB made their first appointment of a woman as deputy medical officer for their South Wales area.[4]

The last pit-brow lass in the Wigan coalfield finished work at Golborne Colliery in 1966 and the very last woman colliery-surface worker in the United Kingdom retired in 1972 from the Harrington No 10 mine in Lowca, Cumberland. One of them, Rita Culshaw from Wigan, told the *Daily Mirror* she had loved the work and, despite being 83, 'would go back to the mine tomorrow'.[5]

It is not known who the last Welsh woman was, but possibly Martha Richards who died aged 93 in 1974, the last woman to have worked in the Stepaside Pits, Pembrokeshire.

Women duly moved to the supportive role, caring, catering, and administrative, and occasionally posed as wives and family members sitting in photos amid hordes of men. There were the Coal Queen beauty competitions as women posed scantily clad and seductively for the male gaze. Some women's work was acknowledged and celebrated, such as the colliery sister at Bargoed Colliery, Betty Barker, who wrote a piece on her 21 years there in the 2011 edition of *Glo*, a magazine about the Welsh coal industry edited by Ceri Thompson at the Big Pit National Coal Museum. Daily attendances to her surgery were high Betty recalled, with men saying, 'Let her do the stitching; she's good at embroidery!'[6] A year later, in the same magazine, Ann Jenkins, wrote of being a clerical officer at Groesfan Colliery in 1965 [7]; and Rosemarie Williams was described as 'the last mineworker in north Wales'. There had been a Miner's Office in Wrexham for over a hundred years and for fifty-three of those years Rosemarie was the secretary.[8]

Gone but Not Forgotten

Despite a number of books having been written about the Wigan Pit Brow Lasses, the Tip Girls of Wales were mostly forgotten but a few did remember them. In 1978, Welsh artist Nicholas Evans (1907–2004) from Aberdare, produced the art work, *Women Working Windlass (Pit Top)* and *My Mother was a Pit Girl* (1990). In 2020, Hilary Barry exhibited *Merched Pwll* (Pit Girls) at Cyfarthfa Castle Museum & Art Gallery.

When working on my book *A History of Women in Men's Clothes* I wrote extensively about women passing as men in various hard labours, or those who were criticised for wearing trousers, including the Wigan women, and this resulted in my interest in the Welsh Tip Girls. Having chatted to Ceri Thompson at the Big Pit National Coal Museum he was keen to increase the knowledge and coverage of these women and so together we planned an exhibition. It consists of twelve exhibition boards full of information and images and a mannequin dressed as a tip girl. Ceri and I also asked the Craft Club, a group of volunteers at St. Fagans Museum, if they could replicate one of the Clayton images. Like many people, they had never heard of the tip girls and so we gave them images and descriptions to aid in the interpretation and the resulting costume was included in the exhibition.[9] However, all this happened just as the COVID lockdown took place meaning little could be done to launch or celebrate the exhibition. In September 2022 the exhibition moved to the Waterfront Museum, Swansea where it remained until March 2023. Further plans are being considered for display in other parts of Wales.

Nevertheless, it is a beginning, as it is the first exhibition to celebrate Welsh women in coal mines and, as much of the research collected by myself and Ceri Thompson could not fit into this book, it leaves the possibility of a great deal more work to do.

Today

Since the late twentieth century UK laws restricting women's employment, and their pay, have changed to keep them more in line with men's work and pay, but gender employment and pay gaps still persists. Following the Employment Act 1989 women are now allowed to work underground, but few do so.

In 2021 a study was done by Natural Resource Governance Institute (NRGI) and World Resources Institute (WRI) on women working in extractives, those industries extracting raw materials from the earth, and found that 60 countries still have laws on the books that restrict women's employment in mining, mostly in the sub-Saharan Africa areas. Most of these laws originated from the British Mines and Collieries Act of 1842 that banned women and girls from working underground which spread across the British Empire and elsewhere.

In the 1920s and 1930s, the International Labour Organization (ILO) adopted several protectionist conventions around women's labor in the mining industry, prohibiting women's underground work and limiting women's ability to work at night. These provisions became enshrined in the governing documents of ILO member states, pushing women further into lower-status, lower-wage work, particularly in the global south. Limits on women's participation and narrow definitions of what it means to work in the sector have rendered women's work throughout the extractives value chain largely invisible. This has translated into lack of unionization, poor organization and poor policies and protections.[10]

Today, women's overall participation in the global workforce is 47%, but only 14% of the global industrial mining workforce, and few are in the higher paying jobs being left predominantly in administrate fields. There are women miners, particularly in the USA, and occasionally articles appear about them and their work – but many speak of being hampered by discrimination and the attitudes of men who believe such work is unsuitable for women.

Women's rights still have a long way to go. Similarly, women's history is still playing catch-up to men's history and so it is important we know about, and celebrate, the extraordinary women who were the Tip Girls of Wales.

Notes

Chapter 1: Degrading Labours
1. National Mining Hall of Fame & Museum, *Lou Henry Hoover*. Available online.
2. Hoover, Herbert (1912) *De Re Metallica, Translated from the First Latin Edition of 1556 by Georg Agricola* (New York, Dover Publications, Inc., 1912) Accessed online via Project Gutenberg
3. Ibid
4. Owen, George, 'A History of Pembrokeshire.' *The Cambrian Register*, Vol. 2, 1796. Accessed online.
5. *Haverfordwest and Milford Haven Telegraph*, 10 January, 1917
6. Edwards, George, 'The Coal Industry in Pembrokeshire' *Field Studies*, Vol 1, Issue 5, 1863
7. Lloyd-Morgan, C. "Temperance to Suffrage", in Angela V. John, (ed.), *Our mothers' land: chapters in Welsh women's history, 1830–1939* (Cardiff: University of Wales Press; 2nd edition (28 Feb. 2011)
8. Anon, *A collection of Welsh tours* (London: G. Sael, 1798)
9. Mein, John, *Extract of coroners' inquests in the coalfield of eastern Pembrokeshire, 1786–1830* (GenUKI, 2008) Accessed online.
10. Thompson, Ceri, *From the cradle to the coalmine: the story of children in Welsh mines* (Cardiff: University Wales Press, 2014)
11. Clarke, Edward Daniel, *Travels in various countries of Europe, Asia and Africa* (London, 1818)
12. Simonin, Louis, *Underground Life: Mines and Miners* (London: Chapman and Hall, 1869)
13. Evans, John Rev., *Letters written during a tour through south Wales, in 1803, and at other times* (London, 1804)
14. Chris Mounsey, *Developments in the Histories of Sexualities in Search of the Normal, 1600–1800* United States: Bucknell University Press., 2013
15. Pountney, Jon *Blaenavon: stories from an industrial town* (YouTube, 2018). Accessed online.
16. Glamorgan Gazette, 22 November 1907
17. *Aberdare Leader*, 6 June 1903
18. *Weekly Mail*, 10 October 1903
19. *Aberdare Leader*, 25 June 1904
20. Anon, *The condition and treatment of the children employed in the mines and collieries of the United Kingdom* (London, 1842). Accessed online.
21. Anon, Children's Employment Commission on the mines, *Reports from Commissioners: Children's Employment (Mines) Vol VX, 1842* (London: Parliamentary paper, 1842). Widely available online.
22. Ridd, Tom, 'Pits and Pit Boys in the Swansea Area Gower' *The Journal of the Gower Society*, Vol 17, 1966

Chapter 2: The 1841 Census
1. Higgs, Edward, *Making Sense of the Census Revisited*, (London: Institute of Historical Research, 2005)
2. Census of Great Britain, 1841, Abstract of the answers and returns made pursuant to acts 3 & 4 Vic. c.99 and 4 Vic. c.7 intituled respectively "An act for taking an account of the population of Great Britain", and "An act to amend the acts of the last session for taking an Account of the Population". Occupation abstract, 1841. Part I. England and Wales and Islands in the British Seas. British Parliamentary Papers 1844 XXVII (587)
3. Lloyd, Val, 'Attitudes to Women at North Wales Coalmines c1840–1901', *Llafur the journal of the Society for the Study of Welsh Labour History*, Vol, 5 no. 2, 1989

Chapter 3: A Great Many Girls
1. Commissioners for Inquiring into the Employment and Condition of Children in Mines and Manufactories, *The condition and treatment of the children employed in the mines and collieries of the United Kingdom* (London: William Strange, 1842)
2. Thompson, Ceri (2014)
3. Commissioners for Inquiring into the Employment and Condition of Children in Mines and Manufactories (1842)
4. Ibid
5. Ibid
6. Ibid
7. Ancestry, *About 1841 Wales Census*. Accessed online.
8. Thompson, Ceri (2014)
9. Commissioners for Inquiring into the Employment and Condition of Children in Mines and Manufactories (1842)
10. Ibid
11. Ibid

Chapter 4: Lucy Thomas and Eos Vach
1. *Cardiff Times*, 11 June 1910
2. *Tarian Y Gweithiwr*, 14 February 1901
3. *Ancestry.com*. 1841 *Wales Census* [database on-line].
4. Wilkins, Charles *The South Wales Coal Trade and Its Allied Industries from the Earliest Days*, (Cardiff, Daniel Owen and Co. Ltd, 1888)
5. *Evening Express*, 25 June 1909
6. *Pioneer*, 7 April 1917
7. *Glamorgan Morgan and Brecon Gazette and Merthyr Guardian*, 22 June 1839
8. *Cardiff Times*, 11 June 1910
9. *Cardiff Times*, 6 October 1906
10. Vincent, James Edmund *John Nixon, Pioneer of the Steam Coal Trade in South Wales* (London, 1900)
11. *Monmouthshire Merlin*, 2 October 1847
12. *Cardiff Times*, 10 June 1899
13. *The Times*, 18 March 1898
14. *The Times*, 23 March 1898
15. *The Times*, 28 March 1898
16. Nevill, R. J. *The Early Welsh Coal Trade*, National Library of Wales journal, Cyf. 10, rh. 1, Haf 1957
17. Morgan, W. T., 'A Note on Lucy Thomas of Waunwyllt' *National Library of Wales journal*, Cyf. 10, rh. 4, Gaeaf 1958
18. *Cardiff Times*, 11 June 1910

19. *Merthyr Telegraph*, 26 January 1861
20. *The Cambrian*, 3 December 1836
21. *Monmouthshire Merlin*, 3 December 1836
22. *Glamorgan Monmouth and Brecon Gazette and Merthyr Guardian*, 21 October 1837
23. Schreiber, Charlotte, Lady, *Lady Charlotte Guest; extracts from her journal, 1833–1852* (London, Murray, 1950)
24. *Monmouthshire Merlin*, 13 October 1838
25. *The Cambrian*, 6 April 1839
26. *Glamorgan Monmouth and Brecon Gazette and Merthyr Guardian*, 13 April 1839
27. *Monmouthshire Merlin*, 23 August 1845
28. *The Atlantic Monthly*, March 1858

Chapter 5: They are Murdered by the System
1. Commissioners for Inquiring into the Employment and Condition of Children in Mines and Manufactories (1842)
2. Ibid
3. Ibid
4. *Good Words*, 1 January 1869
5. Commissioners for Inquiring into the Employment and Condition of Children in Mines and Manufactories (1842)
6. Ibid
7. Ibid
8. Anon, *Physical and moral condition of the children and young persons employed in mines and manufacturing* (London: Her Majesty's Stationary Office, 1843)
9. Ibid
10. *Morning Chronicle*, 15 July 1842
11. *Cardiff and Merthyr Guardian*, 18 June 1842
12. Anon, *The Physical and Moral Conditions of Children and Young Persons Employed in Mines and Manufactures* (1843)
13. Ibid
14. *Cardiff and Merthyr Guardian*, 4 June 1842
15. Commissioners for Inquiring into the Employment and Condition of Children in Mines and Manufactories (1842)
16. Wynne Evans, Leslie, 'Colliery Schools in South Wales in the Nineteenth Century', *National Library of Wales journal*. 1957, Winter. Volume X/2. Available online.
17. Ibid
18. Commissioners for Inquiring into the Employment and Condition of Children in Mines and Manufactories (1842)

Chapter 6: Getting around the Act
1. Pinchbeck, Ivy, *Women Workers and the Industrial Revolution 1750–1850*, 3rd edition, (London: Virago, 1981)
2. Browning, Elizabeth Barrett, *The Cry of the Children* (1843) Available online.
3. Hansard, HC Deb 07 June 1842 vol 63 cc1320–64
4. Hansard, HL Deb 30 June 1842 vol 64 cc783–5
5. Hansard, HL Deb 08 July 1842 vol 64 cc1166–8
6. Hansard, HL Deb 14 July 1842 vol 65 cc101–24
7. Ibid
8. Hansard, HL Deb 25 July 1842 vol 65 cc571–88
9. *The Economist*, 28 September 1844
10. Hansard, HL Deb 01 August 1842 vol 65 cc891–3

11. Edmonds, O. P., & Edmonds, E. L., *An Account of The Founding of H.M. Inspectorate of Mines and The Work of The First Inspector Hugh Seymour Tremenheere* British Journal of Industrial Medicine., 1963. Available online.
12. Bates, Denise 'The scandal of female miners' *History Extra* online blog, 3 October, 2012. Available online.
13. *Monmouthshire Merlin*, 3 June 1843
14. Commissioners for Inquiring into the Employment and Condition of Children in Mines and Manufactories (1842)
15. *The Ipswich Journal*, 7 June 1845
16. *The Times*, 28 November 1846
17. *Northern Star*, 7 October 1843
18. *Liverpool Mercury*, 7 November 1845
19. *Cornwall Chronicle*, 26 July 1845
20. *Royal Cornwall Gazette*, 27 August 1858
21. *Sheffield & Rotherham Independent*, 29 August 1869
22. *Evening Express*, 10 April 1899
23. *South Wales Echo*, 28 December 1895
24. *Aberdare Times*, 5 April 1862
25. *Carmarthen Weekly Reporter*, 11 October 1901
26. Gordon, *Penal Discipline* 1922
27. Hansard, HC Deb 07 June 1842 vol 63 cc1320–64
28. Lane, David, *Pit Brow Lasses Scrapbook*. Internet edition, 3rd Revision, Feb 2007. Available online.
29. ibid
30. Richardson, Joshua *On the Prevention of Accidents in Mines* (London: Longman and Company) 1848 P.23–24
31. Tremenheere, Seymour, 'Reports from Commissioners' in *The Sessional Papers of the House of Lords, Session 1846, Vol. xxxvi* (London: House of Lords, 1846)
32. *The Times*, 9 August 1850.
33. Jon Mein, (2008)
34. Hughes, Basil H.J., *Pembrokeshire Parishes, Places & People*. Available online via Academia. ed.
35. Coflein, *Garden Pit, Landshipping Colliery*. Available online.
36. Tremenheere, Seymour 1846
37. Val Lloyd, 1989
38. Lingen, R. R. W., Symons, Jellynger C., and Johnson, H. R. Vaughan, *Reports of the Commissioners of Inquiry into the State of Education in Wales*, Great Britain Committee on Education, 1847–1848. Available online.
39. Ibid
40. Ibid
41. Romano, Rossana Barragán, and Leda Papastefanaki. 'Women and Gender in the Mines: Challenging Masculinity Through History: An Introduction.' *International Review of Social History* 65 (2): 191–230, 2020

Chapter 7: Unsexing Themselves
1. Milburn, Amanda Janet Macdonald (2013) *Female employment in nineteenth-century ironworking districts: Merthyr Tydfil and the Shropshire Coalfield, 1841–1881* thesis, Swansea University. Available online.
2. *Monmouthshire Merlin*, 13 October 1854
3. *Merthyr Telegraph*, 4 October 1856

4. Anon, *Labour and the Poor Volume VIII: Wales, The Mining and Manufacturing Districts*, (Liverpool: Ditto Books, 2019)
5. *Monmouthshire Merlin*, 12 December 1857
6. *Monmouthshire Merlin*, 20 September 1856
7. *Morning Chronicle*, 21 March 1850
8. *Monmouthshire Merlin*, 20 September 1856
9. *Merthyr Telegraph*, 30 January 1858
10. Symons, Jelinger Cookson, *The Industrial Capacities of South Wales* (London: Longman, Brown, Green, and Longmans, 1855)
11. *Morning Chronicle*, 21 March 1850
12. *Morning Chronicle*, 18 March 1850
13. *Morning Chronicle*, 21 March 1850
14. *Morning Chronicle*, 18 March 1850
15. O. P. Edmonds & E. L. Edmonds 1963
16. Tremenheere, Hugh Seymour Report of the Commissioner Appointed Under the Provisions of the Act 5 & 6 Vict., C.99. to Inquire into the Operation of that Act and Into the State of the Population in the Mining Districts, 1850
17. Ibid
18. Tremenheere, Hugh Seymour Report of the Commissioner Appointed Under the Provisions of the Act 5 & 6 Vict., C.99. to Inquire into the Operation of that Act and Into the State of the Population in the Mining Districts, 1854
19. *The Times*, 14 January 1858
20. *Merthyr Telegraph*, 4 October 1856
21. *Morning Chronicle*, 21 March 1850
22. *Merthyr Telegraph*, 5 September 1857
23. *Merthyr Telegraph*, 16 January 1858
24. *Merthyr Telegraph*, 26 July 1856
25. *Monmouthshire Merlin*, 20 September 1856
26. *Merthyr Telegraph*, 19 December 1857
27. *Morning Chronicle*, 21 March 1850
28. Coal Mining Accidents and Death Index, 1878–1935. Accessed via Ancestry.
29. *North Wales Chronicle*, 8 December 1855
30. Coal Mining Accidents and Death Index, 1878–1935. Accessed via Ancestry.
31. *Silurian, Cardiff, Merthyr, and Brecon Mercury, and South Wales General Advertiser*, 29 November 1851
32. *Merthyr Telegraph*, 3 January 1857
33. *Merthyr Telegraph*, 17 January 1857
34. *Monmouthshire Merlin*, 20 October 1855
35. *Merthyr Telegraph*, 28 August 1858
36. *Illustrated Usk Observer*, 2 May 1857
37. *Merthyr Telegraph*, 7 March 1857
38. *Monmouthshire Merlin*, 25 August 1854

Chapter 8: The 1851 Census
1. Census of Great Britain, 1851, Population Tables, II. Ages, civil conditions, occupations and birth-place of the people with the numbers and ages of the blind, the deaf-and-dumb, and the inmates of workhouses, prisons, lunatic asylums, and hospitals. Vol. I. BPP 1852-53 LXXXVIII Pt [1691.I]
2. Census Office, *The Census of Great Britain in 1851* (London: British Government, 1854)
3. Hunt, Robert *Mineral Statistics of the United Kingdom of Great Britain and Ireland* (London: H.M. Stationery Office, 1855)

Chapter 9: Should Female Labour be Employed?

1. Menelaus, William, & Jenkins, William. *Reports by William Jenkins and William Menelaus addressed to G.T. Clark on possibility of improving coal sales*, Glamorgan Archives DG/D/1/8/1.2
2. John, Angela V. *By the sweat of their brow: Women workers at Victorian coal mines* (London: Routledge, Kegan, and Paul, 1984)
3. Her Majesty's Stationery Office *Census of England and Wales for the Year 1861 Population Tables Vol. II* (London: Her Majesty's Stationery Office, 1863)
4. National Association of coal, lime, and ironstone miners of Great Britain, *Transactions and results of the national association of coal, lime, and ironstone miners of Great Britain*, (London: Longman, Green, Longman, Roberts, and Green, 1864)
5. *Aberystwyth Observer*, 3 September 1864
6. John Plummer, 'A Real Social Evil', *Once a Week*, 27 August, 1864
7. *Merthyr Telegraph*, 7 January 1865
8. *Merthyr Telegraph*, 14 January 1865
9. *Merthyr Telegraph*, 28 January 1865
10. *Merthyr Telegraph*, 4 February 1865
11. *Merthyr Telegraph*, 11 February 1865
12. *Merthyr Telegraph*, 18 February 1865
13. *Merthyr Telegraph*, 25 February 1865
14. *Merthyr Telegraph*, 4 March 1865
15. Longe, Mr. 'Metal Trades in South Wales' in *Children's Employment Commission: Third report of the Commissioners*, Parliamentary Papers (London: HMSO, 1863)
16. 'A Saunterer' 'A vacation at Merthyr' *Merthyr Telegraph*, 16 June 1866
17. *Y Glorian*, 23 March 1867 quoted by John, Angela V. 'A Miner Struggle: Women's Protests in Welsh Mining History' in *Llafur the journal of the Society for the Study of Welsh Labour History*, Vol. IV, 1, 1984. Available online at the National Library of Wales, Welsh Journals
18. Good Words, *Toiling and Moiling: Some Account of our Working People, and How They Live: 1. The Merthyr Iron Worker*, 1 January, 1869

Chapter 10: The Clayton Images

1. *Merthyr Telegraph*, 14 October 1865
2. *Western Mail*, 12 November 1884
3. *South Wales Daily News*, 9 October 1894
4. Baylis, Gail, 2006
5. *Merthyr Telegraph*, 11 February 1865
6. Hudson, Derek, Munby, Man of Two Worlds: The Life and Diaries of Arthur J. Munby, 1828 1910 (London: J. Murray, 1972)
7. Amgueddfa Cymru – National Museum Wales, Industry Collection, No. 28.119/4
8. Shopland, Norena *A History of Women in Men's Clothes: from Cross-dressing to Empowerment* (Pen and Sword Books, 2021)
9. Gail Baylis, 2006
10. *Monmouthshire Merlin*, 1 May 1874
11. Amgueddfa Cymru – National Museum Wales, Industry Collection, No. 28.119/6
12. *Western Mail*, 27 April 1874
13. *Cambrian*, 18 October 1872
14. Her Majesty's Stationery Office, *Children's Employment Commission*, (London: Her Majesty's Stationery Office, 1862)
15. Blaenau Gwent Access to Heritage Project, Facebook group, 9 September 2014

16. *Merthyr Times*, 31 October 1895
17. Gail Baylis, 2006

Chapter 11: Sackcloth and Ashes
1. *Western Mail*, 7 October 1871
2. Census of England and Wales, 1871. *Population Abstracts. Ages, Civil Condition, Occupations, and Birth-places of the People.* Vol. III. (London: HMSO, 1873).
3. John, Angel V. 2006
4. *Cardigan Observer*, 4 October 1879
5. Hudson, Derek, 1972
6. *Cardiff & Merthyr Guardian*, 12 March 1870; *Cardiff & Merthyr Guardian*, 26 February 1870
7. *The Times*, 28 May 1870.
8. Camden, Charles *The Travelling Menagerie* (London: Henry S. King, 1873)
9. *Graphic*, 1 February 1873
10. John, Angel V. 2006
11. Ibid
12. *Evening Express*, 1 January 1909
13. Ibid
14. Ibid
15. *South Wales Daily News*, 27 June 1872
16. *Merthyr Telegraph and General Advertiser*, 28 June 1872
17. *Cardiff Times*, 29 June 1872
18. *South Wales Daily News*, 29 August 1872
19. *South Wales Daily News*, 3 September 1872
20. *Belfast News*, 30 January 1873
21. Morris, H. and Williams, L. J. *The South Wales Coal Industry 1841–1875* (Cardiff, University of Wales Press, 1958)
22. *Merthyr Telegraph*, 12 February 1875
23. *Western Mail*, 9 Mar. 1875
24. *Aberdare Times*, 12 April 1873
25. *Monmouthshire Merlin*, 29 May 1875
26. *Wrexham Advertiser*, 6 March 1875
27. *Weston Mail*, 1 August 1877
28. *Western Mail*, 31 March 1877
29. *Monmouthshire Merlin*, 1 May 1874
30. *Wrexham Advertiser*, 19 August 1876
31. *Aberdare Times*, 13 July 1878
32. *Monmouthshire Merlin*, 6 December 1872
33. *Merthyr Express*, 16 September 1871
34. *Merthyr Telegraph*, 1 November 1872
35. *Monmouthshire Merlin*, 4 October 1872
36. *Merthyr Telegraph*, 6 September 1872
37. *Cambrian*, 2 May 1879
38. *South Wales Daily News*, 26 February 1874
39. *South Wales Daily News*, 21 April 1875
40. *Pontypool Free Press*, 27 July 1872
41. *County Observer*, 22 June 1878
42. *South Wales Daily News*, 28 January 1881

Chapter 12: 1881 Census
1. *Wrexham and Denbighshire Advertiser*, 17 September 1887
2. Hunt, Robert, *Mineral Statistics of the United Kingdom of Great Britain & Ireland* (London: H.M. Stationery Office, 1883)
3. Hansard, HC Deb 08 March 1888 vol 323 c563
4. *Weekly Mail*, 15 July 1882

Chapter 13: Angels of Humanity
1. *Wrexham Advertiser*, 14 April 1883
2. *Cardiff Times*, 21 July 1883
3. *Cardiff Times*, 14 April 1883
4. Lever, Ellis 'A real social evil' *The Times* (5 October 1885)
5. Lever, Ellis 'Female labour at collieries' *The Times* (5 October & 20 October 1885)
6. *Daily Colonist*, 4 November 1882
7. Angle V. John 1984; Val Lloyd 1989
8. St Fagans National Museum of History Recording No. 2370
9. Sikes, Wirt *Rambles and Studies in Old South Wales* (London: Sampson Low, Marston, Searle, & Rivington, 1881)
10. *South Wales Echo*, 22 April 1886
11. *Manchester Times*, 27 March 1886
12. *Leeds Mercury*, 22 March 1886
13. *Liverpool Mercury*, 12 April 1886
14. *Cardiff Times*, 15 May 1886
15. *Cambrian News*, 20 August 1886
16. *South Wales Daily News*, 11 February 1887
17. *Western Mail*, 14 February 1887
18. Morgan, D. 'Correspondence' *South Wales Daily News* (13 May 1887)
19. *Western Mail*, 18 May 1887
20. Hansard, HC Deb 14 February 1887 vol 310 cc1406-7
21. *Cardigan Observer*, 28 May 1887
22. *Weekly Mail*, 21 May 1887
23. Mabon 'The miners regulation bill' *South Wales Echo* (8 Jun. 1887)
24. *Western Mail*, 24 June 1887
25. *Cambrian News*, 1 July 1887
26. *South Wales Daily News*, 9 June 1887
27. *South Wales Daily News*, 25 June 1887
28. *Western Mail*, 18 May 1887

Chapter 14: Rough Grace
1. *Weekly Mail*, 9 July 1887
2. *Cardigan Observer*, 9 November 1887
3. *Wrexham and Denbighshire Advertiser*, 17 September 1887
4. *Weekly Mail*, 28 March 1891
5. John, Angela V. 2006
6. *Merthyr Times*, 17 December 1896
7. Welsh Government, *Digest of Welsh Historical Statistics 1700-1974: Chapter 5 - Coal*. Accessed online.
8. *Evening Express*, 26 March 1897
9. *South Wales Daily News*, 3 March 1888
10. *Western Mail*, 27 March 1897

11. *Western Mail*, 27 March 1897
12. *South Wales Daily Post*, 7 May 1895
13. *South Wales Echo*, 27 August 1897
14. Owen, David, *South Wales Collieries*, Vol. 3, (Stroud, The History Press Ltd, 2002)
15. Personal comment
16. Thomas ap Noreh, John 'Coal Dispute' (*South Wales Daily News*, 2 August 1898)
17. *County Observer*, 25 March 1882
18. *South Wales Daily News*, 1 August 1898
19. *Carnarvon and Denbigh Herald*, 28 September 1894
20. *Western Mail*, 23 November 1892
21. *Chester Courant*, 16 February 1898
22. *South Wales Echo*, 18 August 1886
23. *South Wales Daily News*, 22 September 1898
24. *Evening Express*, 20 May 1898
25. *Cardiff Times*, 8 April 1882; Criminal Register 1791–1892
26. *Western Mail*, 25 February 1890; *South Wales Daily News*, 27 February 1890; *South Wales Daily News*, 3 March 1890; *Pontypridd Chronicle*, 7 March 1890
27. *Western Mail*, 9 June 1887
28. Glamorgan Archives, *Glamorgan Court of Quarter Sessions 1790–1971*, Q/S/R/1767/B/35
29. Glamorgan Archives, *Glamorgan Court of Quarter Sessions* 1790–1971, Q/S/D/2/593
30. Ibid Q/S/D/2/921
31. *Glamorgan Free Press*, 11 September 1897
32. *Merthyr Telegraph*, 26 April 1862
33. *Merthyr Telegraph*, 5 August 1865
34. *Merthyr Telegraph*, 20 February 1869
35. *The Cambrian*, 15 February 1895
36. *Merthyr Express*, 16 September 1871
37. *South Wales Daily Post*, 3 November 1893
38. *South Wales Daily News*, 20 August 1897
39. *South Wales Echo*, 24 April 1896
40. *Cheshire Observer*, 7 June 1902
41. *Evening Express*, 8 October 1904
42. *Evening Express*, 12 March 1909
43. Llewellyn, Richard *How Green is my Valley* (Harmondsworth: Penguin Books, 1939) Accessed via Internet Archive
44. Jenkins, R. T., (1959). *James, James (Spinther) (1837 - 1914), Baptist historian*. Dictionary of Welsh Biography. Available online.
45. *Seren Cymru*, 27 March 1891
46. *Evening Express*, 25 June 1896
47. *Pall Mall Gazette*, 6 February 1899

Chapter 15: Diminishing Numbers
1. Welsh Government, *Digest of Welsh Historical Statistics 1700–1974: Chapter 5 – Coal*. Accessed online.
2. HMSO, Census of England and Wales 1901 (63 VIct. c. 4) County of Merioneth, (London: HMSO, 1903)
3. Brace, William 'Workmen's Notes' (*Weekly Mail*, 12 August 1905)
4. *Flintshire Observer*, 26 August 1910
5. 1911 Census of England and Wales, Census Returns of England and Wales, Occupations and Industries, Part II, 1913

6. *Hawera & Normanby Star*, 7 October 1911
7. Evans, George Brinley 'Working on the screens' *Glo Coal*, Vol 5, 2011
8. Hansard HC Deb 05 December 1911 vol 32 cc1234–83
9. Angela V. John, 2005
10. *Cambrian Daily Leader*, 6 July 1915
11. Pritchard, Katie Olwen, *Gilfach Goch in Cameo*, Vol. 2 (Newport: Starling Press, 1873)
12. *Cardiff Times*, 24 February 1900
13. *Cardiff Times*, 26 January 1901
14. *Rhondda Reader*, 12 November 1904
15. *Carmarthen Weekly Reporter*, 31 August 1906
16. Corrop-Price, Martin, *Pembrokeshire the Forgotten Coalfield* (Ashbourne: Landmark Publishing Ltd, 2004)
17. *Evening Express*, 8 January 1908; *Cardiff Times*, 11 April 1908
18. *Chester Courant and Advertiser for North Wales*, 8 May 1901
19. Lloyd, Val, 1989
20. *Evening Express*, 16 May 1907

Chapter 16: Endings and Beginnings
1. Angela V. John, 2005
2. Hansard, HL Deb 26 October 1954 vol 189 cc626–724
3. Hall, Chris 'The women miners of Virginia' *Observer Magazine*, 24 September 2019
4. Angela V. John, 2005
5. Pidd, Helen, 'Why 'pit brow lasses' were coal mining's unsung heroines' (*Guardian*, 14 October 2018)
6. Barker, Betty 'Embroidery and ear syringing' *Glo*, Vol. 5, 2011
7. Jenkins, Ann 'You had to be fit' *Glo*, Vol. 5, 2011
8. McKay, Ted 'The last mineworker in north Wales' *Glo*, 2012
9. Craft Volunteers, *The Making of the Tip Girl*, Amgueddfa Blog, 2021. Available online.
10. Menard, Aubrey, *Women in Mining: A History of Legal Invisibility and Exclusion*, Natural Resource Governance Institute blog, available online.

Bibliography

Anon, *The Condition and Treatment of the Children Employed in the Mines and Collieries of the United Kingdom* (London:,William Strange, 1842). Accessed online.
Anon, *Children's Employment Commission on the mines, Reports from Commissioners: Children's Employment (Mines) Vol VX, 1842* (London, Parliamentary paper, 1842). Widely available online.
Anon, *Physical and Moral Condition of the Children and Young Persons Employed in Mines and Manufacturing* (London, Her Majesty's Stationary Office, 1843). Accessed online.
Baylis, Gail, 'Visual Cruising in South Wales in the 1860s: Tredegar Patch Girls' in *Visual Culture in Britain*, Vol. 7, No. 2, 2006
Bates, Denise 'The scandal of female miners' (2012, 3 Oct.) *History Extra*, Available online.
Browning, Elizabeth Barrett, *The Cry of the Children* (1843) Available online.
Clarke, Edward Daniel, *Travels in various countries of Europe, Asia and Africa* (London, 1818)
Corrop-Price, Martin, *Pembrokeshire the Forgotten Coalfield* (Ashbourne, Landmark Publishing Ltd, 2004)
Edmonds, O. P., & Edmonds, E. L., 'An Account of The Founding of H.M. Inspectorate of Mines and The Work of The First Inspector Hugh Seymour Tremenheere', *British Journal of Industrial Medicine.*, 1963. Available online.
Edwards, George, 'The Coal Industry in Pembrokeshire' *Field Studies*, Vol 1, Issue 5, 1863
Evans, John Rev., *Letters written during a tour through south Wales, in 1803, and at other times* (London, 1804)
Higgs, Edward, *Making Sense of the Census Revisited*, (London, Institute of Historical Research, 2005)
HMSO, *Census of Great Britain, 1851, Population Tables, II. Ages, civil conditions, occupations and birth-place of the people with the numbers and ages of the blind, the deaf-and-dumb, and the inmates of workhouses, prisons, lunatic asylums, and hospitals.* Vol. I. BPP 1852–53 LXXXVIII Pt [1691.I]
HMSO, *Census of England and Wales, 1871. Population Abstracts. Ages, Civil Condition, Occupations, and Birth-places of the People.* Vol. III. (London, HMSO, 1873).
Hoover, Herbert (1912) *De Re Metallica: Translated from the First Latin Edition of 1556 by Georg Agricola* (New York, Dover Publications, Inc., 1912) Accessed online via Project Gutenberg
Hughes, Basil H.J., *Pembrokeshire Parishes, Places & People*. Available online.
Hunt, Robert, *Mineral Statistics of the United Kingdom of Great Britain and Ireland* (London, H.M. Stationery Office, 1855)
Hunt, Robert, *Mineral Statistics of the United Kingdom of Great Britain & Ireland* (London: H.M. Stationery Office, 1883)
John, Angela V., 'A Miner Struggle? Women's Protest in Welsh Mining History' *Llafur the journal of the Society for the Study of Welsh Labour History* Vol. 4, 1, 1984
John, Angela V., *By the Sweat of their Brow: Women workers at Victorian Coal Mines* (London, Routledge, 2005)
Anon, *Labour and the Poor Volume VIII: Wales, The Mining and Manufacturing Districts*, (Liverpool, Ditto Books, 2019)

Lane, David, *Pit Brow Lasses Scrapbook. Internet edition*, 3rd Revision, Feb 2007. Available online.

Lloyd-Morgan, C. "Temperance to Suffrage", in Angela V. John, (ed.), Our mothers' land: chapters in Welsh women's history, 1830–1939 (Cardiff: University of Wales Press; 2nd edition (28 Feb. 2011)

Lloyd, Val 'Attitudes to women at north Wales coalmines, c.1840–1901' *Llafur the journal of the Society for the Study of Welsh Labour History* Vol. 5 No. 2 1989. Available online at Llyfrgell Genedlaethol Cymru – The National Library of Wales

Longe, Mr. 'Metal Trades in South Wales' in *Children's Employment Commission: Third report of the Commissioners, Parliamentary Papers* (London: HMSO, 1863)

Mein, John, *Extract of coroners' inquests in the coalfield of eastern Pembrokeshire, 1786–1830* (GenUKI, 2008) Accessed online.

Milburn, Amanda Janet Macdonald (2013) Female employment in nineteenth-century ironworking districts: Merthyr Tydfil and the Shropshire Coalfield, 1841–1881 thesis, Swansea University. Available online.

Morgan, W. T., 'A Note on Lucy Thomas of Waunwyllt' *National Library of Wales journal*, Cyf. 10, rh. 4, Gaeaf 1958

Morris, H. and Williams, L. J., *The South Wales Coal Industry 1841–1875* (Cardiff, University of Wales Press, 1958)

Mounsey, Chris *Developments in the Histories of Sexualities in Search of the Normal, 1600–1800* United States: Bucknell University Press., 2013

Nevill, R. J. 'The Early Welsh Coal Trade', *National Library of Wales journal*, Cyf. 10, rh. 1, Haf, 1957

Owen, George, 'A History of Pembrokeshire.' *The Cambrian Register*, Vol. 2, 1796. Accessed online.

Owen, David, *South Wales Collieries*, Vol. 3, (Stroud, The History Press Ltd, 2002)

Pinchbeck, Ivy, Women Workers and the Industrial Revolution 1750–1850, 3rd edition, (London, Virago, 1981)

Pritchard, Katie Olwen, *Gilfach Goch in Cameo*, Vol. 2 (Newport: Starling Press, 1873)

Richardson, Joshua, *On the Prevention of Accidents in Mines* (London, Longman and Company) 1848

Ridd, Tom, 'Pits and Pit Boys in the Swansea Area Gower' *The Journal of the Gower Society*, Vol 17, 1966

Romano, Rossana Barragán, and Leda Papastefanaki. 'Women and Gender in the Mines: Challenging Masculinity Through History: An Introduction.' International Review of Social History 65 (2): 191–230, 2020

Schreiber, Charlotte, *Lady, Lady Charlotte Guest; extracts from her journal, 1833–1852* (London, Murray, 1950)

Shopland, Norena, *A History of Women in Men's Clothes: from Cross-dressing to Empowerment* (Pen and Sword Books, 2021)

Simonin, Louis, *Underground Life: Mines and Miners* (London, Chapman and Hall, 1869)

Thompson, Ceri, *From the cradle to the coalmine: the story of children in Welsh mines* (Cardiff, University Wales Press, 2014)

Tremenheere, Seymour, 'Reports from Commissioners' in The Sessional Papers of the House of Lords, Session 1846, Vol. xxxvi (London, House of Lords, 1846)

Vincent, James Edmund. *John Nixon, Pioneer of the Steam Coal Trade in South Wales* (London, 1900)

Wilkins, Charles, *The South Wales Coal Trade and Its Allied Industries from the Earliest Days*, (Cardiff, Daniel Owen and Co. Ltd, 1888)

Wynne Evans, Leslie, 'Colliery Schools in South Wales in the Nineteenth Century', *National Library of Wales journal*. 1957, Winter. Volume X/2. Available online.

Index

1842 Children's Employment (Mines) Report, 4, 6, 13, 14, 15, 16, 20-22, 26, 41, 45, 47, 50, 54, 55, 61, 72, 83

1842 The Condition and Treatment of the Children Employed in the Mines and Colliers of the United Kingdom Report, 7, 8-10, 12

1842 Mines and Collieries Act (first gender specific act of parliament), vii, 59, 63, 68, 69, 74, 77, 78, 85, 87, 163, 179, 181, 183

Abraham, W. 'Mabon' MP, 149-151
Accidents of females at mines, 4, 7, 20, 24, 45, 77, 78, 81, 131, 155, 157, 158, 177, 180
Ages of working females, 2, 8, 11, 15, 16, 17, 20-23, 26, 28, 29, 38, 46, 47, 56-58, 59, 60, 63, 67, 68, 75, 77, 84-85, 89, 91, 99, 118, 119, 132, 134-135, 140, 142, 172, 174
Attire, 100, 147, 148, 156, 167
  Aprons/pinafores/smocks, 33, 100, 101, 102, 105, 112, 113, 114, 115, 119, 130, 144, 160, 167, 172
  Belts, 50, 100, 112
  Bloomer costume, 120, 121, 124, 126
  Bonnets and hats, 79, 80, 94, 105, 110, 111, 152, 167
  Boots/clogs/shoes, or lack of, 26, 49, 50, 76, 79, 93, 100, 105, 112, 113, 119, 120, 130, 141, 167, 173, 175
  Dress, 2, 28, 43, 79, 99, 100-102, 105, 112-115, 119, 120, 121, 123, 124, 130, 140, 143, 144, 145, 147, 152-153, 156, 157, 162, 167, 170, 183
  Dressed as men, 50, 61-63, 93, 126, 141, 162
  Earrings, 110, 112
  Feathers, 101, 105, 110, 144
  Handkerchiefs/head coverings/headdress, 79, 100, 101, 105, 110, 111, 119, 124, 126, 130, 144, 154, 167
  Jackets, 62, 93, 124, 167
  Necklace, 94, 110
  Parasols, 140
  Petticoats, 76, 112, 129, 160
  Ribbons, 80
  Scarf, 100, 109, 110-112, 115, 125
  Shawls/mantels, 100, 109, 111-113, 125, 140, 152
  Skirt/frock, 81, 105, 113, 119, 120, 124, 144, 167
  Stockings, 68, 79, 100, 101, 105, 108, 109, 113, 145
  Trousers, 50, 62, 93, 100, 109, 113, 119-120, 121, 122, 124, 129, 141, 144, 152, 153, 170, 183

Being naked, vii, 2, 48-49, 55, 60, 139
Browning, Elizabeth Barrett, 55-56
Bruce, Henry Austin MP, 120-121

Callen, Ann, colliery owner, 4
Churchill, Winston, Home Secretary, 167
Clayton, William (Tredegar photographer), 103-104, 107, 108, 109-110, 115
Crisp, C.B., 104-107, 108, 113
Cooper, John (Wigan photographer), 106-107

Deaths of females at mines, 4, 5, 6, 7, 8, 20, 25, 45, 56, 65, 66, 80-81, 130-131, 157-158, 177-179
Dickens, Charles, 7, 55
Disraeli, Benjamin, 55, 75
Domestic servitude, 43, 44, 50, 66, 69, 73, 74, 90, 91, 95, 106, 108, 126, 136, 139, 142, 155

Education and schools, 8, 11, 24, 30, 32, 36, 37, 42, 52-54, 64, 67, 74-75, 77, 80, 99, 100, 101, 142, 147, 151

Factory Acts and work, 8, 69, 74, 90, 97, 118, 139, 153, 156, 172, 173
Female coal mine owners, 31, 89, 91, 136, 137
Female forenames (most common), 134
Female surnames (most common), 15, 134
Fiction, 161-164
Food and drink, vii, 44, 46, 66, 67, 73, 94, 125, 126, 140, 175, 178

Bacon, 14, 44, 128, 172
Beer, 17, 44, 54, 66, 82
Bread, 21, 26, 30, 44, 76, 145
Breakfast, 30, 44, 99, 127
Butter, 30, 44, 76
Cheese, 21, 26, 44, 76
Dinner, 26, 44, 76, 78, 99, 129, 145, 154, 155
Meat, 14, 44, 76, 127
Milk, 44
Potatoes, 44
Supper, 44
Tea, 44, 67, 76, 167, 176
Franks, Robert Hugh, 1842 Report commissioner, 10, 25, 29, 30, 47, 52, 53, 58

Gaskell, Elizabeth, 55
Gordon, Mary Louisa, 63
Guest, Lady Charlotte, 38, 175

Health
  Bad breath, pneumonia silicosis, 27, 30, 47, 138, 178-179
  Deformed limbs and spine, 46, 47, 48
  Disabled, 29, 30, 179, 180
  Hernias, 47, 157, 179, 178
  Physical stature, 46-47, 78
  Pregnancy and miscarriages, 48, 57, 137, 158, 159, 176
  Strength, 27, 28, 29, 43, 70, 145, 173
Hoover, Herbert & Lou, 1-2
Hours worked, 8, 9, 10, 24, 25, 27, 29-30, 41-42, 43, 45, 49, 53, 75, 76, 79, 95, 119, 121, 154, 155-156, 181

John, Angela V., 101, 113, 117, 141, 153, 178
Jones, Hugh Herbert, 1842 Report commissioner, 9, 21, 28, 44, 45, 46, 48, 51

Language used to describe the women:
  Creatures, 2, 50, 57, 71, 143
  Femininity, or lack of, 69, 70, 71, 75, 94, 99, 101
  Immorality, 51, 55, 69, 72-74, 89, 90, 92, 93, 95, 98, 109, 117, 122, 123, 126, 131, 139, 143, 149, 152, 158, 163, 168, 176
  Indecency, 50, 51, 55, 66, 127, 129
  Masculinity, 162, 62, 70, 73, 79, 80, 101, 112, 116, 126
  Morals, vii, 9, 41, 46, 49, 51, 57, 69, 70, 73, 78, 93, 123, 129, 139, 140, 143, 145, 150, 151, 153, 176
  Repulsive, 50
  Unfit for duties of women, vii, 66, 73, 139, 140, 145, 150

Unladylike, 62, 101, 156
Unsexed, 43, 44, 50, 69, 70-71, 73, 102, 122, 123, 143, 151
Unwomanly, 93, 146
Lodgers, living as, 15, 16, 17, 18, 24, 76, 85, 87, 88, 89, 91, 135, 138
Lord Ashley, MP and social reformer, 8, 9, 56, 57, 59, 61, 63, 66, 78

Mabon, see *Abraham, W. 'Mabon' MP*
Marquess of Londonderry, MP and coal owner, 58, 59
Matthews, Henry, Home Secretary, 148-149, 151, 164
Menelaus, William, manager of the Dowlais Ironworks, 90, 120
Mine explosions, 6, 29, 62, 104
Munby, Arthur Joseph, 107-108, 109, 118, 152

National censuses
  1841 – 10, 11-19, 20, 21-23, 32, 60, 61, 83-91, 133, 134
  1851 – 22, 23, 65, 83-89, 90, 91, 92, 133, 134
  1861 – 91, 111, 114
  1871 – 103, 117, 165
  1881 – 92, 103, 132-138, 144
  1891 – 103
  1911 – 83, 91, 92, 154, 165-166

Occupation Abstracts Reports, 12-13
  1841 – 14, 19
  1851 – 83-84
  1861 – 111
  1901 – 165

Page, Raissa, photographer 182
Photographs, 92, 93, 100, 103, 106, 107, 108, 109, 115, 116, 117, 120, 152, 153, 162, 167, 176, 182
Pinchbeck, Ivy, 55
Pit Brow Lasses, 83, 103, 106, 143, 182

Queen Victoria, 9, 39, 103, 117

Religion, or lack of, 15, 24, 30, 50, 52, 53, 54, 60, 74, 87, 115, 120, 142, 145, 159, 163, 172

Sackcloth and Ashes, Thomas Henry Thomas painting, 131
So Green was my Valley, novel by Richard Llewellyn, 163
Schools, see *Education*

Statistics of working women, vii, 12, 13, 15, 65, 66, 84, 90, 99, 118, 119, 132, 133, 135, 151, 154, 155, 165, 178, 179, 181-182
Strikes, 64, 123-126, 141, 142, 157, 178
Suffrage, 96, 147, 150, 152, 166

Thomas, Lucy, mother of the Welsh steam coal trade, 31-36
Thompson, Ceri, Curator, Big Pit: National Coal Museum, vi, viii, 114, 157, 182, 183
Treachery of the Blue Books, 53, 67-68
Tredegar women, 103-116, 119, 120, 125, 152, 162, 163, 183
Tremenheere, Hugh Seymour, 64-65, 66, 72, 74, 77-78, 80
Types of employment,
  Carrying coals on their backs, 3, 4, 5, 6, 7, 59, 173
  Carrying tools, 25, 26, 42, 43
  Cleaning coal, 5, 128, 136
  Cleaning mines and roads, 17, 18, 21, 28, 43, 45, 84, 86, 88, 89, 114, 129, 131, 154, 166
  Door keeping, 16-18, 21, 23-24, 27, 42, 45, 54, 68, 85-86
  Drammer/trammer (moving coal drams/trams), vii, 8, 14, 20, 24, 25, 26, 27, 28, 30, 41, 42, 43, 45, 47, 48, 54, 77, 79, 80, 81, 89, 105, 114, 119, 123, 140, 142, 144, 146, 147, 152, 154, 158, 162, 169, 170, 172, 174
  Fillers (filling trams), 3, 17, 18, 23, 24, 25, 26, 28, 76, 82, 84, 85, 88, 89, 144, 120, 127, 130
  Girdle and chain (children dragging trams), 26, 50, 69
  Hauliers (working with horses), 17, 22, 24, 27, 43, 62, 122, 136, 155
  Labourers, 12, 13, 18, 19, 61, 71, 84, 87, 88, 91, 94, 98, 117, 135, 136, 137, 138, 154, 172, 173

Oiling trams, 17, 27, 28, 43, 86, 89, 112, 136, 154
Sorting, sizing and screening coal, 2, 5, 8, 28, 29, 33, 90, 123, 129, 136, 141, 142, 144, 154, 155, 158, 166, 170-171, 177, 180, 181
Tip girls (generic term for those working on the pit heads), 6, 7, 37, 40, 75, 79, 80, 82, 83, 89, 90, 100, 101, 102, 104, 108, 109, 119, 120, 123, 124, 126, 127, 128, 129, 130, 131, 135, 136, 142, 143, 144, 145, 155, 157, 158, 160, 161, 163, 176, 178, 182-184
Tippers (emptying trams), 17, 25, 77, 81, 88, 89, 105, 114, 127, 135, 136, 141, 142, 157, 170
Weighing coal, 17, 43, 81, 88, 89, 136
Windlass women, 4, 14, 25, 29-30, 42-43, 47, 49, 54, 76, 77, 183
Working underground, vii, 3, 5, 7, 9, 10, 16, 23, 24, 25, 26, 28, 40, 42, 47, 49, 57, 58, 59, 60, 64, 65-66, 68, 77-78, 86, 89, 91, 92, 138, 152, 157, 163, 174, 175, 181, 182, 183, 184

Vach, Eos, 31, 36-40

Wages, 10, 18, 24, 29, 37, 38, 41, 42-44, 46, 49, 52, 59, 60, 61, 63, 64, 65, 66, 67, 68, 75, 82, 86, 87, 94, 117, 118, 119, 120, 121, 122, 123-126, 139, 141, 142, 144, 148, 149, 154, 156, 170, 171, 174, 175, 176, 178, 183, 184
Widows, 4, 15, 16, 21, 34, 61, 65, 85, 86, 87, 88, 89, 99, 129, 135, 136, 143, 144, 155, 157, 165, 173
Women as heads of households, 15, 16, 17, 18, 85, 87, 88, 89, 135
World War I, vii, 68, 171-174
Wynne, Francis Elizabeth, amateur artist, 4